LAMENTATIONS
and the
SONG OF SONGS

BELIEF

*A Theological Commentary
on the Bible*

GENERAL EDITORS

Amy Plantinga Pauw
William C. Placher[†]

LAMENTATIONS
and the
SONG OF SONGS

HARVEY COX and STEPHANIE PAULSELL

WESTMINSTER
JOHN KNOX PRESS
LOUISVILLE · KENTUCKY

© 2012 Harvey Cox and Stephanie Paulsell

First edition
Published by Westminster John Knox Press
Louisville, Kentucky

12 13 14 15 16 17 18 19 20 21—10 9 8 7 6 5 4 3 2 1

Book design by Drew Stevens
Cover design by Lisa Buckley
Cover illustration: © David Chapman/Design Pics/Corbis

Library of Congress Cataloging-in-Publication Data

Cox, Harvey Gallagher.
    Lamentations and the Song of songs : a theological commentary on the Bible /
Harvey Cox, Stephanie Paulsell.
      p. cm. — (Belief)
    Includes bibliographical references and indexes.
    ISBN 978-0-664-23302-0 (alk. paper)
1. Bible. O.T. Lamentations—Commentaries. 2. Bible. O.T. Song of Solomon—
Commentaries. 3. Bible. O.T. Lamentations—Theology. 4. Bible. O.T. Song of
Solomon—Theology. I. Paulsell, Stephanie, 1962- II. Title.
    BS1535.53.C69 2012
    223'.907—dc23
                                                                2011039955

Contents

COMMENTARY

LAMENTATIONS

THE SONG OF SONGS

Publisher's Note

William C. Placher worked with Amy Plantinga Pauw as a general editor for this series until his untimely death in November 2008. Bill brought great energy and vision to the series, and was instrumental in defining and articulating its distinctive approach and in securing theologians to write for it. Bill's own commentary for the series was the last thing he wrote, and Westminster John Knox Press dedicates the entire series to his memory with affection and gratitude.

William C. Placher, LaFollette Distinguished Professor in Humanities at Wabash College, spent thirty-four years as one of Wabash College's most popular teachers. A summa cum laude graduate of Wabash in 1970, he earned his master's degree in philosophy in 1974 and his Ph.D. in 1975, both from Yale University. In 2002 the American Academy of Religion honored him with the Excellence in Teaching Award. Placher was also the author of thirteen books, including *A History of Christian Theology*, *The Triune God*, *The Domestication of Transcendence*, *Jesus the Savior*, *Narratives of a Vulnerable God*, and *Unapologetic Theology*. He also edited the volume *Essentials of Christian Theology*, which was named as one of 2004's most outstanding books by both *The Christian Century* and *Christianity Today* magazines.

Series Introduction

Belief: A Theological Commentary on the Bible is a series from Westminster John Knox Press featuring biblical commentaries written by theologians. The writers of this series share Karl Barth's concern that, insofar as their usefulness to pastors goes, most modern commentaries are "no commentary at all, but merely the first step toward a commentary." Historical-critical approaches to Scripture rule out some readings and commend others, but such methods only begin to help theological reflection and the preaching of the Word. By themselves, they do not convey the powerful sense of God's merciful presence that calls Christians to repentance and praise; they do not bring the church fully forward in the life of discipleship. It is to such tasks that theologians are called.

For several generations, however, professional theologians in North America and Europe have not been writing commentaries on the Christian Scriptures. The specialization of professional disciplines and the expectations of theological academies about the kind of writing that theologians should do, as well as many of the directions in which contemporary theology itself has gone, have contributed to this dearth of theological commentaries. This is a relatively new phenomenon; until the last century or two, the church's great theologians also routinely saw themselves as biblical interpreters. The gap between the fields is a loss for both the church and the discipline of theology itself. By inviting forty contemporary theologians to wrestle deeply with particular texts of Scripture, the editors of this series hope not only to provide new theological resources for the church, but also to encourage all theologians to pay more attention to Scripture and the life of the church in their writings.

We are grateful to the Louisville Institute, which provided funding for a consultation in June 2007. We invited theologians, pastors, and biblical scholars to join us in a conversation about what this series could contribute to the life of the church. The time was provocative and the results were rich. Much of the series' shape owes to the insights of these skilled and faithful interpreters, who sought to describe a way to write a commentary that served the theological needs of the church and its pastors with relevance, historical accuracy, and theological depth. The passion of these participants guided us in creating this series and lives on in the volumes.

As theologians, the authors will be interested much less in the matters of form, authorship, historical setting, social context, and philology—the very issues that are often of primary concern to critical biblical scholars. Instead, this series' authors will seek to explain the theological importance of the texts for the church today, using biblical scholarship as needed for such explication but without any attempt to cover all of the topics of the usual modern biblical commentary. This thirty-six-volume series will provide passage-by-passage commentary on all the books of the Protestant biblical canon, with more extensive attention given to passages of particular theological significance.

The authors' chief dialogue will be with the church's creeds, practices, and hymns; with the history of faithful interpretation and use of the Scriptures; with the categories and concepts of theology; and with contemporary culture in both "high" and popular forms. Each volume will begin with a discussion of *why* the church needs this book and why we need it *now*, in order to ground all of the commentary in contemporary relevance. Throughout each volume, text boxes will highlight the voices of ancient and modern interpreters from the global communities of faith, and occasional essays will allow deeper reflection on the key theological concepts of these biblical books.

The authors of this commentary series are theologians of the church who embrace a variety of confessional and theological perspectives. The group of authors assembled for this series represents more diversity of race, ethnicity, and gender than any other commentary series. They approach the larger Christian tradition with a critical respect, seeking to reclaim its riches and at the same time to acknowledge its shortcomings. The authors also aim to make available to readers a wide range of contemporary theological voices from many parts of the world. While it does recover an older genre of writing, this series is not an attempt to retrieve some idealized past. These commentaries have learned from tradition, but they are most importantly commentaries for today. The authors share the conviction that their work will be more contemporary, more faithful, and more radical, to the extent that it is more biblical, honestly wrestling with the texts of the Scriptures.

William C. Placher
Amy Plantinga Pauw

Acknowledgments for
the Song of Songs

I am very grateful to William C. Placher for inviting me to be a part of this commentary series. Like all the authors he recruited for this project, I have felt his absence and missed his counsel as I worked.

For close reading, careful editing, and constant support, I thank Donald McKim of Westminster John Knox and Amy Plantinga Pauw, the general editor of the series.

I am grateful to all the communities that invited me to share parts of this commentary as it was taking shape: Christmount Christian Assembly in Black Mountain, North Carolina; the monthly faculty seminar hosted by the Center for the Study of World Religions at Harvard Divinity School; Fourth Presbyterian Church of Chicago; the Memorial Church at Harvard University; All Hallow's College of Dublin City University in Dublin, Ireland; the Bethany Fellows of the Christian Church (Disciples of Christ); the Boston Ministers Club; and the Baptist Seminary of Kentucky. The conversations I had about the Song in all these places had a tremendous influence on my thinking about how to read the Song devotionally in our own day.

I am grateful to Loulie Kent, whom I met at the Memorial Church at Harvard. Loulie generously shared with me her memories of sending messages from the Song of Songs to her husband when he was serving on a U.S. submarine in the 1970s. I also offer thanks to Laura Sterkel and Mary Kay Wysham, whom I met at Fourth Presbyterian Church, for their insight into Song 1:17. I am grateful to Debra Bendis at *The Christian Century,* who accepted several essays from me on the Song of Songs.

I have learned a great deal from teaching the Song of Songs with Francis X. Clooney during the last two years and from reading his own work on the Song. Paul J. Griffiths allowed me to read his *Commentary on the Song of Songs* before it was published, and I thank him for his generosity.

I am grateful to the friends, family, and colleagues who read portions of this commentary in draft, discussed the Song with me at crucial points, recommended books and articles for me to read, and invited me to share my work with the communities they serve, especially Dorothy Austin, Elizabeth Myer Boulton, Matthew Myer Boulton, François Bovon, Jamie Brame, Francis X. Clooney, Harvey Cox, Kristine Culp, Diana Eck, Bernadette Flanaghan, Paul J. Griffiths, Taylor Guthrie Hartman, E. Glenn Hinson, Amy Hollywood, Richard Holton, Father Matthew Kelty, O.C.S.O., Karen King, David Lamberth, Rae Langton, Jon Levenson, Kevin Madigan, Kay Northcutt, John O'Donnell, Michael O'Sullivan, Sally Paulsell, William O. Paulsell, Joyce Shin, and John Stendhal. I am grateful to Dean William A. Graham of Harvard Divinity School for his support of this project and for the time he gave me to work on it.

I am especially grateful to my parents, William O. and Sally Paulsell, who have accompanied me on many trips to speak about the Song and whose delight in each other has not diminished after more than fifty years of marriage. I thank my daughter, Amanda Madigan, and my husband, Kevin Madigan, for all that they have taught me, and are still teaching me, about love.

Abbreviations

AB	Anchor Bible
ACW	Ancient Christian Writers
JPS	Jewish Publication Society Version
KJV	King James Version
NIV	New International Version
NLT	New Living Translation
NRSV	New Revised Standard Version
OBT	Overtures to Biblical Theology
OTL	Old Testament Library
REB	Revised English Bible
RSV	Revised Standard Version
TNIV	Today's New International Version

LAMENTATIONS

Introduction:
Why Lamentations? Why Now?

The book of Lamentations is one of the shortest in the Bible. It is also one of the most poignant and evocative. A piercing cry of pain from the broken heart of a ruined city, it can reach deeply into the heart of anyone familiar with the stories or the photographs of Dresden, Stalingrad, Warsaw, and Hiroshima, or even of Lower Manhattan after 9/11, of Port-au-Prince after the 2010 earthquake, or New Orleans after Katrina. It pulsates with an urgent contemporary tone, but its voice and style can sound angular and odd at times to today's ears. It calls out to us from another era and evokes, along with the pain and sympathy, a certain distance and strangeness. Still, reading it today with an active imagination makes it as relevant as tomorrow's headlines. It is, in a true sense, a classic.

How then should a commentary on this text proceed? In her splendid book *Lamentations and the Tears of the World*, Kathleen O'Connor writes, "Lamentations hardly needs interpretation for people who live in the ruins of destroyed cities, whose societies are decimated by genocide, or who barely subsist in the face of famine and poverty."[1] I agree with O'Connor. Therefore what I write here is not an attempt to interpret what needs no interpretation. Rather it is more of a considered appreciation of a timeless masterpiece, an effort to invite the reader into my unreserved admiration, maybe even love, for this jagged, undying elegy.

I have found that although Lamentations sometimes requires an awkward scrambling back and forth between then and now, it also

---

1. Kathleen M. O'Connor, *Lamentations and the Tears of the World* (Maryknoll, NY: Orbis Press, 2002), xiv.

opens the mind to a kind of free association. There is nothing wrong with that. We cannot escape our present, and we read the past in terms of what we live with now. But also we can often grasp the inner meaning of what lies before our eyes or lingers in our recent memories only by hearing a faint rumble from a distant past. When approached in this manner, Lamentations becomes a shockingly current text. It is a rare day whose newspapers and newscasts on TV or the Web do not deliver images of hungry mothers and children, pictures of streets corroded by car bombs and strewn with dead bodies lying in grotesque postures, or wrenching accounts of rape and torture. This is the world we live in. But it is also the world of Lamentations, a book that bears an unnerving resemblance to our own times.

This text is a poem. For reasons I will explain below I will refer to its writer as "The Poet." Also, in part because it is a poem, it is not my intention to write a historical-critical commentary. There are many excellent ones already in print, and I have learned from a number of them. Rather I intend to offer what the editors have called a "theological" commentary. Therefore it may be useful for me to say a word about my approach to theological reflection.

For most of my life as a teacher who is also a minister, I have thought of my calling as offering whatever help I can to making the message of the gospel known. I relish the responsibility to preach when the occasion presents itself. Like many other preachers, I have found that standard commentaries are helpful, even essential, in preparing a sermon, but only up to a point. I have discovered that often what helps me most in penetrating into a biblical text is to engage in a kind of free association. I let the text stir up the embers of my mind. Then I try to correlate it with what is going on in the life of the congregation, in the world, and in my own life, often drawing on a wide variety of literary and artistic expressions. This is why the reader of this commentary will find an array of references to poetry, novels, films, paintings, and even photography, which I consider an especially potent art form.

But as a professor at a university I also think about a biblical text with reference to both classical and current philosophical and theological currents. Hence the reader will discover allusions to thinkers from Plato to Tillich, and even to more recent philosophers of the European deconstructionist and postmodern schools. Are these sources theological? I think they are, and they are not just hauled in. These writers roam the intellectual world we live in. I believe they belong in a twentieth-first-century commentary just as the church fathers, Augustine, Luther, and Calvin felt free to call upon the sources they knew in their time. Remember, Paul was perfectly willing to quote to the Athenian crowd "some of your poets" on Mars Hill (Acts 17:22–31).

I have also chosen not to comment on Lamentations in a traditional, sequential, verse-by-verse style. The reason, quite simply, is that it is not a sequential text. Its scattered and furrowed contours discourage such a line-by-line approach. Its idiom is more like the sputtering and fuming of the dazed victims of any disaster whose capacity for sequential thinking has been fractured and undermined. In Lamentations, The Poet stammers and then becomes eloquent in turns. Themes appear then disappear, only to surge up again and again. Consequently, I have commented on this text thematically, exploring the motifs it presents, leaves, and then returns to, themes like suffering, exile, war, revenge, and many others.

There is something else to be said about this text: it is bound to unsettle some modern religious sensibilities. *The God whose visage appears in it is not very nice.* Here, in the voice of the city of Jerusalem, is a sampling:

> "The Lord treated with scorn
> all the mighty men within my walls;
> he marshalled rank on rank against me
> to crush my young warriors.
> The Lord trod down, like grapes in the winepress,
> the virgin daughter of Judah."
>
> (1:15 REB)

What kind of God is this? He is not the smiling superhelper who will lift us from our worries. He is not the friendly companion standing by to lighten our burden or put a smile on our faces. Those seeking that kind of God are advised to look elsewhere. On the other hand, such spiritual happiness seekers might do well to allow Lamentations to speak to them, if only to balance the books, to discover how vacuous and puerile many of our present images of God have become. I have not heard many sermons drawn from Lamentations. But having now lived with this powerful poem for a while, I think there should be a lot more of them.

Warning: it took time for Lamentations to resonate with my own life. But once it began to do so, it pierced through to a level few other books have. It pushed me to recall experiences from many years ago that I had almost forgotten, and it brought them back with a clarity I thought had fled. They were not all pleasant memories. But I am grateful that this harsh, even relentless book helped me exhume them from the dim recesses of my memory and lend them a sometimes disquieting lucidity.

It has also become clear to me that this book speaks not only, or not even mainly, to individuals. Collectively, we as an American nation need its message. We are the victims of a continuing amnesia about our wars and their aftermaths. The only things certain about any war are that it will not go as expected and it will result in horrors few anticipated, even though we should have. Also every war, small or large, has an aftermath. Lamentations is about an aftermath, what happens after the war is supposedly over. It does not read like "good news," but I am sure that if its awful implications can be grasped, either by reading this often-overlooked text itself or by studying the many others that convey the same urgent message, we as a nation can shake off our amnesia and think much more carefully before we plunge onto yet another battlefield.

Ruined Cities: A Personal Note

Why have I been so drawn to the book of Lamentations? Maybe it is because I have seen more than my share of ruined cities. I was introduced to them very young. I first set foot in Germany in July 1946, just one year after the end of World War II. I say "set foot," because it was not much more than that. My footstep was onto a landing platform in Kiel, Germany. It took place during the short time needed to raise the SS *Robert Hart*, the merchant marine vessel on which I was a youthful crew member, to the level of the Baltic Sea as we were entering the Kiel Canal though a lock. Two of my young shipmates and I had clambered down a ladder the captain and first mate had set up to confer with canal authorities. But we were quickly sent back up the ladder by a no-nonsense local policeman. Still, I at least felt the satisfaction that, for the first time in my life, I had indeed "set foot" in a foreign land.

What I noticed most about the area around the lock was how utterly devastated it appeared. The arms of sunken cranes still hung at precarious angles. The buildings near the locks looked charred and shattered. Rusting hulks of ships protruded awkwardly from the water at the edges. Canals, after all, are valuable strategic assets, and this one had been a favorite target for both the American and the British bombers for years. The Kiel Canal and the area around it had not escaped either. Kiel, Germany, in 1946 was a ruined city.

Two days later I climbed ashore for a longer visit in a city that was even more devastated: Danzig (later renamed Gdansk when it was made part of Poland after the war). Danzig had been a "free city," with a population made up of Poles and Germans. It is the setting of Gunther Grass's zany antiwar novel, *The Tin Drum*. Hitler demanded it be integrated into the Third Reich. Poland resisted. Tensions escalated and World War II began. Danzig had been both bombed and shelled many times over. When our ship tied up in its port area, called Gdynia, to unload our cargo, the crew was allowed to visit what was left of it. There was not much.

At first I just stood and stared at the blackened timbers and the gawky chimneys rising over piles of debris where houses once stood. Endless blocks of skeletal ruins stretched in every direction. The acrid smell of smoke still hung on the air, not from the wartime attacks but from the fires the shivering populace built in the rubble to keep warm. The moment we stepped onto the dock crowds of young prostitutes—some of them barely teenagers—swarmed around us, pathetic in their ragged skirts, torn stockings, and ridiculous makeup. Hordes of scruffy children dogged us, begging for food.

All her people groaned,
they begged for bread;
they bartered their treasures for food
to regain their strength.
"Look, LORD, and see
how cheap I am accounted."
(1:11 REB)

The only traffic in the town were antique trolleys, an occasional furtive taxi, and military vehicles crowded with cherubic young Polish soldiers carrying the kind of submachine guns I had seen before only in gangster movies. The Soviet-installed Communist government had already taken over, but the population was not pacified. Shouts and the crackle of gunfire could be heard every night. Shops had little to offer. There was a shortage of dogs or cats—they had all long since been eaten. It was not a city in which you would have to *interpret* Lamentations.

Back home, I developed a lasting interest in World War II. In college I studied German and majored in modern European history. After my first year in seminary I worked for a summer with a church youth program among the Cockneys in the Lime House area of east London. Here was another ruined city, even seven years after the incendiary bombs and V-2s of the blitz had leveled whole blocks. The church I worked in was 90 percent destroyed. It had not been rebuilt, and the small congregation huddled for worship in an adjacent parish hall.

"From heaven he sent down fire,
which ran through my bones;
he spread out a net to catch my feet,
and turned me back."
(1:13)

A few years later, in 1956, when I was the campus minister at Oberlin College, I accompanied a group of students to Germany, France, and Poland on a study tour. In Berlin I left the group in the relative safety of the western part of the city and made my way to the eastern sector. The infamous Berlin wall was not yet built, so it was possible but "not advisable," as the American occupation authorities informed me, to make the trip. But I did anyway. Between the western and eastern parts of the city lay a vast wilderness of wreckage. The Americans, the British, and the French jointly administered the west. The Russians controlled the east. But none of them had any interest in rebuilding the large swath of wasteland that lay between them. In the east, the area around Friedrichstrasse and in the west the streets along the Kurfurstendamm were coming to life. But in between lay nothing but twisted metal, piles of bricks, loose wires, and ruptured streets. At night the lack of street lights made it Hades dark.

Still, I was fascinated by Berlin. I admired the way people on both sides continued to live despite all they had been through. So when I received an invitation to spend a year there in 1962/63 as an Ecumenical Fraternal Worker, I accepted it. By then the wall, which the East German regime had thrown up in 1961, cut an ugly scar through the old center of the city. The United States was still at that time, along with France, Great Britain, and the USSR, one of the "occupying powers." Therefore, according to the agreement reached at the war's end among them, I was permitted, as the holder of an American passport, to cross over into the Soviet-occupied sector as long as I returned to the West within twenty-four hours. My assignment in the city was to facilitate communication between the two parts of the severed city, and this required me to travel back and forth through "Checkpoint Charley." Consequently I was exposed to the acres of urban desolation three times a week.

I also noticed something I will return to later. Places of worship, or sometimes just segments of them, remained here and there, and some had become symbols of community and hints of possibility. Just inside the wall on the eastern side stood a church building that bore the ironic name, "Church of the Reconciliation," even though the banks of barbed wire on top of the wall partially obscured it from view. In the heart of West Berlin, near Bahnhof Zoo, stood the jagged tower of the old Kaiser Wilhelm Memorial Church.

Blasted by allied bombers, its splintered steeple still loomed above the surrounding shops and restaurants. It remains there today. After the war, Berliners decided not to remove the wreckage but to allow it to stand as a permanent reminder of what war does. But was that cracked tower a reminder of what "they" had done to us or of what "we" brought on ourselves? Standing there, silent and ghostly, it allowed anyone seeing it to read his own message into it. Every time I passed its serrated stone profile, I thought about what had happened to this fabled city, and why.

In 1945, as the war drew to a close, four million soldiers of the Red Army poured into the eastern parts of the Third Reich. All the themes of Lamentations were in play: for the Russian soldiers, bitter memories of blackened Stalingrad and other burned cities all over their country, and the humiliation of initial defeat now crowned with triumph had curdled into an appetite for revenge. These men killed and burned and raped in resentful fury. Thousands of civilians died, and German military casualties in that one month alone exceeded the total British and American losses in the entire war. Burrowed in his reinforced bunker far below the surface, Hitler refused to surrender, declaring that the German people had failed him and deserved annihilation. In a paroxysm of fury, just before he shot himself, he ordered that the subway system, where many thousands of people had taken refuge, be flooded. But the German general to whom he issued the command quietly refused to carry it out. We can be thankful that something similar happened in Paris. Hitler had ordered that its bridges and historic buildings should be piled with high explosives so that when his army left, the city on the Seine could be destroyed. The dynamite was all set in place, and as the Nazis pulled out Hitler kept asking his aides, "Is Paris burning?" It was not. The German commander, who had lived there during the occupation, had quietly neglected to carry out the führer's command.

The sentiment in Germany just after the war was complicated. The Allies had expected that after the surrender they would encounter continued resistance from "Werewolves," die-hard Nazis and SS veterans. But this did not happen. Most Germans were too preoccupied with rustling for food and finding shelter for their families amid the wreckage. They were in no mood to resist.

> We must buy the water we drink;
>   our wood can be had only at a price.
> Those who pursue us are at our heels;
>   we are weary and find no rest.
> We submitted to Egypt and Assyria
>   to get enough bread.
> Our fathers sinned and are no more,
>   and we bear their punishment.
>   (5:4–7 NIV)

Some people on the Allied side believed that once the Germans learned all the gruesome facts about the extermination camps at Auschwitz and Bergen-Belsen they would be wracked with remorse. But they were not. Looking around them at the debris in their own cities, and into their empty larders, shuddering in the cold, they thought they had already been punished enough. When the Italian Jewish writer Primo Levi stepped off the train to look around Munich in 1945 on his way back to Turin from Auschwitz, where he had been penned up for two years, he was troubled by what he saw. Later he wrote, "I felt I was moving among throngs of insolvent debtors, as if everybody owed me something, and refused to pay."[2] The Germans in fact were numb. When Rudolf Hess, Hermann Göring, and other Nazi leaders were put on trial for crimes against humanity in Nuremburg, few Germans had any sympathy for them. Weren't they the ones who had brought this all on?

But, unlike the voice in Lamentations, there were few cries for revenge against those who had devastated their cities. The Germans seemed to accept their situation grimly and set to work to rebuild what had been destroyed. Still, eventually many Germans began to feel that they owed the world an accounting. The Protestant churches

---

2. Quoted in Tony Judt, *Reappraisals: Reflections on the Forgotten Twentieth Century* (New York: Penguin, 2008), 51.

took the lead. They issued an official apology for their complicity and silence during the Nazi reign. A different tone began to emerge. The government put aside millions of deutschmarks to compensate Jewish survivors whose property had been taken, and eventually to help support Israel. Prime Minister Willi Brandt famously fell on his knees before a memorial to the Warsaw ghetto uprising during a visit to Poland. Within a generation Germany became the country that, more than any other, paid real attention to facing up to its past sins. There is little doubt that the moral leadership of the churches played a decisive role in this remarkable national self-searching.

Since my sojourns to London and Berlin I have also visited Hiroshima, in some ways the ultimate ruined city, vaporized in an instant one clear morning in August 1945 along with seventy thousand of its inhabitants. It has now declared itself a "peace city," with many of its people accepting a special responsibility to ensure that nothing like what happened to them ever happens again.

Ruined cities have become the icon of the twentieth century. T. S. Eliot, probably the finest poet of that century, features them in a searing passage in his masterpiece, "The Waste Land."

> What is that sound high in the air,
> Murmur of maternal lamentation
> Who are those hooded hordes swarming
> Over endless plains, stumbling in cracked earth
> Ringed by the flat horizon only
> What is the city over the mountains
> Cracks and reforms and bursts in the violet air
> Falling towers
> Jerusalem Athens Alexandria
> Vienna London
> Unreal[3]

Eliot's poem is made even more pertinent for this commentary because of its mention of Jerusalem and the way he explicitly aligns

---

3. Quoted from T. S. Eliot, *The Complete Poems and Plays 1909–1950* (New York: Harcourt, Brace & World, 1952), 48.

it with the long tradition of laments, even of "maternal laments." Also in the poem, which was first published in 1922, the poet inserts the line, "London Bridge is falling down," a line from a children's song but also a Cassandra-like prophecy of what lay ahead for the city.

Then, of course, there is 9/11. As Americans we had thought of ruined cities, but always *elsewhere*. Now the misshapen girders and warped frames were piled up in the heart of our largest city. The myth of America's invulnerability, tucked between two oceans, was punctured. It is startling to read in Lamentations that the people of Jerusalem were enduring the same destruction of a similar myth.

> No one, neither the kings of the earth
> nor any other inhabitants of the world,
> believed that any adversary, any foe
> could penetrate within the gates of Jerusalem.
> (4:12 REB)

The people of Jerusalem were shocked to discover that their city, protected (they thought) by God, could be penetrated. But it was. Also, they were horrified that even the temple itself could be razed by their enemies. Likewise the 9/11 attack leveled what some considered the "temple" of the American market "religion," the World Trade Center. The towers that fell were not just the highest buildings in a nation proud of its skyscrapers, they were also proud symbols of financial power, not just for Americans, but for the attackers. But the pieces of those proud towers was now scattered through the streets.

> How dulled is the gold,
> how tarnished the fine gold!
> The stones of the sanctuary lie strewn
> at every street corner.
> (4:1 REB)

The twentieth-century world is pockmarked by the scar tissue of ruined cities. Some have been rebuilt, a few in a masterful manner, like the "old city" of Warsaw, a brick-for-brick replica of what it looked like before. Others, like downtown Berlin, have been rebuilt with gleaming signature buildings designed by the world's most famous architects. Still, when one adds the Twin Towers of 9/11 to Eliot's invocation it is hard to avoid two disturbing thoughts. The first is that indeed we have just lived through the era of the ruined city, but the second is that that era may not yet be over. Singly and together these cities pose the unavoidable questions put to us by Lamentations: What, if anything, have we learned from this suffering and horror? Where, if anywhere, is God in it? Are there any grounds to hope and pray that it will not happen again?

PART 1

HOW TO READ LAMENTATIONS

How should a twenty-first-century person read Lamentations? I recommend what I call a "participatory mood." I believe that if one reads it this way, rather than in an "objective" way, something happens. Since the book paints a picture of intense suffering on a small but concentrated canvas, it makes us reflect on how we—or anyone else—respond to suffering. Whatever the historical-critical approach to the Bible has contributed, and it has contributed much, one of its side effects may have been to deprive some readers of an element of empathy. This lack of empathy is especially present in those who have been trained to read things with a critical eye or even with what is now called a "hermeneutics of suspicion." But our question now is: what does such a "distanced" reading miss?

We can be sure that The Poet of Lamentations did not compose it merely to be analyzed, dissected, and classified at arm's length. What did The Poet expect from us? If we meet someone who is in obvious pain and is complaining, sobbing, and at times even screaming at us, we can be certain the person does not expect us to stand back and analyze what she (or he) is saying. We might grab her by the shoulders and tell her to cut out the sniveling. We might begin to cry along with her. We might run away as fast as possible. But none of these responses is the same as the "detached gaze" of the uninvolved observer. By adopting such a distancing mode, we may lose what is most essential in what the person is trying to communicate. My premise throughout this commentary is that the "meaning" of any biblical text is not simply "there." Rather it *happens*. It arises from the interaction of the text and the reader. Is it possible that the victory of the historical-critical approach to the Bible, at least in some circles, has been a Pyrrhic one, and that it has—perhaps unintentionally—carried with it a virus that can anesthetize readers to what the writer is trying to say?

Of course the historical-critical approach to the Bible has not triumphed everywhere. But where it has not carried the day it has often evoked an even more lethal countervirus, a fundamentalist insistence on the literal accuracy of every word in every verse. These two ways of opening the Bible—the historical-critical and the literalist—may appear to be opposites, and in many ways they are. But what they both miss is that the Bible is more poetry than prose, more saga than history, more evocation than description. Both fundamentalist literalism and the historical-critical approach to the Bible embrace a flat, pedestrian view of a text, shorn of nuance and overtones. Neither calls for any bold act of imagination or empathy, which is what Lamentations seems to cry out for.

It is not this way everywhere. One of the reasons the Bible has played such a powerful role in the Christian base communities of Latin America, and in the liberation theology they spawned, is that the participants in those communities had not been affected by either historical-critical scholarship or literalistic fundamentalism. They gathered and read the Scriptures, especially the Gospels, as gripping narratives, and they allowed them to evoke reflection about similar experiences in their own lives.

In our historical era we may have a special difficulty entering into a text like Lamentations in part because we are perched at a cusp of transition in which the culturally powerful, objective-distancing view of the world has not completely displaced the participatory one. One can stand, for example, in front of Pablo Picasso's masterpiece *Guernica* and look at it in different ways. The picture was inspired by the bombing of a small Basque village by the fascists during the Spanish Civil War. Distorted limbs, gaping mouths, and dismembered bodies litter the scene. A large print of this painting hung on the wall of the living room in the home of my teacher Paul Tillich in Cambridge. He called it the greatest example of religious art of the twentieth century, not because its theme was explicitly "religious" in any conventional sense (it was not) but because the moral rage and indignation of the artist seemed to Tillich an authentic religious vision. *Guernica* and Lamentations have much in common.

But does *Guernica* pack the same power today, even after the instantaneous destruction of Hiroshima and the firebombing of Dresden make the incident that inspired it pale by comparison? What about those people who can look at *Guernica* solely through the eyes of art historians, admiring (or shaking their heads over) the brush strokes, color choice, or overall design? And what about the art dealer, who looks at this or any other canvas as dollar signs prance in his head as he wonders what it might sell for at Sotheby's? In short, *Guernica*, like any other work of art that depicts suffering, does not speak for itself. What it "says" is determined in part by what we bring to it. I say "in part" because one can imagine a dealer or an art critic looking at this canvas when suddenly something happens. It breaks out of the categories they have imposed on it. It leaps through perceptual structures and seizes them by the throat. That is the power of truly great art. This is also true of biblical texts, like Lamentations. What we find in it is due in large measure to what we bring to it, but not entirely, because it is also due to what is "there."

I have said that we stand at a transitional point in the cultural sensibility of our era. We have been inundated, especially through technology, by distancing mechanisms, while parts of us still nurture the participatory mode. But this tension often proves to be a painful place to live. In Federico Fellini's great film *La Dolce Vita*, the Italian director focuses on this contradiction and on how it cripples us. The antihero, played by Marcello Mastrioni in one of his best performances, is Marcello Rubini, a reporter for a gossipy tabloid in Rome that takes him to the swank haunts of the Via Veneto in search of juicy stories. In his work he is constantly accompanied by a covey of paparazzi who gleefully snap pictures of the antics of celebrities. One day an editor calls and asks him to drive into the countryside near Rome to cover the alleged appearance of the Virgin Mary to two children. He goes, followed by the paparazzi, and he takes along his girlfriend, who suspects that the way he is going about his job is making him cynical. At the site, where crowds have gathered and brought sick friends hoping for miracles of healing, TV crews are standing by with klieg lights. Symbolically Marcello climbs up a lighting tower to survey the scene from a distance while his girlfriend mingles with the crowd. He is "above it all," while she becomes part of the event. At first mainly curious, the girlfriend eventually kneels and prays to the Virgin to return Marcello to the person he once was. When a rainstorm interrupts the scene and one of the sick people dies, Marcello coolly writes it down in his notebook. This infuriates the girlfriend, who pounds Marcello with her fists. Meanwhile the paparazzi snap pictures. But one of them, after taking a picture of the dead man, pauses and crosses himself. This brief moment catches the point of the whole film. What is our first impulse? To objectify what lies before us or to empathize? Can we balance the two? Must one supplant the other? Like any great artist, Fellini does not answer the question for us.

This short scene also tells us something vital and painful about our culture, namely that the art form that amplifies the contradiction better than any other is photography. In 1977 the American writer and critic Susan Sontag published a discerning book titled *On Photography*. Her thesis was that the flooding of our world with photographic images has created a "chronic voyeuristic relation"[4] to the people and things around us. She claims it fosters an attitude of nonintervention. One cannot, she argues, both intervene and record. But is Sontag right about this? Her observation brings to mind the controversy that arose in the 1930s around the famous photograph of a bloodstained baby sitting and crying amid the wreckage of the Shanghai railway station during the war between China and Japan. On the one hand, the picture aroused considerable sympathy in those who saw it. On the other, some people asked, "Why didn't the photographer simply pick the child up and comfort it?" What the picture does is to dramatize the dilemma we all feel in an age of mass media and of immense human misery.

Sontag also argues that photography exerts a leveling influence as events with important significance are constantly juxtaposed with those that are merely trivial. A quick glance though today's magazines, where pictures of smiling swimsuit models share the page

---

4. Susan Sontag, *On Photography* (New York: Farrar, Straus and Giroux, 1977), 10.

with those of hungry children clutching their mothers' skirts, bears out her indictment.

I agree with Sontag to some extent. But the context does make a difference. When photography becomes one more tool in the market economy's kit of gadgets to promote consumer spending, it can do great damage. But when properly used, photography, including TV, can also nourish empathy. When they saw police beating non-violent marchers on the bridge in Selma, for example, literally thousands went there to join the next march. Graphic TV coverage of the Vietnam War catalyzed public opposition to it. Paradoxically, when he wanted to protest how picture taking can numb us to human sensitivity, Fellini did so by making a film.

Today's reader of Lamentations has an important choice to make. *How* should one approach the text? I suggest a two-step process. First, one should indeed know something about the source, dating, structure, and provenance of the text. This commentary and many others will help with this initial step. But that is only the beginning. The next step, the most important one, is to *enter* the text, allow its powerful images to reach below the cognitive level. How should we read Lamentations? Maybe we should read it aloud. In any case: *Let it speak!*

1 ✳

Stepping into Lamentations

Overall Structure of Lamentations

The book of Lamentations consists of five chapters, all in Hebrew verse. In the Hebrew canon it is placed in the Writings, as the third of the Megilloth ("Scrolls") between Ruth and Ecclesiastes. This might suggest that some compilers thought it bears a kinship to the wisdom tradition. In the Christian canon it is placed between Jeremiah and Ezekiel. This position implies that Lamentations can also be thought of as a "prophetic" utterance. There is no reason, however, that it cannot be thought of as related to both these scriptural genres. Also, its position among the prophets in the Christian Bible follows that of the Latin Vulgate, which in turn followed the Greek Septuagint. This positioning may be due to a tradition we discuss below that once attributed its authorship to the prophet Jeremiah, "the weeping prophet."

There are five laments in Lamentations. The first two and the last two seem to be based on the fall of Jerusalem to the Chaldeans in 587 BCE. The third lament does not have this explicit focus, but its style and language strongly suggest the same author. Unlike many other biblical books, Lamentations gives little or no evidence of having been edited or of having supplemental material added.

I have included a section below on the interesting structure of the Hebrew poetry of Lamentations. Chapter 5 displays a standard Hebrew poetry structure, three-beat lines paralleled by the next line. The first four chapters, however, are composed in the so-called *qinah* meter, which I have characterized as "potholed poetry" because of its irregular, bumpy rhythm. Some scholars have argued that this poetic form is derived from earlier funeral laments. I have included a section relating Lamentations to the wider and deeper history of laments, and especially of the decisive role women have played in this form of mourning.

Theologically, as well as in its literary form, Lamentations is a unity. Although it raises a number of different pressing theological and ethical concerns, its religious vision is consistent throughout. The text has been well preserved, and there are few disputes about translation. There has never been a serious question about its worthiness to be included in the canon. Since this text has been read and chanted aloud for centuries, the serious student of Lamentations might find it rewarding to read it aloud the whole way through.

Authorship

Let us begin at the beginning. Who are we listening to? In other words, who wrote Lamentations? Was it a woman or a man? In the Septuagint version (often referred to as the LXX) it begins, "And it came to pass, after Israel had been taken away into captivity and Jerusalem had been laid waste, that Jeremiah sat weeping and lamented this lamentation over Jerusalem and said. . . ." But scholars agree that this sentence was never in the original Hebrew text, and most also agree that Jeremiah was not its author. Therefore this opening attribution does not appear in modern translations, including the English-language ones. But if the author was not Jeremiah, then who was it?

Many readers feel that the voice of the book sounds at times like that of a woman. There is some evidence for this possibility. The writer obviously knows firsthand the special plight of the women of the defeated city. Lamentations is, after all, a "lament," and although the need to lament knows no temporal or geographical or gender boundaries, women have been its chief practitioners. The lament is one of the oldest literary forms, perhaps even preliterary. Laments, mostly for warriors who have been lost in what seemed to them and their loved ones to be an endless and pointless war, are threaded through the *Iliad*. Women are the great virtuosi of lament, and the most recent scholarship on lament reveals that they have played a much larger role in creating them than was previously thought.[5]

Some scholars have made a persuasive case that the oral tradition on which the Greek classics are based arose from the plaintive songs and keening of the women whose husbands and sons had been killed. Frequently even in works written by men, abandoned women have created the most memorable laments. Were these men mainly formalizing a genre they learned from women? There are many examples. Ariadne's howl of angry protest and misery after she has been abandoned by Theseus on the island of Naxos was captured centuries later by Monteverdi's opera *Arianna*. Richard Strauss followed him with his *Ariadne auf Naxos*, but redrafted it into a play within a play, perhaps because he felt a straightforward presentation of Ariadne's agony might be more than an audience could bear.

Another of the most famous of these abandoned women is Dido, the queen of Carthage whom Aeneas visits on his way to Italy after the Trojan War. She offers generous hospitality to Aeneas, then falls in love with him. He seems to reciprocate, but then—believing he is following his fate—sets sail and leaves. Dido has her servants pile up the weapons he has left behind, lying to them that by burning the shields and swords she will purge herself of the rancid memory of her false lover. But then she climbs to the top of the pyre, pierces herself with Aeneas's own sword, ignites the flames, and dies.

That women, both in real life and in artistic and musical creations, are often the principal lamenters lends some support to the speculation that the author of Lamentations, or at least the creator of the oral tradition on which it is based, may well have been a woman.

Why is the lament such a permanent fixture in the human drama? No one escapes some encounter with shipwrecks, large or small, in the course of a life. Women and men, the high and the low, young and old: no one is immune from catastrophe. In Lamentations the tragedy strikes all classes and age cohorts.

---

5. Linda M. Austin traces the literary rhetoric evoking a voice crying in "The Lament and the Rhetoric of the Sublime," *Nineteenth-Century Literature* 53, no. 3 (1998): 279–306.

Princes are hanged up by their hand:
the faces of elders were not honoured.
They took the young men to grind,
and the children fell under the wood.

(5:12 KJV)

Sometimes disasters creep up on us gradually; sometimes they pounce suddenly like a thief in the night. Traffic accidents strike when we least expect them. Loved ones—parents, spouses, siblings, and children—die unexpectedly. Divorce or unemployment disrupts our life plans. Disease stalks us at all ages. Sometimes the personal catastrophe storms ashore as part of a national disaster, like a war, a depression, a famine, or an epidemic. At other times it seeks us out individually. The book of Lamentations gains much of its power by fusing these two—the individual and the corporate—into a single sustained work of despair, humiliation, and—eventually—a kind of wild hope against hope, all sentiments that both men and women feel.

Of course it would be useful to know, if we could, whether it was a man or a woman who wrote this book. It is anything but an irrelevant consideration. But since it is unlikely that we will ever know the answer to this riddle, we must content ourselves with the recognition that Lamentations to some extent transcends gender. Its status as a literary jewel continues because not only nations and empires rise and fall, so do individual men and women. In any case, I have not tried to resolve this issue here. Still, it is clear to me, as it will be to any careful reader, that Lamentations is a *poem*. For the most part, I refer to its writer simply as "The Poet." This avoids the awkward "he/she" construction. In a sense this is not a debate that is relevant to the present commentary. It is like the meaningless argument of whether Homer wrote the *Odyssey* or Shakespeare wrote *Hamlet*. Even the fact that

> The book of Lamentations gains much of its power by fusing these two—the individual and the corporate—into a single sustained work of despair, humiliation, and—eventually—a kind of wild hope against hope, all sentiments that both men and women feel.

Lamentations may have been written a long time after the destruction of Jerusalem detracts not one whit from its spiritual power. It even enhances it. Like the *Iliad*, which was composed long after the fall of Troy, but whose deeds of courage and sacrifice still resonate, Lamentations is not time bound or event bound. It bemoans the tragedy that has fallen upon all classes and ages alike. It has become timeless.

2

The Poet of Divine Punishment

In order to get inside the world of Lamentations it is important to ask: Where is The Poet coming from? This is not easy to answer. At first sight it appears that this poet's historical and cultural heritage is in many ways quite different from ours. The Poet assumes what scholars call the "Deuteronomic" paradigm of God's relationship to his covenant people. According to that ancient code, Yahweh will bless and protect his people, but only so long as they faithfully fulfill their covenant obligations and dutifully obey all his precepts. This principle is most sharply stated in the famous *Parshat Bechukotai* in the book of Leviticus:

> If you follow My laws and faithfully observe My command-
> ments, I will grant your rains in their season, so that the earth
> shall yield its produce and the trees of the field their fruit. Your
> threshing shall overtake the vintage, and your vintage shall
> overtake the sowing; you shall eat your fill of bread and dwell
> securely in your land. . . .
>
> But if you do not obey Me and do not observe all these
> commandments, if you reject My laws and spurn My rules, so
> that you do not observe all My commandments and you break
> My covenant, I in turn will do this to you: I will wreak misery
> upon you—consumption and fever, which cause the eyes to
> pine and the body to languish; you shall sow your seed to no
> purpose, for your enemies shall eat it. I will set My face against
> you: you shall be routed by your enemies, and your foes shall
> dominate you. You shall flee though none pursues.

And if you do not obey Me, I will go on to discipline you sevenfold for your sins. (Lev. 26:3–5, 14–18 JPS [the translation often used in synagogue services])

The covenant is thus a tit-for-tat arrangement. God will stand by and bless his people, but only if they hold up their side of it. Therefore The Poet insists that, even in the midst of all the destruction piled upon Jerusalem, God was in the right. Speaking with the voice of the city, The Poet says:

> The LORD was in the right,
> for I rebelled against his command.
> (1:18 REB)

The first thing God did was to withdraw his protection of his people:

> In his fierce anger he hacked off
> the horn of Israel's pride;
> he withdrew his protecting hand
> at the approach of the enemy;
> he blazed in Jacob like flaming fire
> that rages far and wide.
> (2:3 REB)

God not only "withdrew his protecting hand" from his people, he actually actively entered into the punishment.

> In enmity he bent his bow;
> like an adversary he took his stand,
> and with his strong arm he slew
> all those who had been his delight.
> He poured out his fury like fire
> on the tent of the daughter of Zion.
>
> The Lord played an enemy's part
> and overwhelmed Israel,

overthrowing all their mansions
and laying their strongholds in ruins.
To the daughter of Judah he brought
unending sorrow.

(2:4–5 REB)

Think of The Poet of Lamentations as a poet of divine punishment. This is not a trivial league to belong to. Dante was also a poet of divine punishment. Also, while this pact of mutual responsibility with God may at first seem antiquated to many readers, it is not all that far from the religious mentality—whether conscious or unconscious—of many people today both in America and elsewhere. Any minister, priest, or rabbi can testify that when tragedy strikes an individual or a family—disease, an accident, a premature death—people more often than not will feel that God is punishing them and that therefore they must have done something wrong. When they articulate this feeling it is hard to persuade them that what has happened—cancer, a house fire, or an offspring who has "gone bad"—is not a divine punishment. Somehow or other the Deuteronomic construction of God punishing us by inflicting divine retribution has seeped deeply into the marrow of countless people.

> Somehow or other the Deuteronomic construction of God punishing us by inflicting divine retribution has seeped deeply into the marrow of countless people.

This mentality was particularly evident in many sermons preached in America just after 9/11. Desperate to find some reason for what appeared to be a senseless attack on America, some preachers seized upon the divine punishment motif. America had obviously done something that was immensely displeasing to God. The preachers differed on exactly what that was; for example, the Reverend Jerry Falwell famously blamed it on gays and feminists. But whatever the sin that was being punished, there was no doubt in the minds of many pulpiteers that God had brought it on. I monitored some of the many sermons preached during those turbulent days, but I was surprised not to find any that used Lamentations 2:5 (quoted above). It would have been easy to extrapolate "mansions" into "skyscrapers," and "strongholds" into the Pentagon. In this case I felt grateful that the self-described "Bible-faithful" preachers were not as familiar with the Bible as they might have been.

It is not only "religious" people who think and feel this way. There is a secular analog. One of the most curious but common ways that punishment motif functions is in the widespread conviction that particular diseases strike people in an organ or system in which they have been doing something questionable. This is true in the case of throat cancer and smoking or of excessive drinking and sclerosis of the liver. But the theory is taken to wild extremes. For much too long a time after the AIDS pandemic struck, some Christian preachers declared it was God's punishment on homosexuals. Of course, already then it was widely known that the HIV virus could be transmitted through hypodermic needles and blood transfusions, but that did not deter the zealots who interpreted illness as divine judgment. This cruel canard only began to slacken after it became clear that babies were being born with the HIV virus.

A somewhat more subtle but still invidious version of this theory is the deployment of illness as a metaphor. After her own diagnosis with cancer, from which she ultimately died, the American writer and critic Susan Sontag wrote a book in 1978 entitled *Illness as Metaphor* in which she launched a crusade against using sicknesses as metaphors for anything. Calling a group of people or a societal trend, for example, a "cancerous growth" injures those people who have the actual disease, which Sontag insisted was just that, a disease. Later Sontag revised and expanded the book, entitling it *Aids and Its Metaphors* (1988).

There is no basis in current Jewish or Christian biblical studies or theological ethics to interpret diseases as divine punishment. To do so seems to most of us today to be reprehensible. The residual tendency among some Christians to engage in this ugly polemic should be called sharply into question. But to understand the mentality that still moves people to interpret "bad things" as divine punishment, there is no better case study than Lamentations. Let us now take a step into the text itself.

The first word in the original Hebrew version of the book is *Ekah*

("How . . ."), an exclamation that conveys both stunned astonishment and an imponderable query. In the Hebrew Bible, Lamentations is called *Ekah* because of this first word, which appears in the first, second, and fourth chapters.

> How deserted lies the city,
>> once so full of people!
> How like a widow is she,
>> who once was great among the nations!
> She who was queen among the provinces
>> has now become a slave.
>
> (1:1 NIV)

The book contains only six chapters and is wedged into the Christian canon just after Jeremiah and before Ezekiel. Some English versions still title it "Lamentations of Jeremiah" because the old tradition, mentioned above, says it was written by the seventh-century prophet. The rabbis customarily called it *Qinot*, meaning "Elegies." Greek translations followed this usage and called it *Threnoi*, for which the Latin is *Threni*, "Laments."

The biblical book of Lamentations is neither the first nor the last lament in history. We have already mentioned the Greek classics. Researchers have unearthed earlier laments for cities in Sumer ravaged by war and for the dying god Tammuz. Clearly The Poet who composed Lamentations was not inventing a new form. In the Bible itself David sobs out his remorse about the loss of his son Absalom ("O my son! Absalom my son, my son Absalom! Would I had died instead of you," 2 Sam. 18:33 REB). And his lament over those lost in battle is one of the most eloquent chapters in the entire Bible:

> The beauty of Israel is slain upon thy high places: how are the mighty fallen! Tell it not in Gath, publish it not in the streets of Askelon; lest the daughters of the Philistines rejoice, lest the daughters of the uncircumcised triumph. . . .
>
> How are the mighty fallen, and the weapons of war perished! (2 Sam. 1:19, 20, 27 KJV)

The mothers of Bethlehem lament over the innocent children King Herod has slain in his desperate effort to kill the infant he fears may threaten his throne:

> In Ramah was there a voice heard, lamentation and weeping and great mourning, Rachel weeping for her children, and would not be comforted, because they are not. (Matt. 2:18 KJV)

Over the centuries people have crafted thousands of songs and poems for soldiers slaughtered in now nameless battles, for nameless dead children, and for lovers lost or stolen. The blues, one of the most precious creations of African Americans, carry this theme into the heart of American and, more recently, global life. Reading the biblical Lamentations inevitably brings to mind songs like "The St. James Infirmary Blues" with its lyric of a lover "stretched out on a long white table." The livid anger of Lamentations recalls all the war songs that describe the awful fate that will be visited on the enemy, and its shrieks conjure Allen Ginsberg's almost hysterical but strangely religious poem "Howl."

> I saw the best minds of my generation destroyed by madness,
>   starving hysterical naked,
> dragging themselves through the negro streets at dawn
>   looking for an angry fix,
> angelheaded hipsters burning for the ancient heavenly
>   connection to the starry dynamo in the machinery of
>   night,
> who poverty and tatters and hollow-eyed and high sat up
>   smoking in the supernatural darkness of cold-water flats
>   floating across the tops of cities contemplating jazz,
> who bared their brains to Heaven under the El and saw
>   Mohammedan angels staggering on tenement roofs
>   illuminated,
> who passed through universities with radiant eyes
>   hallucinating Arkansas and Blake-light tragedy among the
>   scholars of war.[6]

---

6. Allen Ginsberg, "Howl," *Collected Poems 1947-1997* (New York: HarperCollins, 2006), 134.

It is significant that Ginsberg not only stems from a Jewish family heritage but has written several poems drawing on his heritage, including his "Kaddish." Given the liturgical function of Lamentations, it is important to note that "Howl" was first composed as a performance piece for a coffeehouse in Berkeley, California. It was to be recited with musical accompaniment and was something like a secular liturgy. Maybe one way to read either "Howl" or Lamentations today would be to play a CD of sad screeching music in the background as it is read aloud. This would help recreate its original intended effect.

The theme of lamentation plays a significant role in Christian visual art. Painters and sculptors have depicted time and again scenes of the removal of Christ's body from the cross, the grieving of the disciples, and especially of Mary weeping over the body of her dead son, the pietà. It appears frequently in black spirituals and hymns. One has only to recall Bach's "O Sacred Head Now Wounded" or "Were You There When They Laid Him in the Tomb?" to be reminded of countless other musical laments.

No one escapes some encounter with tragedy, large or small, in the course of a life. There is a critical theological question at stake here: Does God suffer and lament? We will return to this issue in a later section.

3

Potholed Poetry

I have already noted that since Lamentations is a poem, it should be read as a poem. But it should also be mentioned that its versification is peculiar. Indeed, one of the most fascinating features of Lamentations is the meter of its Hebrew poetry. It is written in a form that has three significant words in the first line and two in the second. This is not just a comment on its style. It has to do with much more than mere packaging. The meter gives the poem what is sometimes called a "limping" quality. In Hebrew it can sound uneven, rutted, and bumpy, like a potholed road. When someone is hit by catastrophe they can easily lose balance, stumble, or collapse. The staggering meter turns out to be a nearly perfect medium for the content of the lament. The poem veers back and forth between despondency and—here and there—faith. In the midst of a desperate passage suddenly there flashes a tiny spark of hope, only to fade away quickly.

> He has made my teeth grind on gravel,
> and made me cower in ashes;
> my soul is bereft of peace;
> I have forgotten what happiness is;
> so I say, "Gone is my glory,
> and all that I had hoped for from the LORD."
> The thought of my affliction and my homelessness
> is wormwood and gall!
> My soul continually thinks of it
> and is bowed down within me.

> But this I call to mind,
> and therefore I have hope.
> (3:16–21)

Notice that in verse 18 the writer has lost all hope. But in verse 21 hope has returned. Consistency is not a feature of this poem, nor is it a quality of people in the grip of a heartbreaking situation. When a new confidence in God returns, as we shall see, it does not last long.

> The steadfast love of the LORD never ceases;
> his mercies never come to an end;
> they are new every morning;
> great is your faithfulness.
> (3:22–23)

Like its meter, Lamentations is disjointed, and like all human beings, The Poet is inconsistent—moods come and go. Kierkegaard once wrote gnomically that "suffering is precisely the consciousness of contradiction."[7] If he is right, then Lamentations is the perfect vehicle for a meditation on suffering. Contradictory sentiments erupt, disappear, and creep back in. The book leaves the reader confused, momentarily hopeful, then vaguely unfulfilled, but this is the way one usually feels in the grip of suffering.

Scholars, as they are wont, continue to argue about why the book is so full of clashing and incompatible sentiments, and some feel its placement may provide a clue. For example, Mark Leuchter contends that Jeremiah 26–45 represents an attempt to refute the theology of Ezekiel.[8] Whether or not this is true, it reminds us that the entire Bible is a cacophonous melee of voices stretching over many centuries and many genres. Those who claim there is a single "biblical theology" are just not paying attention. Many parts of the Bible in this way (though not in all ways) resemble a Zen koan. They are not intended merely to convey information but to stun the reader/

---

7. Soren Kierkegaard, *Concluding Unscientific Postscript to Philosophical Fragments*, vol. 1, ed. and trans. Howard Hong and Edna Hong (Princeton, NJ: Princeton University Press), 483.

8. Mark Leuchter, *The Polemics of Exile in Jeremiah 26–45* (New York: Cambridge University Press, 2008).

listener into a recognition. They generate cognitive dissonance, which pushes us toward newer thresholds of awareness. Lamentations is a superb example of this, but the parables of Jesus have a similar resonance. They are not morality tales like Aesop's Fables. Rather, they plop listeners into unfamiliar situations they might never otherwise encounter: the return home of a n'er-do-well son, or a carefully planned banquet no one shows up for. Like the parables, Lamentations is not for children.

Lamentations also projects no unified worldview, no coherent image of God. It does not depict what we "ought" to be like in the face of tragedy: noble, stoic, patient, long-suffering. It reflects what we really *are* like—miserable, enraged, confused, and vindictive. Life may be like a road, of course, but it often seems to be a road pitted with ruts and crevices, like the lurching poetry of this text.

Though its setting is the aftermath of the defeat and destruction of Jerusalem in 586 BCE by the Babylonians, Lamentations' searing evocations of disaster and agonized expressions of suffering, rage, and despair, and its occasional sparks of hope have transformed it into a poem for the ages. Indeed, many scholars believe it was written years, possibly even centuries, after 586. The book mentions no names and gives no historical details. If it were not for what else we know about ancient Hebrew history and Jerusalem, it would be impossible to know what the writer is talking about. But why is the book so devoid of historical specifics?

I think the reason it does not provide dates and place names is that to the suffering mind these are irrelevant. The victim does not want to dissipate any of your attention. She is saying, indeed screaming, "*Look* at me! *Listen* to me! *Pay attention* to me! To *me*." Thus The Poet calls out in anger to God:

> LORD, look and see:
> who is it you have thus tormented?
> (2:20 REB)

The answer to her demand arrives soon, not from God, but from her own depths.

> It is I whom he led away
> and left to walk
> in darkness, where no light is.
> Against me alone he has turned his hand,
> and so it is all day long.
>
> (3:2–3 REB)

As this verse shows, sometimes the sufferer blocks out what others are undergoing in an obsessive concentration on his/her own hurt. Yes, here The Poet almost seems to be babbling, but that is the way victims of catastrophe talk. It is this naked humanness of the poem that suggested the approach to the commentary that I have chosen. Instead of following a verse-by-verse course, I have located some of the major themes of Lamentations and discussed them in more depth, with reference to the theological issues they raise, issues like mourning, revenge, exile, war, torture, and the significance of suffering. The careful reader will find, however, that I have commented on nearly every verse, on some of them more than once in different contexts.

4

Acrostics and Rituals

Among classical and modern laments Lamentations displays some unique characteristics. There is one important feature of Lamentations as a poem that someone reading it in English will not notice. In the original Hebrew text, the first four of the elegies that constitute the book are acrostics, that is, the verses are arranged with the first letter of each verse appearing in alphabetical order. The English translations do not preserve this formal structure, but the question that arises in the mind of anyone who knows about this pattern is: why? Of course an acrostic ordering makes the poem easier to remember and recite, which is further evidence that it was originally intended for oral presentation. But is this the only reason? I do not think so. We must go on to ask, what is the religious and theological significance of the acrostic structure? Consider this graphic depiction of what mourning involves:

> See, O LORD, how distressed I am;
> my stomach churns;
> my heart is wrung within me,
> because I have been very rebellious.
> In the street the sword bereaves;
> in the house it is like death.
>
> (1:20)

> My eyes are spent with weeping;
> my stomach churns;

> my bile is poured out on the ground
> because of the destruction of my people,
> because infants and babies faint
> in the streets of the city.
>
> (2:11)

This inner roiling can cause loss of balance, staggering, and faint-ing, cogently mirrored in the lurching rhythm of the poetry. On the mental level this giddiness wipes out normal parameters of percep-tion and thinking. We can go blank or forget who we are or where we are. In individuals as well as in societies, grieving is viewed both as a necessity and as a danger. People can fall to pieces, and maybe they need to, at least for a time. But how long can either an individual or a society survive in such a condition?

Grief is wrenching and demanding. The sadness wells up from the entrails. It can shake one's whole body, churn the stomach, turn saliva sour, and freeze the limbs.

> [God] has forced me aside, thrown me down,
> and left me desolate.
> He has bent his bow
> and made me the target for his arrows;
> he has pierced right to my kidneys
> With shafts drawn from his quiver.
> . . . .
> He has given me my fill of bitter herbs
> and made me drink deep of wormwood.
> He has broken my teeth on gravel;
> racked with pain, I am fed on ashes.
>
> (3:11–13, 16–17 REB)

Grief shakes us to the core. It spews forth in moans, tears, and sometimes in whimpers. The heartfelt expression of grief, as anyone who has ever attended a funeral or wake in cultures in which it is not repressed knows, involves the whole body. Both in individuals and in societies, grieving is viewed as a necessity, but also as a danger. If

people can fall to pieces, so can a society, and no society can survive
for long in such a condition. Everything in the world looks foreboding and dangerous.

> This is why we are sick at heart;
> all this is why our eyes grow dim:
> Mount Zion is desolate
> and overrun with jackals.
>   (5:17–18 REB)

This is obviously a perilous state to remain in for very long. What
can be done? The stiff-upper-lip school views all but the most refined
and subdued expressions of grief as abnormal, even pathological.
"Straighten up" or "Pull yourself together" are the prescribed remedies. But trying to suffocate or bottle up grief only leads to more serious conditions. People are understandably afraid to give way to the
ocean of emotions they feel within them because that might cause
them to lose control of themselves. They put the cork on the bottle
and push it in tight. But the experience of history has demonstrated
that this is the wrong way to cope with grief. Psychotherapists have
turned out shelves of books about the damage people do to themselves when they do not permit themselves (or are not permitted) to
vent their distress.

In his famous treatment of mourning in *Mourning and Melancholia,* Freud shows how the process of grieving requires the piece-by-piece surrender of the connections we have had with the lost person.
He called this "the work of grieving," and anyone who have lived
through it knows it is hard work indeed. But this cutting of ties is
necessary in order to make room for the new affective bonds that we
must forge if we are to continue to live. What Freud, with his deep
antireligious bias, did not recognize, however, is that the traditional
mourning rituals facilitate exactly this gradual shedding and rebuilding process

For millennia, religions have sculpted responses to this enduring
human dilemma: rituals. This is where the acrostic structure of Lamentations comes in. Before people are willing to give way to their

emotions they want to feel safe. Rituals, in this case mourning rituals, provide that space. They allow the explosion but put limits on its destructive potential. The Jewish custom of "sitting shivah" is a good example. The word *shivah* means seven. When someone dies, family members stay at home and customarily sit on the floor. They do not cook. Friends bring food. They repeat traditional prayers. After seven days, however, the mourners are required to stand up, leave the house, and walk for a short time. Life goes on. They return to the world. They stroll around the block. One month later they engage in traditional prayers for the *sheloshim* (30 days of mourning). At every Sabbath service for a year they stand and pray the "mourner's kaddish." Then on the anniversary of the person's death, they mark it with the ritual of *yahrzeit*. After that they no longer pray the kaddish on the Sabbabth but on the yahrzeit each year. This old ritual pattern, dating from long before modern psychotherapy, facilitates passage through what psychologists recognize today as the emotional stages of mourning.

Other religions and traditions have similar rituals. The point they have in common is that they permit what scholars have called a "limbic" interval, a time when a certain emotional thrashing around can go on because the context in which it occurs is safe and familiar. Traditional Christian funeral rituals do the same. We know they are bounded spaces. They have a beginning and an ending. The eating and drinking, even boisterous conversation, that sometimes go on at the wake or at the reception after a funeral sometimes offend people. But they can be useful signals to everyone that life does go on. They are like the stroll around the block.

An acrostic is like a ritual. It is a pattern. It delineates a safe space/structure within which what might sound like excessive expressions of rage, despair, and anger can well up without wreaking permanent damage on the person or on the community. With an alphabetical acrostic there is a beginning and an end. You always know where you are, and therefore you can give yourself—and others—both space and permission to vent emotion.

5

When Is Mourning "Real"?

> The elders of Zion
> sit on the ground in silence;
> they have cast dust on their heads
> and put on sackcloth.
> The maidens of Jerusalem
> bow their heads to the ground.
>
> (2:10 REB)

Sitting in silence, piling dust on one's head, donning special garments, touching the head to the earth: what we see here is the description of a mourning rite. For many people with a modern or secular sensibility, of course, all ritual is suspect, and this includes rituals of mourning. Today many people tell friends that when they die they want "no weeping and wailing." They do not want a traditional funeral; they want a party, a "celebration" of their life. They want stories, humorous anecdotes, and lots of wine and good food. No black armbands or veils please, and no dirges. Keep the music light and innocuous.

Such sentiments are understandable. But they miss something important about the human reaction to death and deprivation. These losses evoke mixed feelings. They make people sad, so they need an acceptable way to express the sadness, sense of privation, and anger. But the survivors often harbor feelings of ambivalence about the deceased. When someone close dies they almost always feel a sharpened awareness of their own mortality. These are all powerful feelings that need to find an acceptable outlet. Sharing amusing yarns is something that surely belongs somewhere in a mourning ritual. But something else is needed as well.

The black and Creole people of New Orleans who invented jazz had a deeper insight. After the church ceremony, on the way to the cemetery they played sad, tender music. Then, after the body had been lowered into the grave, the prayers said, and the earth strewn on the coffin, they returned to town. But on the way back they beat out "Oh Didn't He Ramble!" with trumpets riffs, flatted fifths, and trap drum breaks. While listening to the cool improvisations of Miles Davis, the coloratura flights of John Coltrane, or the big band standards of Count Basie today, we should never forget that jazz was born out of this instinctively perceptive insight into what human beings need when loss strikes.

One of the problems the modern reader meets in trying to grasp the thrust of Lamentations is that it reflects the mourning rituals not just of ancient Jews but of traditional cultures in general. How such people mourn can be puzzling and upsetting to moderns. Screaming, howling, cutting garments, pouring dust over their heads! Such emotionally explicit behavior seems somehow uncivilized. But what is especially troublesome for many is that people in premodern societies often seem to be (and in fact are) crying on cue, and this means that their sadness cannot possibly be "real." Indeed, there are even professional mourners, usually women, who are called upon to lead the weeping even if they hardly know the deceased or the family. Are they just faking it? Do they really *feel* any grief? Modern people tend to believe that mourning should be heartfelt and spontaneous. It should not be put on or involve mere acting. This means among other things that the role of professional mourners becomes highly suspect. How could they actually be mourning if they are paid to cry?

Some years ago, Gail Holst-Warhaft, a professor of classics and comparative literature at Cornell, addressed this and other related questions in a book aptly titled *Cue for Passion*.[9] By examining traditional mourning rites, both as they continue to exist in some places and in classical sources, she argued persuasively that the expression

9. Gail Holst-Warhaft, *Cue for Passion* (Cambridge: Harvard University Press, 2000).

of grief need not be spontaneous to be genuine. From before birth until after death, people in ritual societies live lives that are delineated by rituals. They express their most authentic selves through and by means of those rituals. Rituals evoke, channel, and express real emotion.

Holst-Warhaft also explores another issue that bears directly on a contemporary reading of Lamentations: Having set aside age-old ways of mourning, how do people in the modern world cope with tragic loss? Using traditional mourning rituals as an instructive touchstone, she explores the ways sorrow is managed in our own times and how mourning can be drawn upon for social and political ends. Since ancient times political and religious authorities have been alert to the dangerously powerful effects of communal expressions of grief, even while they value mourning rites as a controlled outlet for emotion. But today grief is often seen as a psychological problem: the bereaved are encouraged to seek counseling or to take antidepressants. At the same time, we have witnessed some striking examples of the deployment of shared grief for political purposes. One instance is the unprecedented concentration on recovery of the remains of Americans killed in the Vietnam War. In Buenos Aires the Mothers of the Disappeared forged the passion of their grief into a political protest. Similarly the gay community in the United States, transformed by grief and rage, not only lobbied effectively for AIDS victims but channeled their emotions into fresh artistic expression.

One might argue that, in contrast to earlier cultures, modern society has largely abdicated its role in managing sorrow. But this is not true. In *Cue for Passion* and similar treatments we see that some communities, like those mentioned above, when moved by the intensity of their grief, have harnessed it to gain ground for what they consider worthwhile social objectives. Still, this does not answer our original question: how can mourning be real if it happens "on cue"?

Readers of Shakespeare might spot where the phrase "cue for passion" comes from. Toward the end of act 2 of *Hamlet*, the prince of Denmark, rankling with hatred for his uncle who has murdered his father and married his mother the queen, engages a traveling troupe of actors to present a play. He wants the skit to "catch the conscience of the king." In a sort of tryout the players present a scene from the fall of Troy in which Priam weeps for Queen Hecuba amid the flames of the defeated city. Later Hamlet muses that he himself must be some sort of "rogue and peasant slave" because he is unable to summon up the passion actually to kill the usurping king. His thinking reminds us that a play is something like a ritual. The words and actions are patterned. Any "naturalness" is expressed within the structure, which both elicits and delimits it. Hamlet wonders, how can an actor in a play weep real tears for a mere character in that play? He goes on:

> For Hecuba!
> What's Hecuba to him, or he to Hecuba,
> That he should weep for her? What would he do,
> Had he the motive and the cue for passion
> That I have? He would drown the stage with tears
> And cleave the general ear with horrid speech,
> Make mad the guilty and appal the free,
> Confound the ignorant, and amaze indeed
> The very faculties of eyes and ears.

Challenged by the sight of theatrical emotions to confront his own listlessness, Hamlet is pushed toward resolution. Here we witness two themes that plait their way through Lamentations: mourning and revenge.

> O, vengeance!
> Why, what an ass am I! This is most brave,
> That I, the son of a dear father murder'd
> Prompted to my revenge by heaven and hell,
> Must like a whore unpack my heart with words,
> And fall a-cursing, like a very drab,
> A scullion.

Hamlet is heaping abuse on himself because he believes that, even though he has genuine reason to weep and to hate, his feelings remain elusive, while this mere actor in a play sheds real tears. As it turns out, the play not only catches "the conscience of the king," it also focuses Hamlet's passion. Although it takes him two more acts to kill his father's assassin, the drama of Priam and Hecuba has served its purpose.

Human emotions, including sorrow, may seem at first to belong to an individual. They seem internal. But emotions are actually social. We mourn with and for other people. Those who lead ritual mourning know this. They weep because they are part of the larger community of mourning. True, sometimes in the modern world this sense of relatedness can become suspect. How close to her were those thousands of people who piled up floral tributes at Buckingham Palace for Princess Diana? How much of it was "real"? How much of it was a fad hyped by the media? The same might be asked about the wave of mourning that erupted after the death of Michael Jackson. But when someone dies in a car or plane crash, even though people today may consciously eschew ritual, they stack up flowers, notes, souvenirs, and teddy bears at the site. Despite our protestation, we are still ritual animals, and because we sometimes mourn "on cue," this does not mean that our mourning is unreal. We do not easily outgrow the ritual dimension of our being.

We probably never will. We have much more in common with The Poet of Lamentations than first meets the eye. When we bear that in mind, the book becomes much more accessible.

> Despite our protestation, we are still ritual animals, and because we sometimes mourn "on cue," this does not mean that our mourning is unreal. We do not easily outgrow the ritual dimension of our being.

PART 2

THEOLOGICAL ISSUES

When we move into the core theological issues of Lamentations, we notice that three require our attention. The first is what I call "the absence of God." The second is the spiritual significance of memory. The third is the persistent problem of evil, what theologians refer to as "theodicy."

6

The Absence of God

The LORD abandoned me to my sins,
and in their grip I could not stand.
(1:14 REB)

What do I do when God abandons me? This question is one that has a long and continuous history in the idiom of the Bible. Jesus croaks it out on Golgotha while dying on the cross, and his words are so charged that translators preserve the original Aramaic: "*Eli, Eli, lema sabachthani,*" before they translate it, "My God, my God, why have you forsaken me?" (Matt. 27:46). The deepest sorrow The Poet of Lamentations faces is that God is gone, or seems to be gone. She feels abandoned.

This wrenching sense of God's absence was once only the province of the most daring of saints, like John of the Cross, or mystics, like the anonymous writer of *The Cloud of Unknowing.*[10] But what was once the experience of a spiritually privileged few has in modern times become much more general, if in a somewhat different key. The saints felt the absence of God as a heart-stopping terror. Today many people sense God's absence with a shrug of regret or indifference.

The "dark night of the soul" robbed John of the Cross of his

> The saints felt the absence of God as a heart-stopping terror. Today many people sense God's absence with a shrug of regret or indifference.

---

10. See the edition by Halcyon Backhouse (London: Hodder & Stoughton, 1985).

sleep. It bothers today's casual atheist or agnostic only occasionally. He or she does not agonize over it.

Still, what both Lamentations and the writings of John of the Cross reveal is that an acutely felt awareness of the absence of God can itself be a religious experience. There is something awe-full about it, in the sense of awe inspiring. For a significant number of people the question today is not *whether* one experiences the absence of God, but what one does in response to that experience. Like staring at the sun or contemplating one's own death, it is not an experience that invites one to stay with it for long. Consequently, for many people, the typical response is to pursue distraction. The result is the proliferation of instant communication devices. A recent study discovered one teenage girl who sends 2,700 text messages a month. But this is only one symptom of a culture-wide attention deficit disorder.

Still, as the twentieth century fades and the twenty-first rushes on, something else is happening. For more and more people the absence of God has sharpened into an awareness that something—it is not clear what—is missing from their lives. Surveys in the United States do not reveal any substantial growth in the number of atheists. They remain a small minority. But the surveys do reveal a steady growth in the number of people who declare that they are "spiritual but not religious." This self-designation means different things to different people. For most it implies that they have not forsaken some hope for a relationship to God, transcendence, or mystery. But they do not trust the institutional scaffolding or doctrinal wrapping in which the religious institutions they are familiar with teach or preach about this mystery. They do not want to accept something on someone else's authority, whether the authority is wearing a clerical collar or a white lab coat. They are "seekers." They want to find out for themselves, to test things out in the petri dishes of their own lives. The writer of Lamentations would understand them. She does not trust the sanctified representatives of her religion, and if there had been scientists in that time she would not have trusted them either:

> there is no direction from priests,
> and her prophets have received
> no vision from the LORD.
>> (2:9 REB)

One of the most startling aspects of this often-overlooked biblical book is that the religious experience it describes replicates in an almost uncanny way the experience of both modern and postmodern humanity. For The Poet the awareness of God's remoteness is made more vivid by the stabbing recognition that it was not always this way.

> Why do you always forget us?
>> Why do you forsake us so long?
> Restore us to yourself, O LORD,
>> that we may return;
>> renew our days as of old
> unless you have utterly rejected us
>> and are angry with us beyond measure.
>> (5:20–22 NIV)

The big question here is, Has God rejected us, or have we rejected God?

I can still remember the shock I felt when I picked up *Time*'s April 8, 1966, edition and saw on its cover: "Is God Dead?" The article was an oversimplified and even sensationalized story about four then-current Protestant theologians, William Hamilton, Paul van Buren, Gabriel Vahanian, and Thomas Altizer. The four worked in very disparate ways. Hamilton derived much of his perspective from Dietrich Bonhoeffer's suggestion of a "religionless Christianity."[11] Van Buren was influenced by analytic philosophy and by the dialectical theology of Karl Barth. Vahanian was steeped in European cultural history and linguistic studies but was also influenced by Barth. Altizer

---

11. Dietrich Bonhoeffer, *Letters and Papers from Prison,* ed. Eberhard Bethge, enlarged ed. (New York: Macmillan, 1972), especially 280–82.

came to his position from a very different direction. A student of
Asian religions, he was fascinated by the emphasis on "nothingness"
in Buddhism and saw in it a connection to Western nihilism. All four
found in Nietzsche's announcement of the death (or rather murder)
of God in *Thus Spake Zarathustra* a powerful metaphor that seemed
to bring their disparate thoughts into focus.[12] The so-called death of
God movement these men represented made a considerable splash
for a time. But within a couple years it had faded away and was often
even dismissed as a fad.

But rightly understood this movement was not just a vogue.
What these thinkers were attempting to do was to respond to something that, at that time at least, appeared to be an indisputable fact.
Whereas for centuries of Western history the reality of God had
seemed to be a commonplace, increasingly this was no longer the
case. In his massive study, *A Secular Age*, the Canadian philosopher
Charles Taylor argues that our present spiritual situation is "historical."[13] What he means is that we locate ourselves today as having
"overcome a previous condition." This means that our past is contained within our present condition and that we do not understand
ourselves or our present world unless we are clear about where we
came from.

Taylor's insight is critical not just for understanding The Poet of
Lamentations but for understanding our present spiritual situation,
which he calls a "predicament." Who we are today spiritually does
define itself in part by who we once were, and the meaning of that
self-definition varies radically for different people. For some we are
just leaving behind a past of superstition and obscurantism, if not
fast enough. For others we are losing an invaluable heritage, and all
too quickly. Those of us who try to make the message of the Bible
available today must therefore talk to (at least) these two highly disparate audiences. There is also an emerging third public, constituted
in part by the "spiritual but not religious" people mentioned above.

An important distinction must be drawn between "atheism" on
the one hand and the "death" or "absence" of God on the other. For

---

12. See the collection of Nietzsche's writings in *The Philosophy of Nietzsche,* trans. Thomas
    Common et al. (New York: Modern Library, 1937).
13. Charles Taylor, *A Secular Age* (Cambridge: Harvard University Press, 2007).

these theologians, although none of them expressed it explicitly, the late twentieth century was very much like the mood of The Poet of Lamentations. There had once been a God, or at least the widespread belief in God. Now, as The Poet of that book puts it:

> you have covered yourself with a cloud
> beyond reach of our prayers.
> (3:44 REB)

The stark difference between atheism and the loss or absence of God is that in atheism there is no sense of loss. It elicits a shrug or a smile or sometimes enormous anger against all theists. Even the somewhat hyperbolic phrase "death of God" suggests that there was once something that is now missing. How one responds to that empty space is, of course, the daunting question. For Nietzsche it was a kind of liberation, although even for him the "God" who had been killed was the "God" of Western, bourgeois piety. For others the emptiness was something that needed to be affirmed and embraced. For Altizer at least it meant accepting the utter self-emptying (*kenosis*) of God with all its radical implications.[14]

While the brief "death of God" theology wave was cresting, some critics grouped me as one of the writers in this school (if it can be called a "school"). But I never was. I wrote the final chapter of *The Secular City* as a critique of the "death of God" theology.[15] Although I appreciated what these theologians were trying to say, I thought they did not sufficiently grasp how much the "God" whose death they spoke of was a provincial, Western construction, an *idea* of God that was a product of their own somewhat narrow intellectual milieu.

Ironically, at the time they were writing, another powerful view of God was also coming to birth. Among Christians in what was then called the "Third World," now more commonly referred to as the "Global South," an understanding of God as the judge of Western imperial religiosity was coming to birth. The various liberation

14. See John Caputo and Gianni Vattimo, *After the Death of God*, ed. Jeffrey W. Robbins (New York: Columbia University Press, 2007), 66–70 passim.

15. Harvey Cox, *The Secular City: Secularization and Urbanization in Theological Perspective* (New York: Macmillan, 1965), 241–69.

theologies, especially those that sprang up in Latin America, were saying to the death-of-God theologians, "So your God is dead! Well, good riddance. The God we trust is the vindicator of the poor, the one who casts down the mighty from their thrones and raises those of low degree." This theology of liberation not only seemed more biblical but resonated strongly with millions of destitute and struggling people outside the charmed circle of European and American illuminati.

In any case, although the death-of-God thinking seemed to sink out of sight for a few decades, it has recently made a bold new appearance, albeit under different auspices and with a different outcome. Now the discussion has been taken up by a congeries of younger philosophers and theologians. Some seem to be doing both these disciplines or cultivating the space in between them. Two of the key thinkers in this group are the American John Caputo and the Italian Gianni Vattimo.[16] Caputo places himself in the "spiritual predicament" Charles Taylor describes, but he refuses to accept the either/or of atheism or traditional theism. He does not see our postmodern era as either a brave new world of human emancipation (there are still too many forms of bondage around us) or as a plunge into degeneration. Like Vattimo he rejects the words *desecularization* or *resacralization* because they seem merely to be reversing previous patterns.

With reference to current debates between atheists and theists, Caputo draws on his Catholic background. He recalls that Thomas Aquinas taught that God cannot be described either as "existing" or "not existing" since God transcends both these human categories. Caputo also insists on a sharp distinction between Christendom and Christianity, the first being a territorial designation from what was indeed another era, the second being the name of a movement that is still very much on the move. He also cites favorably Søren Kierkegaard's trenchant *Attack upon "Christendom"* and Bonhoeffer's "religionless Christianity" for a "world come of age," which the German pastor and martyr eludes to cryptically in *Letters and Papers*

---

16. For an excellent description and analysis of this trend in philosophy and theology see Richard Kearney, *Anatheism: Returning to God after God* (New York: Columbia University Press, 2010).

from Prison.[17] Caputo believes that with the death of Christendom, Christianity can now shed much of the institutional and doctrinal baggage it carried for centuries, and that it has a vital message to demonstrate and to preach in this new "spiritual situation." He describes this situation as one in which growing numbers of people have lost confidence in both what he calls "scientific positivism" and "transcendent authority." His analysis may sound overly intellectual to some, but he puts his finger on a sentiment that is also widespread among young people today. It was hit upon well in "If I Ever Lose My Faith in You," a song made popular almost two decades ago by Sting, "I lost my faith in science and progress . . . I lost my belief in the holy church."

This is a kind of pop postmodernism, but Caputo would agree. He believes postmodernism has cut the ground from under both traditional theism and atheism since the attacks on God by the deconstructionists critics have now boomeranged back on those critics. It has also undermined the serene confidence some modern people once had in the capacity of science to fashion a brave new world. The postmodern sword cuts many ways. What we see now he says, in a gnomic phrase, is something like "the death of the death of God."

Caputo also believes that Christians have nothing to fear from this seemingly radical, even blasphemous language. The God of the Christian gospel is the one who laid aside his divinity to become man and experience a human death. This is the core of Paul's *kenosis* passage in Philippians 2. God's power, Caputo asserts, echoing Paul again, is a weakness that is stronger than the strength of any human. God's sovereignty is not a matter of grandiose omnipotence but of self-emptying love.

I cannot help feeling that The Poet of Lamentations might find some kinship with these twenty-first-century thinkers. Otherwise how could he or she have combined in a few short verses at the end of the book phrases like, "Lord, your reign is for ever, your throne endures from age to age" with "Why do you forget us?" and "you have utterly rejected us" (5:19, 20, 22 REB)? Could it be that there is a strange kinship between an intense awareness of the absence of God and an intense appreciation of God's reality?

17. Søren Kierkegaard, *Attack upon "Christendom,"* trans. Walter Lowrie (Princeton: Princeton University Press, 1944); Bonhoeffer, *Letters and Papers.*

7

God: From Absent to Assailant

Sometimes the sense of God's absence curdles into a white hot anger against God. It pictures God not as absent but as hostile and malevolent. This hate seems to sound in Lamentations.

> It was I whom [God] led away
> and left to walk
> in darkness, where no light is.
> Against me alone he has turned his hand,
> and so it is all day long.
>
> He has wasted away my flesh and my skin
> and broken my bones;
> he has built up as walls around me
> bitterness and hardship;
> he has cast me into a place of darkness
> like those long dead.
>
> He has hemmed me in so that I cannot escape;
> he has weighed me down with fetters.
> Even when I cry out and plead for help
> he rejects my prayer.
>
> (3:2–8 REB)

This is as dark a picture of God as one can find anywhere in the Bible. Here The Poet sees God (and the Hebrew for "see" means also feel and experience) as an assailant who bludgeons people with "the rod of the wrath of the LORD" (v. 1). The victim feels assaulted but also penned up, constricted, unable to move. This is a kind of claustrophobia often present in deep depression. It seems impossible to stir, as though one were having a nightmare or were chained down. It is dark, and The Poet feels as though she is already buried in Sheol, dead and forgotten. Worst of all, when The Poet somehow summons the strength to call out to God, God rejects the prayer.

This cluster of feelings is not quite the same as that of the modern person who is not even able to shake a fist at God or to cry out against God. The modern experience is rather one of sheer emptiness. God is not hostile or cruel, brutal or ruthless. God is just not there. Only a shadow remains, sometimes not even that. Who can summon the energy to yell out into a void?

The experience of the absence or withdrawal of God is a common one today. Is it something to which we should respond? Or do we just ignore it? Or do we just wait? Spiritually insightful people are of a different mind on these questions. For some of the most sensitive, however, the absence of God need not be the occasion for giving up on faith, or even on theology. For some our bleak era calls for patience. Simone Weil (1909–1943), who struggled with faith and doubt throughout her short life, called it "waiting for God." For her it was a long and harrowing wait. One day she wrote in her notebooks, "If we love God, even though we think he doesn't exist, he will make his existence manifest."[18]

For other contemporary saints, our parched era can become the occasion for purgation, transformation, and renewal. Paul Ricoeur interprets Bonhoeffer's reflections from his prison cell as:

> Ours is without doubt the time when the whole of human beings is connected to God by his silence and his absence. . . . If I assume all of this modern culture, and live—if I dare to say—out of the absence of God, then I can hear the word "God is dead" not as a triumphant thesis of atheism—because I will say that the word "God is dead" has nothing to do with

---

18. *The Notebooks of Simone Weil*, trans. Arthur Wills, 2 vols. (New York: Putnam, 1956), 2:583, quoted in David McLennan, *Utopian Pessimist: The Life and Thought of Simone Weil* (New York: Poseidon, 1980), 191.

the word "God does not exist"—but as the modern expression, on the scale of an entire culture, of what the mystics had called "the night of understanding." . . . "God is dead" is not the same thing as "God does not exist." It is even the total opposite. This means to say: the God of religion, of metaphysics and subjectivity is dead; the place is vacant for the preaching of the cross and for the God of Jesus Christ.[19]

Ricoeur has retrieved this startling insight from one of our most admired Christian martyrs. But Bonhoeffer was prescient. Though faced with a certain death on the gallows at the Flossenburg concentration camp, where he was hanged on April 9, 1945, he could still peer with astonishing acumen into the future. As I have mentioned elsewhere, he recognized that the profoundly purgative experience that had once been the privileged experience of the mystics such as Julian of Norwich, Meister Eckhart, and John of the Cross was now becoming one that the entire culture was passing into.

Bonhoeffer's words are even more telling when we contrast them with some other Christian martyrs, who faced the teeth of lions in the Circus Maximus or were tied to a pillar of flaming faggots or were slowly starved in the gulag. Most of these turned their thoughts to the next world. Not so for Bonhoeffer. He did not fear death. But the closer he came to the gallows, the more Bonhoeffer celebrated life in the world. Within weeks of his execution he wrote:

> I have come to understand more and more the profound this-worldliness of Christianity. The Christian is a not a *homo relogiosus*, but simply a man, as Jesus was a man. . . . I don't mean the shallow and banal this-worldliness of the enlightened, the busy, the comfortable, or the lascivious, but the profound this-worldliness, characterized by discipline and constant knowledge of death and resurrection. . . . It is only by living completely in this world that one learns to have faith. . . . By this-worldliness I mean living unreservedly in life's duties, problems, successes, experiences and perplexities. In so doing

---

19. Paul Ricoeur, "The Non-religious Interpretation of Christianity in Bonhoeffer," in *Bonhoeffer and Continental Thought: Cruciform Philosophy*, ed. Brian Gregor and Jens Zimmermann (Bloomington: Indiana University Press, 2009), 165.

> we throw ourselves completely into the arms of God, taking seriously, not our own sufferings, but those of God in the world—watching with Christ in Gethsemane.[20]

Is it fair to compare Bonhoeffer's personal suffering, which he does not want to dwell on, with the suffering of The Poet of Lamentations? There are real similarities. Bonhoeffer had to be separated from his vivacious young fiancée, Maria von Wedemeyer (whom he had met in his confirmation class), but in prison he realized they would never marry. Like some of the people of whom The Poet writes, he himself had been snatched away from a life of intellectual adventure and material privilege by the National Socialist seizure of power. All his professional plans were dashed. The July 20 plot to assassinate the führer by planting a bomb in his field headquarters behind the front, with which Bonhoeffer had conspired, had failed. By the time he wrote the lines quoted above, many of his co-conspirators had already been arrested and tortured. Like The Poet, he had witnessed fathomless devastation. While he was imprisoned in Berlin in the military stockade at Tegel, he could hear the din of the bombs dropped by the Royal Air Force and the American Air Force, and he could look through the bars in any direction and see his hometown being reduced to smoldering rubble. He knew people were dying by the tens of thousands. While he was being transported south in a wood-burning truck with some other members of the foiled plot to kill Hitler, he could see streams of desperate refugees choking the roads. Yet he never became morose, never seems to have stooped to self-pity.

Was he just trying to put on a brave face to his friend Eberhard Bethge, to whom he wrote those precious smuggled letters? How did he respond when the Gestapo guards actually opened the cell door to conduct him to his own cross and he became a "dead man walking"? Did he falter? The last glimpse we have of him is through the eyes of an English prisoner, Payne Best, who maintains that Bonhoeffer sustained his dignified bearing even as he stepped out of the

---

20. Bonhoeffer, *Letters and Papers from Prison*, 369–70.

cell. Had he in fact found a source of strength in the midst of the chaos of national defeat and personal death?

In any case, Bonhoeffer's affirmation of the reality of God echoes the refusal of The Poet of Lamentations to give up on God, despite a persistent temptation to do so. Admittedly The Poet's affirmation is episodic and inconsistent. Nonetheless here and there it shines like a diamond in the ashes.

> Bonhoeffer's affirmation of the reality of God echoes the refusal of The Poet of Lamentations to give up on God, despite a persistent temptation to do so.

Yet this I call to mind
    and therefore I have hope:
Because of the LORD's great love we are not consumed,
    for his compassions never fail.
They are new every morning;
    great is your faithfulness.
I say to myself, "The LORD is my portion;
    therefore I will wait for him."
The LORD is good to those whose hope is in him,
    to the one who seeks him;
it is good to wait quietly
    for the salvation of the LORD.

                                    (3:21–26 NIV)

Like Bonhoeffer, The Poet somehow saw, at least at times, that deprivation and defeat, far from destroying faith, can even be its prerequisite.

It is good for a man to bear the yoke
    while he is young.
                (3:27 NIV)

Bonhoeffer writes that in Tegel prison he had to learn how to live with solitude. With only severely limited visits from his family and with restricted contact even with other prisoners, he sat for long hours alone in his cell. One of his recent biographers, Ferdinand Schlingensiepen, believes that Bonhoeffer's visits to the Benedictine monastery at Ettal, where he lived for short times in a monk's cell, helped prepare him to appreciate solitude.[21]

> Let him sit alone in silence,
>   for the LORD has laid it on him.
> Let him bury his face in the dust—
>   there may yet be hope.
> Let him offer his cheek to one who would strike him,
>   and let him be filled with disgrace.
> For men are not cast off
>   by the Lord forever.
> Though he brings grief, he will show compassion,
>   so great is his unfailing love.
> For he does not willingly bring affliction
>   or grief to the children of men.
>   (3:28–33 NIV)

The most remarkable feature about this shift in sentiment is that The Poet now begins to consider not only her own suffering but that which is inflicted on other innocent people. She begins to decry tyrants who deny people's rights and those who mistreat the incarcerated.

> To crush underfoot
>   all prisoners in the land,
> to deny a man his rights
>   before the Most High,
> to deprive a man of justice—
>   would not the Lord see such things?
>   (3:34–36 NIV)

Granted, neither Dietrich Bonhoeffer nor The Poet of Lamentations provides easily accessible reading for people whose lives are

21. See Ferdinand Schlingensiepen, *Dietrich Bonhoeffer 1906–1945: Martyr, Thinker, Man of Resistance*, trans. Isabel Best (London: T. & T. Clark, 2010).

cushioned by comfort and freedom. But it is important to remember that neither comfort nor freedom characterizes the lives of countless millions of people around the world. We read them both, however, because we recognize that we all belong to the same body, that pain in one organ causes pain in all the others. We realize, in the words of John Donne, that we need not ask "for whom the bell tolls," because we know at some level that it always "tolls for thee." Our calling, as Bonhoeffer envisioned it, was to plunge into the life of this world and there to "share the suffering of God."

Bonhoeffer died at thirty-nine, before he could develop the hints he throws out in his letters about what he called "living before God as though God did not exist" or releasing the Christian gospel from its "religious outer garments." But during the same war another prisoner of the Germans thought along some of the same lines, but unlike Bonhoeffer, the French Protestant philosopher Paul Ricoeur, of whom we have already spoken, did survive.

Ricoeur knew from his own wartime imprisonment that there would be no way to go back to a secure faith without passing through a long dark night. Now nothing could be taken for granted. Unlike Bonhoeffer, however, Ricoeur had steeped himself in the atheistic and antireligious writings of his century. He not only read Nietzsche and Freud, who in their different ways had declared that God was dead, but he also believed they had rendered a positive service to Christianity. In a justly famous essay titled "Religion, Atheism, and Faith," Ricoeur asks about the religious significance of atheism.[22] To the surprise of many of his friends and colleagues, he insisted not only that these two atheists should be appreciated by Christians but that their thinking had to be incorporated into any Christianity that could pass through the crucible of the present age. He was sure, like Bonhoeffer, that we were headed into a "post-religious" age that would demand radical changes in the church and theology. His thoughts in this essay about the possibility of a "post-theistic faith" were careful and tentative, but he continued to develop them in later writings.

22. Paul Ricoeur, "Religion, Atheism, and Faith," in Alasdair MacIntyre and Paul Ricoeur, *The Religious Significance of Atheism* (New York: Columbia University Press, 1969), 58–98; repr. in a new translation by Charles Freilich in Paul Ricoeur, *The Conflict of Interpretations: Essays in Hermeneutics,* ed. Don Ihde (London: Continuum, 2004), 436–63.

Two particular features of the "religious" form Christianity had assumed historically Ricoeur said needed to be challenged. He called them "taboo" and "escape." The first is a syndrome that dates back to the dawn of religiosity in human beings: the fear of divine punishment and therefore the need to mollify and expiate the gods or God. His observation is confirmed by the presence of sacrificial cults in nearly all religions. The second element, "escape," points to the timeless human yearning for a strong protector, a powerful father-king figure who can shield us from the snares and pitfalls of life. If Christianity is to speak to the world after Freud and Nietzsche, Ricoeur argued, it must leave behind its dependence on the dread of punishment and craving for protection. For Ricoeur, the atheists had done Christianity a service by exposing these destructive elements, which are not essential to it but, on the contrary, contradict its core message. That central Christian message is about a God who sheds his power and becomes human, and about a Christ who not only breaks religious and societal taboos but is not delivered by a deus ex machina from torture and death.

Ricoeur appreciated the atheists, but he suggested they had not gone far enough. They were stuck in a negative mode. They had done the necessary work of demolition, but how and when could the reconstruction begin? Which God, exactly, had they declared dead? His answer is that they had administered the last rites to a "God" who is the product of human wishful thinking, a "God" who was the projection of images of kings and emperors raised to the ultimate level, lawgivers and protectors on a cosmic scale. This "God" was thus a phantasm concocted because of human infantilism. But as Bonhoeffer had said, we were now entering a "world come of age." Ricoeur added that from now on no moral life can be based on "submission to commandments or to an alien or supreme will, even if this will were represented as divine."[23] If the God who is dead is the god of omnipotence, the emperor of the cosmos, and the manager of the universe, then, Ricoeur said, we are well rid of him.

Where, then, do we go from here? Ricoeur modestly declined to go into any detail about this. He thought we needed to go back to

23. Ricoeur, *The Conflict of Interpretations*, 443.

the early origins of both Christianity and Judaism. He pointed out that the exodus, which is a festival of freedom, happened before the giving of the Law. The God of Jesus is not a punisher but one who pours infinite love into his world. And he insisted that the resurrection and ascension of Christ were not about his leaving this world, but about a new and life-giving way he would be in and with the world, not restricted in time and space. Still, moving Christianity in this direction, he argued, could not be the job of theologians or philosophers. It can only be done by people willing to enact this next stage of Christian existence.[24]

One must say today that both Bonhoeffer and Ricoeur may have been premature in their speculations about a "post-religious" age. Predictions about the decline and disappearance of religion, made by them and others during their lifetimes, have not proven true. But even as revivals, fundamentalisms, and new mutations of spirituality spread around the world, it is hard to escape the feeling that both Bonhoeffer and Ricoeur will be seen to be right in the long run. Religion as we have known it and the "Big Daddy" God whose function is to punish and protect will continue to hold on as long as some people live in fear of divine wrath and need an omnipotent security guard, but such a "God," and the religion that enthrones him, will eventually decline in significance.

Here is a key to why we still need Lamentations today. Does it not profile exactly the God both Ricoeur and Bonhoeffer insist we need to outgrow? I think the answer is that *we can only outgrow that protector/punisher God by coming to grips with just how much he has become a part of us.* As the psychoanalysts teach us, we can only outgrow our parents when we fearlessly confront how deeply they are lodged within our psyches, how often we think and act in response to them without even knowing it. The best way, maybe the only useful way, to read Lamentations is to identify with The Poet and to let her rage and her wild hope become our own. Then, and only then, are we ready to open ourselves to the forgiving and loving God that The Poet hopes is still there and will assert himself once again. There is no shortcut. Lamentations, despite its ruthless portrait of God, is in the biblical canon because in their wisdom the rabbis, and later the church fathers, somehow knew we needed it. We still do.

---

24. Quoted from Kearney in *Anatheism,* 73. I have relied on Kearney's excellent discussion of Ricoeur in this book.

8

Memory and Lament: The Presence of the Past

Remember, LORD, what has befallen us;
look, and see how we are scorned.

(5:1 REB)

The second key theological issue of Lamentations is memory. As human beings we live in history, both our individual life trajectory and the annals of our people. The way the 2,500-year-old Lamentations is used in today's Jewish community provides a valuable example. Consider this: a dozen elderly men sit in a small room in a town in upstate New York on a warm day in late July. They all wear *kippahs* (Jewish prayer caps). A young rabbi stands with his back to them reading a text in Hebrew. He bows now and then as his voice rises and falls. The old men pray along with him. In the middle of the room to the left of the men stands a folding screen. On the other side of it a half dozen women listen quietly. It is the Jewish holiday of *Tishah b'Ab* (the ninth day of the Jewish month of Ab), and they are lamenting the destruction of the temple in Jerusalem, which occurred in 586 BCE. The text they are reading, and through which they are praying, is Lamentations.

But why do Jews still mourn the loss and destruction of Jerusalem? After all, it was lost to the Babylonians under Nebuchadrezzar fully 2,500 years ago. Then it was captured by the Romans and razed again in 70 CE. Why the tears today, millennia later, especially since in 1967 it was taken by Israel from Jordan and is now under Israeli control? Moreover, a photograph taken of the paratroops who had stormed into the area and then stood in a clump at the Western Wall with their faces wrapped in astonishment and joy has become one of the iconic pictures of the twentieth century. So why mourn?

Rabbi David Hartman asked himself this question in 1967 when he returned from Israel to the synagogue he served in Canada in time for Tishah b'Ab and found his congregants seated on the floor lamenting the loss of a city that had now been regained. Why? Reflecting on this seemingly contradictory experience eventually taught the rabbi a profound lesson. First, he realized that the fall of the city in 587 BCE was both unprecedented and unexpected. How could God, whose temple stood in its midst, allow this humiliating catastrophe to happen? Why? Also, to the victims, the loss seemed final and irretrievable. It was, in a sense, the end of history, or so it seemed.

But the grating juxtaposition of the reconquest of Jerusalem in 1967 and the congregation's wailing over its loss taught Rabbi Hartman something else. It made him realize that every loss that overtakes us in life brings up the stabbing memory of previous losses. We feel the old pain anew. The death of someone we love recalls previous deaths. Setbacks and losses echo previous defeats. Old wounds are reopened. The griefs and losses of our lives never leave us completely. They wait to pounce.

In his surrealistic novel *The Crying of Lot 47*, Robert Pynchon describes his anti-heroine Oedipa racing through the confusing and fragmented world of Southern California on an errand she often loses sight of. The novel conjures a graphic portrait of the zany disjointedness of much of postmodern life. Like the daughter of Zion in Lamentations, Oedipa's worldview borders on the paranoid. She believes people are mocking her, tormenting her, and treating her shamefully. But small epiphanies break through. In one memorable scene Oedipa bursts into tears in front of a statue that moves her. Then, in keeping with his tragicomic sensibility, Pynchon writes that Oedipa cries into bubble sunglasses, so that any other subsequent tears mix with these, and she sees the whole world through them.

Lamentations is like those sunglasses. It is not just about the sacking and pillaging of Jerusalem. It is about catastrophes, all catastrophes, personal and collective. But more importantly, it is about how we respond to them at both the surface and the subterranean levels of our being.

The twentieth-century rabbi and scholar Abraham Joshua Heschel once wrote that "faith is memory."[25] Memory must of necessity be selective. Otherwise we would suffer like the luckless character in one of Luis Borges's short stories, *Funes el Memorioso*. This hapless hero, due to a riding accident, was unable to forget anything. Try as he would his mind constantly paraded before him everything he had ever seen, heard, or thought, even the memories of his previous vain efforts to forget. He eventually went mad.

> Lamentations is like those sunglasses. It is not just about the sacking and pillaging of Jerusalem. It is about catastrophes, all catastrophes, personal and collective. But more importantly, it is about how we respond to them at both the surface and the subterranean levels of our being.

But, given that we cannot remember everything, what do we remember and why? What is the theological, religious, and spiritual significance of memory?

By far the most significant scholarly work on this issue is Yosef Hayim Yerushalmi's masterful *Zakhor: Jewish History and Jewish Memory*.[26] The author traces the idea of memory in the biblical tradition back to God's commands to the Jews that they should remember and not forget his saving action in their history.

One exemplary passage can be found in Deuteronomy:

> And it shall be, when the LORD thy God shall have brought thee into the land which he sware unto thy fathers, to Abraham, to Isaac, and to Jacob, to give thee great and goodly cities, which thou buildest not, and houses full of all good things, which thou filledst not, and wells digged, which thou diggedst not, vineyards and olive trees, which thou plantedst not; when thou shalt have eaten and be full; Then beware lest thou forget

25. Abraham Joshua Heschel, *Moral Grandeur and Spiritual Audacity: Essays,* ed. Susannah Heschel (New York: Farrar, Straus and Giroux, 1997), 334.
26. Yosef Hayim Yerushalmi, *Zakhor: Jewish History and Jewish Memory* (Seattle: University of Washington Press, 1996).

the LORD, which brought thee forth out of the land of Egypt, from the house of bondage. (Deut. 6:10–12 KJV)

Another is this one from Joshua:

Then Joshua called the twelve men, whom he had prepared of the children of Israel, out of every tribe a man:

And Joshua said to them, "Pass over before the ark of Yahweh your God into the middle of the Jordan, and each of you pick up a stone and put it on your shoulder, according to the number of the tribes of the children of Israel;

That this may be a sign among you, that when your children ask in time to come, saying, 'What do you mean by these stones?'

Then you shall tell them, 'Because the waters of the Jordan were cut off before the ark of the covenant of Yahweh. When it passed over the Jordan, the waters of the Jordan were cut off. These stones shall be for a memorial to the children of Israel forever.'" (Josh. 4:4–7 KJV, slightly modified)

The core idea of these texts is that the Israelites were not to remember myths; they were to recall historical events and God's actions within them for their deliverance and salvation. Of course the Bible also contains many narratives such as the ones we find in 1 and 2 Kings and in 1 and 2 Chronicles. But these were not the principal vehicles for the kind of remembering that God required. Rather, the carriers of memory for the Hebrews were rituals and the holy days on which these events were narrated. The Poet of Lamentations tells us that one of the worst parts about the city's plight is that memories of the holy days and the religious leaders charged with their administration are gone. Clearly, without them memory itself is endangered.

> He stripped his tabernacle as if it were a garden,
> and made the place of assembly a ruin.
> In Zion the LORD blotted out all memory
> of festal assembly and of sabbath;
> king and priest alike he spurned
> in the heat of his anger.
>
> (2:6 REB)

Memory is also threatened because the older people who can pass it on are unable to, and the music that enlivened the festivals has fallen silent. No one dances.

> Old men have left off their sessions at the city gate;
> young men no longer pluck the strings.
> Joy has vanished from our hearts;
> our dancing is turned to mourning.
> The garlands have fallen from our heads.
> Woe to us, sinners that we are.
> This is why we are sick at heart;
> all this is why our eyes grow dim.
>
> (5:14–17 REB)

For centuries the framework of institutional Christianity has been constituted by Scripture, creeds, and confessions. For Jews, the framework is knit together of Scripture, seasons, and holy days. Each one is shaped both to revivify the memory of a historical event and to provoke action. The holiday of Passover, for example, is explicitly described in the various Passover *haggadot* (the prayer books and songbooks used at the Seder) as one in which the participants are to think of themselves as among those being liberated from Egypt, and the ritual meal with its cups of wine, bitter herbs, unleavened bread, and lamb shank all illustrate the story of Moses and Pharaoh and the passage from bondage to freedom. The ritual is also designed to be especially available to children. As we have seen, Lamentations lives on in Judaism today not just as a text but as the fabric of an annual ritual, Tishah b'Ab, in which not just the defeat and destruction of Jerusalem by the Babylonians is mourned but the entire saga of Jewish tragedy.

These two holidays illustrate how memory, and "history" in this ancient Israelite sense, called for two levels. One was to recount the events themselves, but the other—equally important—was to plumb their meaning for the present. The word *zakor* means more than simply "to remember" in the modern English sense. It means both "to remember" and "to act." So when it is said that "the Jews invented history," that is true, but in a particular sense. They invented what might be called "existential history," history as a meaning-bearing reality for a particular people. Although some of the narratives in the Bible are quite detailed, for the Israelites it was the prophets, not the chroniclers, who carried the keys to history. That was because the prophets asked what it *meant*.

Herodotus, sometimes called "the father of history," wrote mainly out of his very characteristic Greek sense of curiosity. The Jews disdained viewing history from mere inquisitiveness. They remembered for a different reason. Consequently they remembered the good and the bad. They remembered things that brought no pleasure or honor to them as a people. This is evident in Lamentations:

> The memory of my distress and my wanderings
> is wormwood and gall.
> I remember them indeed
> and am filled with despondency.
>   (3:19–20 REB)

Contrast this Jewish remembrance of the bad things in the past with the Greeks' understanding of historical memory. In his discerning foreword to Yerushalmi's *Zakhor*, Harold Bloom recalls the words of Leo Strauss about the Epicureans. Strauss points out that the Epicureans took no need of past sorrows, that they recalled only what was pleasurable. Nothing, adds Bloom, could be less Jewish.

Lamentations is clearly not a work of history. It includes no dates and no place names except Jerusalem. It does not even name the nation or the individuals involved in its conquest and pillage. The book may be an appeal for meaning amid a scene of meaninglessness, but even that element is so tightly wrapped in complaint and grievance that it is sometimes nearly obscured. Yet God does still seem to be acting in this unprecedented calamity: The Poet believes God is punishing his people and then adds insult to injury by using a heathen people as the instrument of his wrath. Though dimly, Lamentations still displays the characteristics of this first kind of biblical recollection.

For Yerushalmi, however, something happened to this Israelite style of remembering history after the fall and destruction of

Jerusalem, not the fall The Poet of Lamentations writes about, but the one that took place in 70 CE at the hands of the Romans after the short Jewish revolt against imperial rule. After that defeat there was no more temple. The legions had leveled it except for the western retaining wall. Now, with no temple, the animal sacrifice cult was gone; and since the priests' function was mostly to preside over the sacrifices, there was no more priesthood. The rabbis had to reconceive the holidays. In doing so they invented what we now know as rabbinic Judaism. The Jews did continue to celebrate the holy days, but since they were surviving as a scattered people, there was little awareness of God acting in their current common life. God, the people widely believed, was also in exile. He had acted in the past and would one day in the future redeem his people and restore them to their land. But in the meantime there was little interest in general world history. As Yerushalmi says, after Josephus it would be fifteen hundred years before another Jew would call himself a historian. What the Gentiles did was their business. The great Jewish sage Maimonides thought that writing "history" was a strictly second-rate intellectual endeavor, infinitely inferior to studying Torah or Talmud.

This lack of interest in world history continued, Yerushalmi holds, until the tragic events of 1492, the expulsion of the Jews from Spain by Ferdinand and Isabella. This early example of ethnic cleansing, which also swept out the Muslims, convinced Jewish scholars that for their own good they would do well to attend to what was going on in the outside world, whether God was acting there or not. Some Jews began to ignore Maimonides's dismissal of the historian's art and to write about history in something closer to our modern meaning of the term.

But this new impulse to write history did not last very long. It was quickly overcome for most Jews by the growing popularity of the Kabbalah and other expressions of mysticism such as that of Shabbetai Tsevi (1626–1676), the "false messiah." The result was to introduce a split into Jewish consciousness. On the one hand there was the ritual marking of God's mighty deeds in history, especially at Passover and Purim. On the other there emerged the small beginnings of what was later to become the brilliant tradition of Jewish history writing. But what did the one have to do with the other?

Yerushalmi puts this question but does not answer it. He suggests that today's Jews are not a "people with no history": they are a people who can choose among various histories. But for individual Jews these histories sometimes conflict with one another. For example, the West Bank settlers insist that God has given that land to them and their posterity forever, and that the mandate in the book of Joshua to "conquer and settle" still obtains quite literally. Their reading of "history" conflicts with that of those Jews who trace their history to the command to live at peace with your neighbors or those modern Jews who see themselves as the children of the Jewish Enlightenment and its values of freedom, equality, and fraternity.

Yerushalmi's eloquent book raises a fascinating question for Christians. Did Christian history writing pass through similar stages? The answer, I think, is that it did, but only up to a point. The earliest Christians, as the New Testament makes clear, continued to celebrate the Jewish holidays. The first Pentecost takes place on the Jewish holiday of that name, which means fifty days after Passover, as they were gathered in Jerusalem to mark that holy day in their ancestral calendar. Paul tells the Christians in Rome that if they wish to continue to mark the weekly Sabbath, he has no objections (Rom. 14:15). Of course, as more and more Gentiles streamed into the Christian movement, fewer people wanted to observe the Jewish calendar. Easter and Christmas took their place, a process culminating in the Council of Nicaea in 325.

Then, when Constantine virtually hijacked their movement in the early fourth century, Christians moved into positions of power and Jews found themselves an oppressed minority. Christians, however, saw their churches spreading all around the empire and, with the fall of that empire, soon found themselves in charge of its collapsing institutions. Thus Christian historians, as opposed to Jewish ones, had every reason to study what the Gentile world was up to. They *were* the Gentile world. But they continued to look at history more in the Jewish manner than in the style of Herodotus. They asked not only what had happened but also what it meant. Eusebius wrote his history of the church and his biography of Constantine because, he reasoned, it was Constantine who had handed Christians the reins of power. Augustine's masterpiece, *The City of God,* not only traces the fall of the empire but discerns God's hand at work in it.

This tradition of Christian historiography also had to contend eventually with modern so-called objective history. But the dichotomy has never been as sharp as it became for Jews. Writers of "world history" still looked for clues of God's providence, often without using the word. They searched for hints about the *meaning* of it all. Had Christianity somehow brought about the fall of Rome? Edward Gibbon thought it did. Was the West in irreversible decline? Otto Spengler contended that it was. Or might a spiritual renewal save it from that fate? Arnold Toynbee believed it could.

Even if we accept the canons of modern historical scholarship, however, and the historical-critical approach to the Bible, that does not mean that Lamentations is not historically essential. It is invaluable grist for the historian's mill. Like the letters, journals, and diaries, both of soldiers and of those left behind on the home front, it provides an invaluable "source" that supposedly objective chronicles do not. Some of the richest sources for the history of the American Civil War, of both World Wars, and of the more recent Vietnam and Middle East conflicts can be found in such sources. Historians who ignore them write at their peril. They risk missing some of the most telling dimensions of the struggles they write about. It should be noted, however, that here careful historical-critical study can be of enormous help. By means of lexicography, structural analysis, and comparative study, a text like Lamentations might someday be more accurately dated. It would then illuminate something, not necessarily about the sixth century, which it is ostensibly about, but about the history of the period in which The Poet actually composed it. Still, even if that never happens, the timeless quality of Lamentations confirms its inclusion in the biblical canon.

9

The Mystery of Evil

Can we read Lamentations today with any degree of seriousness without having to confront again the stubborn and seemingly insoluble "problem of evil"? Rape, pillage, starving children, torture all appear in Lamentations. Where was God in all that? And they still go on today. Where, if anywhere, is God? How could egregious evil, especially the suffering of the innocent, continue to tear at a world ruled by a benevolent deity? Puzzling over this question has a long history in the enterprise of Christian theology. Gottfried Wilhelm Leibniz (1646–1716) coined the term *theodicy* in the 1690s. It is derived from the Greek *theos* (God) and *dike* (justice). The word has come to be used to refer to John Milton's desire to "justify the ways of God to men." The question encompasses both the slow death of violated children and the arbitrary, even whimsical destruction wrought by natural disasters. Various answers were advanced, rejected, then advanced again. The debate sometimes seemed circular. Augustine had famously declared evil to be simply an absence of the good. But to other thinkers this seemed a little too easy. Popular theologies attributed evil to Satan and his earthly minions. For the most traditional classical theologies, the question was often shelved by declaring it out of bounds. Evil is a mystery. It was simply not a topic open to the prying of human curiosity. If it is a mystery, then a mystery it shall remain. "The LORD gave and the LORD hath taken away. Blessed be the name of the LORD" (Job 1:21 KJV).[27]

---

27. See Mark Larimore, ed., *The Problem of Evil: A Reader* (Malden, MA: Blackwell Publishing, 2001), for a rich collection of essays on this subject chosen from a religious studies perspective.

In the long saga of American theology, philosophy, and literature, one figure stands out above all others: Herman Melville. His *Moby Dick*, published in 1851, is widely regarded as the greatest American novel. It is also—in my view—our country's most powerful Christian theological novel, a vibrant restatement of powerful biblical themes, not just for the nineteenth but also for the twenty-first century. And it focuses on the old "problem of evil."

Melville was no stranger to theology. His parents were Dutch and Scots-Irish Calvinists. From his youth he was drenched in the doctrines of their church. He opens *Moby Dick* with five quotations from the Bible, drawn from Genesis, Job, Jonah, Psalms, and Isaiah. A lifelong Presbyterian, throughout his years he maintained a vexed and tensile relationship to that tradition. As one of his biographers puts it, Melville engaged in a long "quarrel with God." But his was a kind of lover's quarrel.

Melville once visited Palestine, the "Holy Land" as he called it. On his way he stopped in England to visit his old friend Nathaniel Hawthorne, who was then U.S. consul in Liverpool. They took a long walk together on the sandbanks, and Hawthorne writes of Melville that he began to muse, as was his wont, "of Providence and futurity, and of everything that lies beyond human ken; . . . and I think, he will never rest until he gets hold of a definite belief. It is strange how he persists . . . in wandering to-and-fro over these deserts, as dismal . . . as the sandhills amid which we were sitting. He can neither believe, nor be comfortable in his unbelief."[28]

Many who read this will think immediately of the story of Jesus' healing of the convulsive boy in Mark 9:24. The desperate father of the boy confesses he has some doubts about whether Jesus can heal him. Finally he bursts into tears and cries out to Jesus, "Lord, I believe, help thou my unbelief." That was often Melville's testimony, as it is for many of us today who sometimes find ourselves hovering on the razor's edge of faith and unfaith.

Moby Dick at one level is a rousing yarn of the sea. But it is also enormously more than that. It is an extended meditation on some of

---

28. "Biographical Note," in Melville, *Great Books of the Western World* 48 (Chicago: University of Chicago Press, 1952), vi.

the most basic questions of human existence, especially the persistent dilemma of evil. As the story unfolds we find Ishmael, who is the narrator, and his newfound friend Queequeg walking the streets of Nantucket looking for a whaler they can ship out with. They find the *Pequod* and sign the papers even though the agent, Bildad (who in the Bible was one of Job's "comforters"), voices some doubts about whether he can accept Queequeg. With his fierce face and body tattoos, he appears to be at best an only partially converted heathen, possibly a cannibal. Ishmael assures Bildad, however, that Queequeg belongs to "the First Congregation."

Bildad responds to Ishmael that he must be joking ("skylarking") with him. "What church dost thou mean? Answer me."

Ishmael says, "Finding myself hard pushed, I replied. 'I mean, sir, the same ancient Catholic Church to which you and I and Captain Peleg there, and Queequeg here, and all of us, and every mother's son and soul of us belong; the great and everlasting First Congregation of the whole worshipping world; we all belong to that.'" Ishmael goes on to say that each of us may cherish one or another small corner, but "in the grand belief, in that we all join hands."[29]

Queequeg and Ishmael are both enlisted for the crew, and they all set sail, no one yet having seen the master, who has locked himself in his cabin. Eventually Captain Ahab appears, wearing his tall silk hat and the ivory peg that had replaced the leg bitten off by a whale named Moby Dick. Soon the crew members discover, to the dismay of some but not all, that this captain is not interested in filling the hold with whale oil. He has only one goal in mind: he will find Moby Dick and savor his revenge. After a long and arduous voyage the *Pequod* does find the white whale. Ahab stands in the prow of one of the boats, and as the men hurl their harpoons, he hurls one of his own. But Ahab becomes ensnarled in the line and is dragged to his death. Moby Dick then smashes the boat and heads for the *Pequod* itself and rams it. The ship sinks. Only Ishmael is left to tell the tale, buoyed up by a coffin his heathen friend Queequeg had nailed together for himself, when it bobs up from the whirlpool loosed by the stricken ship.

29. Melville, *Moby Dick*, 66.

Moby Dick has much to say to us today. The men of our time who sometimes lose their lives working on oil rigs, like the now infamous "Wide Horizons" in the Gulf of Mexico, are much like the brave crews who set out for whales in the nineteenth century. Both risk their lives to satisfy our endless and gluttonous appetite for oil. As the great whale smashes the *Pequod* to smithereens, Melville may be asking us: How long do you think Nature will sustain its patience with us while we despoil and destroy her? Moby Dick, the great whale himself, had no argument with human beings. He only resorted to what appeared to be vengeance in self-defense. Enough was enough.

But the deeper core message of *Moby Dick* has to do with the nature of evil. It is a parable of Ahab's obsessive determination to wreak vengeance on an essentially innocent creature of the deep. And it was more than that. In Ahab's fevered mind Moby Dick had come to embody *all the evil in the world.* "I will thrust through him," he says, to all the darkness and distortion in the universe. But Ahab dies in the attempt and takes the whole crew—except for Ishmael—with him.

Ahab thought he could exterminate evil. Melville knew better. He had imbibed entirely too much Bible, and too much Calvin. He not only knew that evil cannot be destroyed—at least not by humans—he also knew that trying to rid the world of evil can make things infinitely worse.

Of course we must fight against evil and injustice, which in Melville's mind included war and racism. About war he once wrote, "The whole matter of war . . . smites common sense and Christianity in the face."[30] On racism we have only to notice that Melville's hero, Ishmael, is friends with the dark-skinned "heathens" on the *Pequod.* But

> When we fuse cosmic evil with something that has wounded us personally, we forget that evil is not just "out there." It also resides stubbornly within each of us. When we set out to destroy it we can sink the whole ship and destroy ourselves with it.

---

30. Herman Melville, *White-jacket: or, The World in a Man-of-War* (New York: Grove Press, 1850), 299.

Melville saw that when we try to destroy evil as such, and especially when we fuse cosmic evil with something that has wounded us personally, we forget that evil is not just "out there." It also resides stubbornly within each of us. When we set out to destroy it we can sink the whole ship and destroy ourselves with it. Calvin would have enjoyed reading *Moby Dick*.

Melville liked to write about the South Pacific tribes he encountered in his journeys as a seaman. Among one of them there is a custom that a person who kills another human being must carry the corpse on his back until it putrefies. What Melville desperately wanted to believe, and I think wants us to believe, is that we do not have to carry a corpse around with us. We do not have to kill ourselves trying to kill off evil, even the evil we ourselves do. God forgives. We can start over again anew.

The symbolism of Ishmael being saved by the coffin that springs out of the dark depth of the ocean is not particularly subtle. It proclaims that death and evil may do their worst, but that life and grace will prevail in the end.[31]

> LORD, turn us back to you and we shall come back;
> renew our days as in times long past.
>
> (5:21 REB)

Melville's stark Calvinist realism about evil was not the only option in the field during his lifetime. In the more liberal theologies of the nineteenth and early twentieth centuries, evil was viewed as something that was gradually, perhaps very gradually, being overcome as the goodness and love of God, and the civilizing mission of Western cultures, spread around the globe. Both the British and the French empires, and to some extent their American successor, held that their imperial reach had the best interests of the "natives" in mind. They would be saved from superstition and witchcraft by the steady advance of Christian civilization. The "more advanced" races were exhorted by Rudyard Kipling (1865–1936) to "take up

---

31. For an insightful treatment of Melville and evil see Andrew Dalbanco, *The Death of Satan—How Americans Have Lost the Sense of Evil* (New York: Farrar, Straus and Giroux, 1995).

the white man's burden" and to "send forth the best you have." For the Kipling and his legions of admirers God was indeed working in history. He was using the great benevolent empires to banish the darkness and savagery of the world. Evil, in short, was in a sense a temporary problem. There would come a time when it would be no more. Discussion of its source and its nature seemed beside the point.

This informal moratorium on theological discussions of evil came to a crashing dénouement when World War I exploded in Europe. Thousands of young men were chopped to pieces by machine guns and shrapnel, and the thud of artillery could be heard even in the studies and classrooms of the most remote scholars. Europe had not lived through a war since 1870, so this war represented evil on a scale no one had seen before. The world pictured by Lamentations had seemed a distant and unreal one, fading further into the past with every passing year. But in his library in the tiny Swiss village of Safenwil in Canton Aargau, a young Reformed pastor, Karl Barth (1886–1968), scanned the newspapers and heard the rumbles. He turned in his reading to Dostoyevsky and Kierkegaard, and he read the Bible with a new set of questions. Out went any theory of the gradual progress of Christian civilization, or images of God as the pleasant benefactor of human needs or the symbol of the highest in human achievement. His *Epistle to the Romans* (German original 1918) was the result, and "dialectical theology" (also sometimes called the "theology of crisis") was born. The question of the meaning of human evil, and of sin and rebellion, were back on the table.

Barth himself was anything but a gloomy person. The music he loved best was not that of the serious Bach or the romantic Beethoven, but the more sprightly works of Mozart. He once said that although the angels may play Bach before the throne of God, when they are playing for their own amusement they undoubtedly play Mozart. Barth's point in his enormously influential commentary on Paul's Epistle to the Romans was not that God was only a God of judgment. God was also a God of love. But Barth insisted that God reveals himself most centrally in the crucifixion of Jesus, and that this means God shares in human suffering. It also means, however, that God cannot be identified with any human achievement and that even the highest human attainments fall short of God's mystery and grace.

As an heir of the Christian Socialist movement and an admirer of one of its principal spokesmen, Christian Blumhardt, Barth was especially doubtful that so-called Western Christian civilization could claim any kind of divine sanction. In the postwar years this conviction earned him many enemies among the strongest advocates of the Cold War. In helping to write the Darmstadt Statement of 1947, which confessed the guilt and responsibility of the German church for the rise of Nazism, Barth pointed out that the church's eagerness to side with antisocialist forces had rendered it a willing tool of Nazi ideology. He vigorously supported the German peace movement and opposed German rearmament. In one of his few references to evil, and in what became one of his most controversial statements, Barth said, "I regard anticommunism as a matter of principle an evil even greater than communism itself."[32] Those are strong words, and one wonders, as more and more evidence of Stalin's atrocities accumulated, if Barth might have reconsidered them. His point, I think, was that to identify any political reality with the very essence of evil—as in "the evil empire" or the "axis of evil"—is a serious error. Barth died in 1968, but it is easy to guess what his feelings would be about current efforts to demonize Islam.

In America another young theologian, a pastor serving his apprenticeship amid the hardfisted labor wars of Detroit in the 1920s, also read his Bible in a new way. Reinhold Niebuhr had been a "liberal" both in politics and theology. But now he changed. He too abandoned fashionable theories of progress because he saw that only power on the other side could ever dislodge the privileged elites. Politically he became more radical and, after moving to New York City to teach at Union Theological Seminary, ran for Congress as the candidate of the Socialist Party.

In theology, Niebuhr read Barth, but he also went back to Augustine and Calvin. He became convinced that sin was not an outmoded category, something to be eclipsed by the spread of literacy

---

32. Karl Barth, "Recapitulation Number Three," *Christian Century* 77, no. 3 (1960): 72.

and education, but that it marked a deep flaw in human nature. It led people to believe they were acting in the common interest when their views of that interest were tinctured by their own unacknowledged social status. Sin, for Niebuhr, arose not from human finitude, but from the desperate ways humans sought to deny that finitude. One suspects that the early "liberal" Niebuhr would have been hard-pressed to make sense of Lamentations, but that the battle-seasoned later Niebuhr would have found it a repellent but accurate portrayal of the world as it really is.

10

The Philosophy of Evil

After the Enlightenment and then until the late twentieth century, philosophers had also shelved any serious concern with "the problem of evil." The logical positivists had little interest in theodicy since none of its key terms was subject to empirical verification. The various schools of philosophy that embraced atheism, such as existentialism and naturalistic humanism, solved it and then abandoned it very easily. Since there was no God with whom to reconcile evil, there was quite obviously no problem.[33]

But then came fascism, Auschwitz, Hiroshima, the gulag—and, even with no God in sight, "the problem" was back with a vengeance. Again the question of why conquerors rape and kill women, why animals feed on human bodies in broken streets, and why "princes are hung by their hands" arose like a leering Dracula from its weed-covered grave. Many believe the twentieth century to have packed in more evil than any other century in history. The question now could not be whether any respectable thinker could ignore this question, but where to begin.

For many writers the answer to this where-to-start question was self-evident. You start with Hannah Arendt's brilliant—and highly controversial—*Eichmann in Jerusalem*.[34] Arendt traveled to Jerusalem in 1961 to witness this trial of the century after Adolf Eichmann

---

33. For an excellent overview of evil in philosophy, see Susan Neiman, *Evil in Modern Thought: An Alternative History of Philosophy* (Princeton: Princeton University Press, 2002). See also Richard J. Bernstein, *Radical Evil: A Philosophical Investigation* (Malden, MA: Blackwell Publishing, 2002).
34. Hannah Arendt, *Eichmann in Jerusalem: A Report on the Banality of Evil,* rev. ed. (New York: Penguin, 1994).

had been captured by the Israelis in Argentina and taken back in order to face trial in the country founded by the people he had helped try to exterminate.

A mental experiment, or an exercise in imagination, will be needed to read Arendt in the light of Lamentations or vice versa. Suppose the Israelites had been able to rally, to recoup, and to defeat the Babylonians and then to bring their leaders back, perhaps to the piles of stone and ashes left where the temple had stood, to try them for their crimes against humanity? How might these defeated leaders have responded to the indictment brought against them? Answering this will open up Lamentations for us in a new way.

If Eichmann gives any clue to how the Babylonians might have pleaded, they would have explained that, like good soldiers before and since, they were merely following orders. They were executing their responsibilities to the best of their abilities. They might even have claimed that they bore no personal animosity toward the Jews, but that as small cogs in a large machine they simply followed procedures. They might even recall for the court individual Israelites they had helped here and there, perhaps even offering the sixth-century BCE equivalent of a cigarette.

What surprised Arendt most about Eichmann as she watched him sitting in the glass-enclosed prisoner's booth, listening to interpreters over earphones, was how terribly ordinary he appeared. He did not look like a monster. He did not seem to be "the kind of person" who would competently administer the transport system that bore millions of innocent men, women, and children to their deaths.

Arendt's point was that, especially in complex modern societies, one does not have to look like a monster, or even to be a monster, to engage in monstrous deeds. Under the Nazis, mass death had become a well-calibrated industry. It relied on thousands of interlocking parts. Someone had to locate or identify the Jews, Gypsies, Communists, gays, and others who were considered enemies of the state. Others had to apprehend them and move them to transport facilities. Someone had to find the engines, engineers, brakemen, and cattle cars and get them to the right stations. At the other end someone else, including trained physicians, had to "make the selections," sending some to immediate death in the gas chambers and others to unendurable toil under grinding conditions, also usually ending in death. The last station of all was the ovens, which of course required their designers, builders, maintenance crews, and cleaners (although this last task was usually left to the prisoners themselves, until they too were gassed and cremated).

The extermination system was so vast and complex that no single person could feel the full weight of the whole ghastly assemblage. Along with the train personnel, railway attendants, and assorted bit players in the drama of death, Eichmann merely slid into a niche, albeit one near the top. He claimed never to have initiated any orders to round up or kill Jews, and never did either himself. He just got them from here to there on the trains, quite efficiently. He did his job.

During the trial Arendt became aware of something: the increasingly complex nature of modern societies would make evildoing more and more faceless. She did not live to see the advent of today's advances in drone warfare, but her observations presaged it. Now men sit at screens in bunkers hidden in a western desert in North America and direct robot planes to precise targets in Afghanistan where they explode into cottages in which some suspected terrorist may be hiding. If children or innocent bystanders are killed too, that is accounted "collateral damage." After their shifts at work the computer-screen warriors can drive home to dinner with their wives and families. No one thinks of them as monsters. They are just doing their duty, or as the current phrase has it, "getting the job done."

But the banalization of evil is not confined to the military. The vast international corporations that spread destitution and dependency to other parts of the world do not depend on the services of cruel people, just of people who are unwilling to look at the end product of their roles in one or another corner of the gigantic apparatus that employs them. Arendt came to the conclusion that, especially in our time, the major cause of evil is not a malicious will or iniquitous intent. It is unawareness. The sin of modern humanity may not be so much pride as sloth, our comfortable willingness to remain unaware. If reading of the evil chronicled in Lamentations opens our eyes to the evil that persists in our own world today, maybe we can become a bit more aware.

PART 3

ETHICAL ISSUES
The Bitter Fruits of War

How bitter is her fate!
Her adversaries have become her masters,
her enemies take their ease.

(1:4b–5 REB)

Lamentations is about memory. But it is about a particular kind of memory: *how* we remember *war*, and *what* we remember. It is, of course, a text about a war that happened a long time ago, but it raises a compelling question for us in America today: How do we remember our past wars? How will we remember the wars we are now engaged in?

In virtually every society in history, remembering and memorializing war have become liturgical, religious, or quasi-religious events, and it is no different in America. We remember our national wars on designated holidays, like Veterans Day and Memorial Day, often in cemeteries or at monuments. Hardly any such occasions pass without some mention of them in Christian churches in Sunday sermons or liturgies. But what is the *content* of these ecclesial exercises?

Lamentations might seem to be a perfect text to draw on in remembering war. But I do not remember ever hearing a sermon at one of these memorial occasions that employs it. Why? Could it be that Lamentations does not express the sentiments we would like to hear? Maybe a careful rereading of this text could inspire someone to preach such a sermon or create such a liturgy.

As a nation there is much to remember, for we have had many wars. Our country was born in 1776 during a long battle that ended in our

independence from England. We still name aircraft carriers for the
critical sites of that struggle: Saratoga, Yorktown, and Valley Forge.
It is also one of the wars that inspires reenactors. Corpulent men
cram themselves into Continental uniforms, put on three-cornered
hats, and assemble to the sound of fife-and-drum corps. The War of
1812 was in some measure a continuation of the fight for independence. Then the young republic wrested control of the North American continent from its indigenous inhabitants by means of a series
of brutal wars and massacres. Next it added the whole southwest as
the booty of a war with Mexico. Our bloodiest war, fought between
1861 and 1865, tested whether the union could be held together in
the face of secession and the running sore of slavery. The Spanish-
American War, scholars today agree, was one of imperial ambition
that made a former British colony into a colonial power itself. In the
twentieth century America has fought two titanic world wars and a
series of smaller but anguishing conflicts in Korea and Vietnam, and,
as I write this, we are still at war in Iraq and Afghanistan.

As a nation we have tried for nearly two and a half centuries to
remember these wars and those who died in them. The Mall in
Washington, DC, is already dotted with monuments to these agonizing chapters in our history. The one to the Korean struggle is
particularly stirring. It catches the grim spirit of this "forgotten war"
by depicting cold, tired men slogging wearily up a hill. It is more
realistic than most such memorials, perhaps because no one can
qualify Korea as a victory. It resulted in a draw at best. The memorial
to World War II is, many visitors admit, not a success. It is grandiose,
pretentious, and uninviting. Engraved with banal slogans, some have
even suggested that it seems almost "Soviet" in its chilly ostentation.
The "good war" does not have a good memorial.

There is one memorial on the Mall, however, that is almost universally acclaimed. Officially it is "The Vietnam Veterans Memorial."
But nearly everyone refers to it as "The Vietnam Wall." Technically
the wall is only part of a complex that includes the "Three Soldiers" statue, the "Vietnam Women's Memorial," and the Wall itself.
Together they honor the 58,260 members of the U.S. armed forces
who died or are missing in action in Vietnam and adjacent Southeast

Asia. Designed by the American landscape architect Maya Lin, it was completed in 1982.

By now hundreds of thousands, if not millions, of people have visited the Wall. Nearly everyone who does reports that they found it intensely moving. I am one of those visitors, and I agree. I also believe that the Wall evokes feelings closer to Lamentations than any of the other memorials. Why?

First, we should remember that from the U.S. perspective, the Vietnam War was neither a victory nor a draw. It was a defeat, and a humiliating one at that, the first in American history. Few who watched on television will ever forget the sight of the knots of terrified people pushing and clawing one another as they sought to board one of the last helicopters leaving the embassy roof after the American forces had evacuated. Try as one will to excuse or rationalize it, Vietnam was a stinging defeat for America. Lamentations is also about what happened after such a defeat.

> All splendour has vanished
> from the daughter of Zion.
> Her princes have become like deer
> that can find no pasture.
> They run on, their strength spent,
> pursued by the hunter.
> (1:6 REB)

The difference is that as Americans we did not have to endure the travail of the people of Jerusalem after their defeat. We were safely ensconced thousands of miles away. It was those citizens of South Vietnam who had sympathized with the Americans or worked for us who bore the brunt, although it turned out to be nothing like the bloodbath of so many grim predictions. Also, the dreaded domino effect that had been advanced as the main reason for waging the war in the first place never happened. After the North Vietnamese reunited the whole country and renamed Saigon "Ho Chi Minh City," no other Southeast Asian country became Communist. Vietnam is now an active trading partner of the United States.

Second, as in Lamentations some voices immediately began to cry for revenge. The *Rambo* films fed this thirst for vengeance by casting Americans as the victims and celebrating a fictional super-warrior who makes war almost single-handedly on the cruel Vietnamese who were allegedly holding hostages in tiny bamboo cages. Others found ways to excuse the defeat ("We should have used nuclear weapons") or blame it on the military or civilian leadership. Still others laid the blame on the antiwar movement, claiming it had sapped the morale of the troops. The country was so full of mixed feelings of bewilderment, frustration, disgust, anger, and shame (all feelings expressed in Lamentations) that as the veterans came back home they were rarely greeted as returning heroes. For years, Americans wondered how, or even whether, to memorialize this divisive war.

Some people commented that Americans had, after all, never been faced with the challenge of how to remember a defeat. This was not quite accurate. It forgets that the American South did experience a defeat in 1865. It was occupied by a conquering army. It did have to come to terms with ignominy and dashed hopes. It is interesting to observe that the American South did so in ways similar to those of The Poet of Lamentations. It constructed the mythical past of an antebellum paradise decked out with white-columned mansions, happy slaves, and mint juleps. For many white Americans, *Gone with the Wind*, especially in its film version, still captures the essence of a charming old Dixie that never existed. How then do we recall the Vietnam War, our one nationwide defeat?

This is a question of tragic import for the veterans of Vietnam. That they could not come home as conquerors with ticker-tape parades and the warm embrace of a grateful nation deprived them of one of the indispensable rituals soldiers need when they return to civilian life. Since normal human beings have a deep aversion to killing, the military must not only desensitize them so that they can kill but also prepare them to reenter a normal environment in which they are not supposed to kill. The reason this can be done is that, as more and more theologians are now realizing, stories and narratives make up the fabric of our lives. The British theologian Don Cupitt has observed that "stories are interpretive resources, models, and scenarios through which we make sense of what is happening to us and frame our action."[35] He adds that stories shape the process of life, and it is through them that our social selves, which are our real selves, are actually produced.

The military knows about stories and narratives too. It prepares men for war by enclosing the killing they must do in battle in a new narrative, different from the civilian one, a narrative that redefines killing. It is no longer murder but is parsed within a vocabulary of patriotism, heroism, and moral sacrifice. But this new narrative must constantly be reaffirmed by rituals such as parades, appreciative recognition (medals and honors), peer support, the gratitude of the nation they serve, and above all the feeling that it was all worth the effort.

But since Vietnam was a defeat, many of these supportive elements were not forthcoming. Even some veterans of World War II shunned the returning Vietnam vets as "losers." They were often not invited to participate in memorial rituals. For some, their medals began to weigh on them as badges of disgrace. But most importantly, they were deprived of the sense that their suffering and sacrifice had been crowned by success. It had not been. The sad result of this dislocation of the normal "civilianizing" required of returned warriors was a wave of depression, suicide, and post-traumatic stress syndrome. Worst of all, since they had no legitimate way of shedding their "killer" socialization, many continued—in their own eyes at least—to think and act as killers. Assaults, homicides, and spouse abuse soared.

> The LORD has . . .
> let the enemy rejoice over you;
> filling your adversaries with pride.
>
> Cry to the Lord from the heart
> at the wall of the daughter of Zion;
> let your tears run down like a torrent
> day and night.

35. Don Cupitt, *What Is a Story?* (London: SCM Press, 1991), lx.

Give yourself not a moment's rest,
let your tears never cease.

Arise, cry aloud in the night;
at the beginning of every watch
pour out your heart like water
before the presence of the Lord.
Lift up your hands to him.

(2:17–19 REB)

In more theological terms, to make them into soldiers, civilians
need to be inducted into a new myth, a new narrative, in order to
overcome their instinctive aversion to killing. Some analysts say they
need this myth, especially after they have killed, and must come to
terms with seeing themselves as killers. In modern history this new
myth is that of the nation-state. I kill, and die if necessary, "for king
and country." But is the myth successful?

In an insightful treatment of the subject Bernard J. Verkamp argues
that it is not. In an earlier age, when men fought under the rules of
the "just war," the church stood by to offer them the opportunity for
penance and forgiveness after they killed. They could divest themselves of their killer identities with the sacrament. But nation-states,
so Vercamp argues, do not have that power. Instead they offer what
he calls "justification," a set of reasons to kill designed to remove the
blame. But do they remove the guilt, the inner destruction, caused
by becoming a killer? Verkamp thinks not, and in the case of Vietnam, since winning the war is integral to the justification system, the
structure fails.[36]

Lamentations unfolds the narrative of a person who—in current psychological terms—is suffering from post-traumatic stress.
As will be noted in a later section on catastrophe, spiritual guides
and therapists testify that in order for healing to occur in such cases
*the opportunity to narrate one's traumatic experience is absolutely essen-
tial.* It is also true that this narration must occur within a larger,

---

36. Bernard J. Verkamp, *The Treatment of Returning Warriors in Medieval and Modern Times*
(Scranton: University of Scranton Press, 1993), cited in Jonathan Tran, *The Vietnam War and
Theologies of Memory* (Malden, MA: Wiley-Blackwell, 2010), 134.

confirming narrative structure. My story must find a place within a larger story. Both are needed. The Poet of Lamentations sobs out her story within the overarching narrative of the longer and deeper story of God and his people.

> The LORD has done what he planned to do,
> he has fulfilled his threat,
> all that he decreed from days of old.
>
> (2:17 REB)

To confess that God has inflicted this horror is a bitter pill to swallow. But at least it gives the tragedy meaning. Suspecting that one's pain is meaningless would add an almost unbearable dimension. The Poet of Lamentations even sees the debacle as providing the occasion for national penance in view of the sins of her people, including its perversion of justice.

> [God] may punish, yet he will have compassion
> in the fullness of his unfailing love;
> he does not willingly afflict
> or punish any mortal.
>
> (3:32–33 REB)

As we have already noticed, now The Poet sees that her suffering is not the only suffering, that many others have been hurt, some by the Israelites themselves.

> To trample underfoot
> prisoners anywhere on earth,
> to deprive a man of his rights
> in defiance of the Most High,
> to pervert justice in the courts—
> such things the Lord has never approved.
>
> Who can command and have it done
> if the Lord has forbidden it?

> Do not both bad and good proceed
> from the mouth of the Most High?
> Why should any man living complain,
> any mortal who has sinned?
>
> (3:34–39 REB)

This leads The Poet to reflection and penitence.

> Let us examine our ways and test them
> and turn back to the LORD;
> let us lift up our hearts and our hands
> to God in heaven, saying:
> "We have sinned and rebelled,
> and you have not forgiven."
>
> (3:40–42 REB)

Lamentations infuses tragedy with meaning, however harsh. But does a visit to the Wall endow the Vietnam War with meaning? Does it therefore become a liturgical act, at least for some people, even "nonreligious" ones? I suspect it does. This is due in part to the inspired design of the Wall itself and to the painfully unresolved feelings many Americans still harbor about Vietnam. I think I understand some of those feelings. I was actively involved in the opposition to the war, inspired in part by Martin Luther King's ringing denunciation of it from the pulpit of Riverside Church. I was even briefly incarcerated at the U.S. Air Force Academy in Colorado Springs for joining with some other protesters, including some novice nuns, in distributing antiwar leaflets at the academy's chapel doors before a Sunday service. But I also found myself admiring the young men who slogged through the jungles of the far-off land to fight what they were told were the enemies of their country. I desperately wanted the war to end, but I did not want to belittle or disparage the soldiers. These sentiments were often at odds within me, and to some extent, after all these years, they still are.

For many people the Vietnam Wall serves as a pilgrimage and ritual site. First, it invokes infinity. Since the wall curves, one cannot take in its whole length at once, so one has the impression of a nearly endless stream of names. Also the polished marble surface allows one to see oneself amid the cascading names of the dead, the Howards and Rileys and Gonzálezes, producing an almost mystical sense of identification with those memorialized. It is important that no ranks are indicated. Colonels and sergeants are treated exactly the same as privates. Death is the great equalizer.

Finally, and perhaps most movingly, there are the physical tributes. Every day visitors place small items along the Wall, often but not always near the name of someone they knew or loved. Knick-knacks, toys, packs of cigarettes, photographs, letters, bottles of scotch or beer line the pavement, and each week park workers carefully gather them and place them in the National Parks Museum where guests can see them. Anyone who has visited a shrine of any faith anywhere in the world recognizes the practice of leaving tributes. It is virtually universal.

One of the main reasons for the immense success of the Wall is that it carries no clichéd inscriptions, no overbearing message we are supposed to go away with. It is what it is: a very long list of the names of tens of thousands (mostly young men) who died. Did they die "in vain"? Whenever I visit the Wall, I feel a stabbing mixture of profound sadness and sharp anger.

> How can I cheer you? Whose plight is like yours. . . ?
> To what can I compare you for your comfort. . . ?
> For your wound gapes as wide as the ocean—
> who can heal you?
>
> (2:13 REB)

Standing at the Wall, invariably I remember that in the shocking film documentary *Fog of War*, Robert McNamara, who was secretary of defense during the war, concedes that it was all "a mistake." He adds that he realized this at the time but did not press his view and did not resign because he wanted to retain his influence with President Johnson. McNamara's admission also makes me think of the decorated Vietnam veteran John Kerry's pointed question to a congressional committee: "Who will be the last man asked to die for a mistake?"

The visions that your prophets saw for you
were a false and painted sham.
They did not bring home to you your guilt
so as to reverse your fortunes.
The visions they saw for you were delusions,
false and fraudulent.

(2:14 REB)

Those who for no reason were my enemies
drove me cruelly like a bird;
to silence me they thrust me alive into the pit
and closed the opening with a boulder;
waters rose above my head,
and I said, "My end has come."

(3:52–54 REB)

Immersing oneself in the book of Lamentations causes one to wonder how we as Americans should remember our many wars.

> Immersing oneself in the book of Lamentations causes one to wonder how we as Americans should remember our many wars.

Of course, we must never forget to mourn and honor the dead, both military and civilian who died during them. But, as Christians, should we not also mourn those who died "on the other side"? The archbishop of Canterbury refused to hold a memorial service in Westminster Abbey for the United Kingdom soldiers and sailors who died during the brief war against Argentina over the Falkland Islands unless the Argentine dead could be honored at the same time. He explained, rightly, that to do otherwise would make the service a tribal pagan rite, not a Christian service. Many protested, but he insisted, and the dignified memorial event paid tribute to all those who had died, regardless of nationality.

That goes at least partway. But could we envision our American memorial services, echoing the book of Lamentations, also becom-ing occasions for national repentance? If not, can we continue to think of these observances as truly biblical, as worship services of the Lord of all history and all peoples? If not, do they remain, at least in some measure, quasi-pagan "tribal" rites? Do ministers, priests, and rabbis have the obligation to insist on what the content of these rituals should include? If they do not, do they become, at least on those days, mere acolytes of a religion of nationalism? Lamentations is a stern and formidable book. But it carries lessons those of us who try to live within the biblical tradition ignore at our peril.

11

Rape

Lamentations catalogs the inevitably brutal fruits of war. Its few pages tell of torture and exile, rape, humiliation, starvation, and even cannibalism. In no other book of the Bible are so many examples of human depravity paraded before the reader's eyes. In this section we will examine some of them more closely. It will not be a pleasant reading experience. We begin with rape.

> Women were raped in Zion,
> virgins ravished in the towns of Judah.
> (5:10b REB)

When cities—or whole countries—are conquered, women are almost inevitably raped. "Rape" is itself only a four-letter word. But what happens? Women, from infants to grandmothers, are seized, thrown down, beaten, stripped, and forcibly entered. All too often the rapist then kills them. This is a gruesome fact of life that those who plan and launch wars—almost entirely men—always fail to take into consideration. Jerusalem was no exception to this lewd reality.

> Jerusalem, greatly sinning,
> was treated like a filthy rag.
> All who had honoured her
> held her cheap,
> now they had seen her nakedness.
> What could she do but groan
> and turn away?
> (1:8 REB)

Surely the saddest part of this quotation is that The Poet sees rape as a kind of divine punishment. Like all too many victims of rape, she looks for a reason and blames herself. And if she does not blame herself, then others often do. "She was wearing skimpy clothes," they may say, or "she was really asking for it." But one should be very clear about this: However they may dress, women *never* ask to be raped.

Sexual violence is not confined to wars. It goes on all the time. The rape of younger and smaller prisoners by guards and fellow prisoners continues to worsen the horror of incarceration. Rape within marriage still continues and is often unreported. "Date rape" is difficult to prevent. Large numbers of women still hesitate to report being raped because of the shame and humiliation it often carries with it. Nowhere is "blaming the victim" more common. Still, rape is a particularly devastating and destructive act. It violates the victim's sense of self-esteem, humiliates her (or him), and causes both spiritual and physical damage.

Of course the raping of women by conquering armies is always "regretted" by official voices, but it is also frequently expected as a normal consequence of war. The warriors are savoring "the fruits of victory." In Lamentations not only are real flesh-and-blood women raped, but the city itself—personified as a woman—is likewise violated and debased. It is often said that rape is not a sexual act but an act of violence. The horrid truth is that it can be both at the same time. This is because the sex act itself can be the focus of many conflicting emotions. It is naive to assume that soldiers who rape women do not enjoy physical pleasure as well as the satisfaction of realizing they are continuing the war by other means. Sometimes rape is more than just a single, dastardly, impulsive affront. It becomes a policy of punishment and terror. The Serbian soldiers who raped hundreds of Muslim women in the recent Balkan conflict apparently took pride in the recognition that they were fulfilling a duty by punishing an "enemy." It is not known whether they realized that their victims were in danger of becoming pariahs in their own families and communities or whether this would have made any difference.

The brutal violation of women has gone on for centuries, but only recently have investigators begun to look systematically into why this happens, what effect it has on its victims, and what can be done both to reduce its scope and to heal the wounds, physical, psychological, and spiritual, that rape inflicts. Here is part of a report by Denis Mukwege, a Congolese gynecologist: "Our first patient . . . was a victim of sexual violence and she was fractured and destroyed in the pelvic region and in the region of the vagina. . . . We saw the number increasing, increasing, and increasing, and now our clinic serves more than 3000 women a year."[37]

The Democratic Republic of Congo is only one of the areas where sexual violence in its ugliest form has broken out in recent years. But for various reasons the DRC appears worse than most other places. In 2005 an organization called the Harvard Humanitarian Initiative (HHI) began to confront this massive crime at all its levels. The program is partially supported by the Swedish Pentecostal Church. The Congolese physician quoted above went on to detail the extent of the damages. The surgery required, he said, often includes repairing internal injuries. Violent rapes can tear the tissue separating the vagina from the bladder and the anus. The result is incontinence, with the woman constantly leaking urine or feces unless the tears, called fistulas, are repaired. "Sadly," he continued, "the weakest can't get to us. They are suffering from paralysis, from broken legs, from compound fractures, so they are unable to walk."

As in Lamentations, the women in the sections of Congo crippled by sexual violence live in constant fear and insecurity. They are not only assaulted when they venture out to the market or to church, but they are also attacked in their homes at night, often with husband and children present. They do not feel safe anywhere. Age is no preventive. Victims as young as three and as old as eighty have been treated.

Adding to the physical injury, the psychological abrasions deepen the agony. Sometimes victims are shunned or excluded as pariahs by their villages or even their own families. ("What could they do but groan and turn away?") They have to cope with searing internal doubt and self-blame. Some contract HIV as a result of the rape. Some become pregnant and struggle with conflicting feelings about the children they bear. A woman named Imani who was treated at

37. Alvin Powell, "Looking Horror in the Face," *Harvard University Gazette*, May 7–13, 2009, 1.

the clinic began recovering from her physical injuries but would require lifelong treatment for the HIV she had contracted. Further, she told the staff she sometimes thought of suicide and felt anger against her only child, a little girl born as a result of rape. She fears she will never have a life with a husband and with children born of love, not violence. Her marriage prospects are indeed poor, and her only family is the child who reminds her of the ghastly days she lived through. "At night when I sleep, I cry," Imani says, "you see my life is just rape, every day."[38]

People working with HHI soon came to recognize that simply treating the thousands of women who are victimized by rapists is not enough. Was there anything that could be done to stop or at least slow down the rate of sexual violence at its source? The people undertaking this task are fully aware of its difficulty and danger. They travel to the villages the soldiers come from to talk with them. They meet with commanders and with groups in the barracks. One man engaged in this staggering assignment said, "I know people make assumption that those who do this are monsters, but if you close your minds to possible reasons people commit atrocities, you're never going to understand why they happen."[39] Inevitably such investigations point back to the underlying reasons for the conflicts that hurl so many young men into what psychologist Robert J. Lifton has called "atrocity producing situations."

For Christians and Jews alike, issues of rape and atrocity become even harder to think about when we discover that both seem to be sanctioned by passages from the Bible. At a time when we often hear that the Koran sanctions violence, Christians and Jews need to come to terms with biblical passages that not only sanction but seem to approve and even to mandate rape. Many such "texts of terror" appear, but here are two of the most notorious ones:

> As you approach a town to attack it, first offer its people terms for peace. If they accept your terms and open the gates to you, then all the people inside will serve you in forced labor. But if they refuse to make peace and prepare to fight, you must attack

38. Ibid.
39. Ibid., 16.

the town. When the Lord your God hands it over to you, kill every man in the town. But you may keep for yourselves all the women, children, livestock, and other plunder. You may enjoy the spoils of your enemies that the Lord your God has given you. (Deut. 20:10–14 NLT)

Then they thought of the annual festival of the Lord held in Shiloh, between Lebonah and Bethel, along the east side of the road that goes from Bethel to Shechem. They told the men of Benjamin who still needed wives, "Go and hide in the vineyards. When the women of Shiloh come out for their dances, rush out from the vineyards, and each of you can take one of them home to be your wife! And when their fathers and brothers come to us in protest, we will tell them, 'Please be understanding. Let them have your daughters, for we didn't find enough wives for them when we destroyed Jabesh-gilead. And you are not guilty of breaking the vow since you did not give your daughters in marriage to them.'" So the men of Benjamin did as they were told. They kidnapped the women who took part in the celebration and carried them off to the land of their own inheritance. (Judg. 21:19–23 NLT)

> The hard truth is that for centuries rape always follows in the train of war, and it always will.

Does Lamentations have something to teach us about rape? Surely those who actually tear the clothes from women and injure them, often for the rest of their lives, must be punished. Neither the heat of battle nor the flush of victory gives them any justification. They have no excuse. But those of us who send them into war also bear some of the responsibility, for the hard truth is that for centuries rape always follows in the train of war, and it always will.

12

Torture

Princes were hung up by their hands;
elders received no respect.

(5:12 REB)

Why did the victors hang people by their hands after the battle for
Jerusalem? Why are people still hung by their hands? Why was Sister Dianna Ortiz, an American Roman Catholic missionary in Guatemala, hung by hers?

> A stench of decay rose from the pit. Rats swarmed over the
> bodies and were dropped onto me as I hung suspended over
> the pit by my wrists. I passed out and when I came to I was
> lying on the ground beside the pit, rats all over me.[40]

Why was this done and why is it still done? Are the tormenters simply punishing the tormented one? Are they trying to extract information ("actionable intelligence" in the fashionable phrase used
today)? Is it a tactic calculated to terrorize the remaining population
into cowering and submitting?

Whatever the answer, what the torturers did and what they do
carries a stinging contemporary bite. Lamentations may have been
written 2,500 years ago, but people are still hung up by their hands
today. Torture continues, although now some call it "enhanced
interrogation."

Torture is also one of the handmaidens of war. Perhaps the most

---

40. Dianna Ortiz quoted in Kerry Kennedy, *Speak Truth to Power: Human Rights Defenders Who
Are Changing Our World,* ed. Nan Richardson (New York: Umbrage Editions, 2000), 50.

famous living torture victim in the world is Senator John McCain, who was a candidate for president of the United States in 2008. While he was a prisoner of war in Vietnam, the young McCain was held in isolation by his captors for long periods of time, beaten and—yes—hung by his hands. As a result of his treatment he is still unable to raise one of his arms over his head. But Senator McCain is merely the best-known survivor of torture. In addition to him thousands and thousands of people have been subjected to a wide variety of torture techniques, and there is no doubt whatsoever that these practices still continue. Amnesty International estimates that fully 81 countries in the world employ torture today, some secretly but some quite openly. Worst of all, for Americans, our own country has not only tortured detainees, but recent laws banning such actions explicitly exempt some agencies, the Central Intelligence Agency in particular, from their provisions. In other words, *torture remains official American policy*.

Torture is defined by international law as:

> any act by which severe pain or suffering whether physical or mental, is intentionally inflicted on a person for such purposes as obtaining from him, or a third person, information or a confession for an act he or a third person has committed or is suspected of having committed, or intimidating him or a third person, or for any reason based on discrimination of any kind, when such pain or suffering is inflicted by or at the instigation of or with the consent or acquiescence of a public official or other person acting in an official capacity. It does not include pain or suffering arising only from, inherent in, or incidental to, lawful sanctions. (UN Convention Against Torture)

Torture has a long history. Its grotesque, twisted trajectory extends from simple kicking and pummeling to modern techniques of electric shock and psychological means. Its history includes such ingenious devices as the rack, on which victims were stretched by pulleys, and the "iron maiden," which enclosed people in sharp metal spikes. The Spanish Inquisition is notorious for its use of torture against suspected heretics, but it is a mistake to suppose that those practices have disappeared. In fact, submerging people in water to the point of drowning, known today as "waterboarding," was passed on in the Spanish battery of tools and was used by them in the Philippines, where the Americans learned about it during the Spanish-American War and then used it against Filipino insurgents. Always in use somewhere, waterboarding surfaced again when Americans began using it against "detainees" in Iraq whom administration officials insisted were not eligible for protection by the Geneva Conventions against "outrages upon personal dignity, in particular humiliating and degrading treatment."

Unfortunately discussions of torture can often sound lofty and bloodless. But the actual testimony of the survivors can bring it into clear and scorching focus. Dianna Ortiz, who is quoted at the beginning of this section, is a Roman Catholic nun, a member of the Ursuline Order. She is an American citizen, a native of New Mexico. In 1989, while serving as a missionary sister in Guatemala, she was arrested by that nation's military and tortured. According to her own testimony, her captors raped her continuously, often in groups. She bears 66 scars from cigarette burns on her back and on other parts of her body. Once she was lowered into a pit containing dead and dying human bodies—men, women, and children, caked in blood, some decapitated.[41]

Reading Sister Ortiz's description of her ordeal side by side with Lamentations is a startling experience. Nothing speaks more clearly of the relevancy of the scriptural text to today. Here, for example, is Sister Dianna crouched in her filthy cell wondering what will happen next:

> When my first rapist, the Police Man, whispered to me, "Your God is dead," he was absolutely right. My God was dead. I sat naked in a cold, dark cell waiting for the next horror to befall me, and I prayed to God, "Please let me die. Free me from this hell." But God would not even do that for me. I was alone, utterly alone. No one listened to my begging prayer.[42]

To the logical mind this account seems contradictory. How can

---

41. Ibid.
42. Dianna Ortiz, "A Survivor's View of Torture," in *Torture Is a Moral Issue*, ed. George Hunsinger (Grand Rapids: Eerdmans, 2008), 23.

someone declare that God is dead one minute, then pray to him the next? But people who have lived in extreme situations know there is no real contradiction. Perhaps the most authentic prayers ever prayed are those that well up out of sheer desperation, prayers that are hurled toward a heaven that seems blank and empty.

Sister Ortiz writes that when one of her women friends, a physician named Dr. Carmen Valenzuela, was led blindfolded into the room where she was to be tortured, the chief torturer said to her, "Doctor, we are not going to kill you, but you are going to beg for us to kill you."[43]

The testimony of survivors of torture makes one thing clear: once someone is tortured, they are always tortured. They never completely recover. The anguish comes back time and again, in restless dreams and in sudden flashes while they are awake. It is a form of what is now clinically described as "post-traumatic stress syndrome." A random sound can trigger it—a door closing, a key jangling. Suddenly the survivor is back in the torture room. Perspiration breaks out; hands tremble; the knees go weak. The Austrian philosopher Jean Amery, who was tortured by the Nazis, writes:

> Anyone who was tortured remains tortured. Anyone who has suffered torture will never again be at ease in the world; the abomination of the annihilation is never extinguished. Faith in humanity, already cracked with the first slap in the face, then demolished by torture, is never acquired again.[44]

But for Sister Dianna two parts of her torture stood out as the worst. One was hearing the screams of others being tormented in the same ways. The second was the sneering assurance her torturers gave her that even if she survived their treatment of her, no one would believe her when she described it later. That was the worst because it left her even more alone.

Fortunately for Sister Ortiz, she is an American citizen, and when she was reported missing and suspected of being abducted, numerous phone calls were made from Washington. She was released, and the head torturer drove her to a place where she could be handed

---

43. Ibid., 24.
44. Quoted in Primo Levi, *The Drowned and the Saved* (New York: Vintage, 1988), 25.

over to American authorities. He even apologized, and said hers was a case of mistaken identity. He and his men had actually been looking for another woman, he said. He asked her to forgive him. Sister Ortiz, however, finds it hard to forgive. She says she has come to the conclusion that Christianity is not just about individual forgiveness, but about justice and speaking the truth. Also she fully realizes that her release was an exception and that hundreds of others had been tortured and many had died in the hands of the same military. She also recognizes that the people who tortured her are hardly exceptions. They are part of a depraved and cowardly worldwide fraternity of those who intentionally inflict pain on defenseless people. Further, some card-carrying members of that fraternity are her fellow American citizens.

After her release Sister Dianna did not simply leave her personal dark night of the soul behind. Instead she founded Torture Abolition and Survivors Support Coalition (TASSC), which is the only organization in the United States that was founded by and for survivors of torture. The organization's main goal today is to seek the repeal of the Military Commissions Act of 2006. Even a cursory reading of this document, signed into law by President Bush, reveals why TASSC members call it "the American torture law." Section F of the law states that the courts it establishes are regularly constituted courts and that therefore they must respect "all the necessary judicial guarantees which are recognized as indispensable by civilized peoples for purposes of common Article 3 of the Geneva Conventions." So far that provision sounds very good, since the Geneva Conventions prohibit torture. But the very next section of the Military Commissions Act carries the title "Geneva Conventions Not Establishing Source of Human Rights," and goes on to say, *"No alien unlawful enemy combatant subject to trial by military commission under this chapter may invoke the Geneva Conventions as a source of rights"* (italics mine). In other words, torturing *some* people is perfectly legal.

In addition to founding TASSC, Sister Dianna patiently pursued the question of the identity of her chief torturer, whom she recalled as speaking accent-free American English. The trail was a long one, but it led upward to General Hector Gramajo, formerly defense minister of Guatemala. He denied all Sister Ortiz's sworn testimony. But she eventually won a civil suit against him in a U.S. District Court. The involvement of Gramajo carried with it a special barb for me, since when she uncovered his identity he was attending graduate school at Harvard, where I was teaching. The disquieting thought came to me that this man might have been in one of my classes, or in one taught by one of my colleagues. By the time I checked this out (he had not been in any of my classes) he was gone. But soon thereafter he gave the commencement address at the notorious School of the Americas, where the United States once trained Latin American military. Torture may begin with a hood over the head in a sound-proof room, but that is only the base of a pyramid that soars upward into well-lighted classrooms, briefing stations, and situation rooms. It is the product not of individual malfeasance but of systematic policy.

Most Americans have a hard time coming to terms with this uncomfortable fact. Indeed, most of us were barely aware of our country's complicity in torture until in April 2004 when the *New Yorker* magazine and *60 Minutes* revealed pictures taken at the prison in Abu Ghraib, Iraq. The photographs showed prisoners being threatened by large dogs, stripped naked, forced to crawl and to climb onto piles of other prisoners, and being degraded in other ways. The most disturbing photograph showed a hooded prisoner standing on a stool with his arms outstretched and wires attached to his body. The first reaction of many Americans was incredulity: "*We* cannot possibly be doing this!" But the fact was that *we* were. Investigations, accusations, denials, and buck-passing ensued. Military and CIA officials insisted that these photos depicted no more than a tasteless prank perpetrated by bored and ill-trained misfits in the lower ranks. They were no more than "a few bad apples." But persistent journalists and conscientious military kept pushing, and as they did the ultimate responsibility for these actions—which it turned out were in no way restricted to Abu Ghraib—reached higher and higher.

Apart from the moral and religious issues that torture raises (see below), even at the lowest level of strategy and of tactics it is a gravely mistaken policy. On August 27, 2010, the *New York Times* printed an editorial titled "Legacy of Torture." It reminded readers that during the presidency of George W. Bush administration officials told Americans that "enhanced interrogation techniques" were necessary to extract information from prisoners and to keep America safe from terrorist attacks. It is now clear, however, that this policy not only did untold damage to America's moral standing in the world, but it also produced very little important information. But it now also turns out that using "enhanced interrogation techniques" (torture) to force confessions has made it very difficult for the courts to try the cases of alleged terrorists. Judges are finding in case after case that, in accordance with American law, the confessions cannot be accepted and that their whole testimony is tainted.

A recent report by *Pro Publica* and the *National Law Journal* indicates that government prosecutors have lost more than half the cases of Guantanamo detainees because they were tortured. Sometimes the torture was administered by American officials, sometimes by foreign governments acting at the request of the United States. Even when government officials have gone back to these prisoners and obtained what they consider to be "clean" confessions, judges have consistently found that these later confessions are also tainted by the earlier methods. The judges are surely right about this. It is not hard to imagine a prisoner who has been tortured being brought back for a new "clean" interrogation remembering what had happened before and tailoring his/her response to be sure it does not start again. Any rational person would probably do the same.

It is possible, of course, that some of the prisoners who were interrogated/tortured are guilty and should stand trial. Still, some are not, and some of these have been released after years of imprisonment. But now, with the record tainted by forcibly extracted confessions, it may be impossible for the government to conduct such trials. The result of this stalemate is a negative one from any point of view. It means both that those actually guilty cannot be legally tried and that those who are not guilty may have to rot in confinement since they cannot be exonerated.

The torture policy has therefore resulted in just the opposite of what its defenders say they intended. For example, the government's case against Farhi Saeed bin Mohammed, who was captured in Pakistan in 2001 and accused of being a fighter for al-Qaeda, may

already have been ruined because its evidence against him was sup-
plied by Binyam Mohamed, who was reported to have been tortured
for two years in Morocco and Pakistan at the behest of the United
States. According to the report, "His genitals were mutilated. He was
deprived of sleep and food.... Captors held him in stress positions for
days at a time. He was forced to listen to piercingly loud music...."[45]
The American government has not denied that Mr. Mohamed was
tortured, and Judge Gladys Kessler of the U.S. District Court for the
District of Columbia ordered him to be released. But at this writing
he is still imprisoned in Guantanamo because the government has
appealed the case. Torture, it seems, is not only wrong and ineffec-
tive; it also produces effects opposite to those intended.[46]

Torture is a tactical question and a political one. It is also surely
a moral issue. But is it, properly speaking, a theological issue? The
answer to this question is a resounding, "Yes, it is."

> Torture is a tactical question
> and a political one. It also
> surely a moral issue. But
> is it, properly speaking,
> a theological issue? The
> answer to this question is a
> resounding, "Yes, it is."

The finest recent exploration of
what might be called "the theology
of torture" is Roman Catholic theologian William Cavanaugh's *Torture
and Eucharist: Theology, Politics,
and the Body of Christ.*[47] Cavanaugh
builds his highly persuasive case on
the Christian doctrine of the church
as the all-inclusive body of Christ.
For him, the Eucharist is the central expression of this body.

The Eucharist is not a mere sign that points to some more con-
crete political reality. Christ's eucharistic body is both *res* and *sacra-
mentum*. Christ does not lie behind the eucharistic sign but saturates
it. Christians do not simply read the sign but perform it. We become
Christ's body in the Eucharist. The Eucharist is the true "politics," as
Augustine saw, because it is the public performance of the true and

---

45. Binyam Mohamed v. The Secretary of State for Foreign and Commonwealth Affairs, No.
   T1/2009/2331 (Court of Appeals, London, 2010), 8.
46. See especially Hunsinger, ed., *Torture Is a Moral Issue.*
47. William T. Cavanaugh, *Torture and Eucharist: Theology, Politics, and the Body of Christ*
   (Malden, MA: Blackwell Publishing, 1998).

eternal city of God in the midst of another city that is passing away.[48]

The most relevant text here is this passage in 1 Corinthians in which Paul is discussing how the many different gifts are distributed in one body.

> All these gifts are the activity of one and the same Spirit, distributing them to each individual at will. Christ is like a single body with its many limbs and organs, which, many as they are, together make up one body. . . . A body is not a single organ, but many. . . . But God has combined the various parts of the body, giving special honour to the humbler parts, so that there might be no division in the body, but that all its parts might feel the same concern for one another. If one part suffers, all suffer together; if one flourishes, all rejoice together. (1 Cor. 12:11, 12, 24–26 REB)

Cavanaugh contrasts the single body of humanity, foreshadowed by the visible body of Christ, as the genuine human community, versus the pseudo-community of the nation-state. Both of course are "imaginary" in one sense. But for Cavanaugh the nation-state as an imaginary community must divide human beings from one another in order to live. Its very existence depends on having an outside threat from which it is ostensibly protecting its citizens. The nation-state relies utterly on the "we-against-them" paradigm. If there were no such threat, the state's raison d'être could disappear and it would collapse. Its existence is a myth that must be ingrained in its people by means of a narrative played out in monuments and rituals. Both the nation-state and the church are founded on dramas in which we enter into the plot, but the plots are radically different. The nation-state plot posits itself against the potent and treacherous other. At the Communion rail everyone is equal. No national or racial or other qualities count. The bread and wine are shared equally. It is an eschatological feast not only of radical economic redistribution but also of universally inclusive community.

---

48. Ibid., 14.

Incidentally, Cavanaugh's point might have been strengthened if he had admitted—perhaps even lamented—that the Christian Communion table has not always been so open and welcoming. It is vital to insist that wherever it is restricted because of denomination or moral status or any other extrinsic factor, its symbolic power is weakened.

The nation-state is also a mythic community. Some would call it an "invented community." It is a newcomer. Its history, on the scale of human history, is a very recent one. But it also requires the people it claims to play parts in a drama, and this is where torture as an instrument of state power appears. Torture is not an aberration in the nation-state. It is required in order to demonstrate to people just what it is protecting them against (Communists, terrorists, etc.). The German political philosopher Karl Schmitt, who eventually became one of the Nazis' chief theorists, claimed that the inherent weakness of all liberal societies is their inability to sharpen the friend-foe dichotomy, the division on which the state's mandate rests. To have a common enemy is the sine qua non of a successful nation-state.

Cavanaugh observes that, paradoxically, by showing what extreme measures it must take (often with feigned reluctance) to protect against this evil enemy, torture serves the purpose of creating and demonizing the dangerous "other." If these people were not so dangerous for us, so the logic runs, why would we have to be doing these (admittedly horrendous) things to them? During the dark years under Pinochet's rule in Chile, military officials sometimes expressed surprise that the "Communists" they were protecting the country against did not really demonstrate much of a danger. They resorted to picking up, torturing, and killing people with no connection to any resistance movement in order to perpetuate the "us-versus-them" scenario. The conclusion is that we must not think of torture as something bizarre and out of the ordinary. It is, rather, integral to everything nations, and others, do to enforce social control.

A pivotal point in the theology of torture is the biblical understanding of the human. From a Christian perspective human beings are not souls temporarily resident in bodies; they are unified entities. Christians do not hold to "the immortality of the soul," which is a Platonic idea, but to the resurrection of the body. Over the centuries, and particularly in recent ones, however, the church has made an unseemly deal with the state. The church was to be the custodian of the soul, but the state was to have jurisdiction over bodies. Human beings were bifurcated. This convenient but fatal arrangement has resulted in Christianity being pushed farther and farther toward the margins of life, while the pseudo-communities known as nation-states have increasingly defined the identities and life meanings of those it claims as its own. When the state uses its authority to torture its people (or anyone falling within its jurisdiction), it is claiming absolute power. Its "right" to inflict humiliation, pain, and death cannot be overturned since even the highest seats of juridical appeal are organs of the same state. Outside it, to retrieve a phrase from an earlier theology, there is no salvation. Torture survivors say that the worst realization that haunted them as they slumped in their cells waiting for the next "interrogation" was that *no one could help them*. Torture is the ultimate paradigmatic enactment of the myth of the nation-state.

Finally, torture is a matter of Christology. A key point in any theology of torture has to be that the Christian gospel centers on a man who died from state-sponsored torture. Unlike the Buddha, the Prophet Muhammad, or any other founder or prophet, the Galilean carpenter was one more person who was hanged by his hands, this time with nails instead of chains or handcuffs. But the gospel is also unlike previous religious myths of conquest, such as that of Gilgamesh. Christians are summoned to identify not with the winner but with the victim. The resurrection of Jesus Christ is, for Christians, a divine affirmation of the just claims of all victims of persecution, tyranny, and torment to ultimate justice and restitution.

Realizing this simple truth of the Christian message, it is hard to understand why Christians often have such a difficult time identifying with the victims of torture. When I was in Argentina during the dark era when the military was picking up "suspects" in unmarked cars and whisking them to torture centers, I asked a Protestant minister in Rio de Janeiro what, if anything, he was doing about it. "Why should I do anything," he answered, "those people are all terrorists anyway." When I tried to explain to him (as subsequent investigations have shown) that they were not "all terrorists," he seemed doubtful. Then when I asked him whether, even if they were all terrorists, he would object to their being tortured (which in that case meant women being gang-raped and men given electric shocks in the testicles), he seemed not to get the point. Had he forgotten about an alleged insurrectionist in first-century Palestine who was humiliated, flogged, ridiculed, and hung up by his hands? I did not ask him. Perhaps I should have.

13

Exile

Judah has gone into exile with suffering
    and hard servitude;
She lives now among the nations,
    and finds no resting place;
Her pursuers have all overtaken her
    in the midst of her distress.

(1:3)

By the rivers of Babylon, there we sat down, yea, we
    wept, when we remembered Zion.
We hanged our harps upon the willows in the midst
    thereof,
For there they that carried us away captive required
    of us a song, and they that wasted us required of us
    mirth, saying, Sing us one of the songs of Zion.
How shall we sing the LORD's song in a strange land?

(Ps. 137:1–4 KJV)

The Poet of Lamentations not only anguishes over the agony of the looted and abandoned city, the result of the Chaldean king Nebuchadrezzar's conquest Jerusalem in 587 BCE. She also laments the lot of those fellow compatriots who have been forced into exile, in what we have known ever since as "the Babylonian captivity." Psalm 137, quoted above, bespeaks the desolation of "displaced persons." Not only are they far from home, but their captors taunt them. They "require mirth" when the exiles are in no mood for it.

That exile ended seventy years later when Cyrus, the Persian king, conquered the Babylonians and allowed the Jews there to "return" to their homeland. I place "return" in quotation marks because in fact no one, or hardly anyone, actually returned. Obviously all the Jews who had been exiled were dead before the "return," with the possible exception of whatever very young children accompanied their parents into exile and lived to over seventy years of age, a rarity in that era. The important point is that with this jarring historical dislocation, the idea of exile entered permanently into the Jewish psyche and from there into Christianity and eventually into a global sensibility. How did this happen?

The great Jewish scholar Gershom Scholem has written: "the historical exile of the Jewish people is none other than the most striking symbol of that state of the universe in which there is no *tikkun* or harmony and by which everything is damaged or harmed. Exile and redemption are thereby transformed into powerful symbols, acquiring the background of a cosmic myth."[49]

No people, in either North or South America at least, have been more gripped by the cosmic myth of exile as have the African people whose forebears were kidnapped and hauled here to toil as slaves. Psalm 137 was one of their favorite texts, even though they did eventually find it possible to "sing the Lord's song" in the strange lands in which they found themselves, and in so doing created two of the most distinctive forms of American poetry and music, the spirituals and the blues. As Allen Callahan, a historian of black American readings of the Bible, points out, the slaves could not cling to a hope of "return." "They would learn to sing their song in a strange land or not at all."[50] Still they loved Psalm 137 and often paraphrased it. Callahan includes this echo of the psalm by an anonymous African American poet:

> By Babylon's streams we sat and wept,
> While Zion we thought upon;

---

49. Quoted in Steven M. Wasserstrom, *Religion after Religion: Gershom Scholem, Mircea Eliade, and Henry Corbin at Eranos* (Princeton: Princeton University Press, 1999), 7.
50. Allen Dwight Callahan, *The Talking Book: African Americans and the Bible* (New Haven: Yale University Press, 2008), 50.

> Amidst thereof we hung our harps,
> The willow trees upon.
> With all the pow'r of skill I have,
> I'll gently touch each string;
> If I can teach the charming sound,
> I'll tune my harp again.[51]

Frederick Douglass liked to quote Psalm 137 as expressing the slaves' heartbreak, "the plaintive lament of a peeled and woe-smitten people." Black American poetry pictures the black man in America beaten to his knees and exiled, but always envisioning a world where none is lonely, none hunted, alien.[52] Thus even when identifying so strongly with the exiles they heard about from the Bible, the African slaves knew there was to be no return. They could dream about Abyssinia and eventually even name their churches for it, but their longing for an end to exile came to focus on two sources of hope. One was that they might escape, "cross over Jordan," to "follow the drinking gourd" and find freedom in the north. The other was that one day, in some way, God would deliver them from their bondage. Sometimes these two hopes were fused in their musical imaginations.

It is important to remember that the wholesale capture and shipment of Africans to the Americas was at its root a business enterprise. They were needed to work the mines of Peru and the plantations of Georgia. Without them the economies of both continents would have shriveled. It is also critical to bear in mind how massive the slave business was. Between 1492 and 1820 five times as many Africans were brought to the Americas involuntarily as white Europeans came voluntarily. This means that the *experience* of exile for the Africans was a wholly different one. It differed from that of the English who crossed the ocean to escape religious persecution or to make a fortune; or the Eastern European Jews who fled to escape the pogroms; or the Sicilians who came simply in search of a living.

51. "Babel's Streams," ed. George Pullen Jackson, *Down-East Spirituals and Others: Three Hundred Songs Supplementary to the Author's Spiritual Folk-Songs of Early America* (New York: J. J. Augustin, 1943), 186.
52. See Henry Louis Gates Jr. and Nellie Y. McKay, eds., *The Norton Anthology of African American Literature* (New York: Norton, 1997), 1508–9.

The slaves had been captured and uprooted from various different locations in West Africa, so there was no "homeland" to which they could hope to return. There were no relatives left behind to whom they could write, at least none they could find out about. Their exile was permanent, and until recently their connections with "Mother Africa" were mainly imaginary ones.

Given this condition of permanent exile, black people in North America developed what theologian Cheryl Sanders calls a "theology of exile."[53] She shows how these African Americans developed a longing for some place, whether geographical or spiritual, where they could "feel at home." For many, the church building itself often became that space. Later it was frequently one of the few spaces the black people in any community actually owned and controlled. It was theirs. Like no other space it served as domicile, meetinghouse, dining hall, and—eventually of great importance—a protected place in which to organize political actions. White people sometimes wonder why blacks seem to spend so much time in church. But their history as a people in exile answers that question.

The South American experience of blacks provides a somewhat different picture, albeit still one of exile. It is not widely recognized that during the centuries of the Atlantic slave trade more Africans were brought to South America and the Caribbean than to North America. Unlike the slaves in North America, many slaves in these areas retained larger swatches of their religion and culture. They created a rich blending of these elements with the folk Catholicism they found in their exile. By fusing the Catholic saints with African deities they constructed a cultural bridge that was usually not available to their counterparts in North America, where Protestantism was more dominant. Religions like Santeria and Umbanda continue to nourish this connection. The Rastafarian faith, however, did eventually develop its own "myth of return." Reggae music characterizes the societies in which they must live now as "The Babylon System," a direct reference to the biblical exile. They still sing and hope for an eventual "return" to an idealized Africa.

53. Cheryl J. Sanders, *Souls in Exile: The Holiness-Pentecostal Experience in African American Religion and Culture* (New York: Oxford University Press, 1996).

Some observers now claim that in the twentieth century this "cosmic myth" of exile extended and amplified itself, and that it has become the characteristic cultural sensibility of our era. A gnawing sense of dislocation and displacement has become not just Jewish but nearly universal. Further, exile need not be the result of finding oneself in a "strange land," unable to "sing the Lord's song." It is a spiritual disquietude, a sense of uprootedness that affects us even in our own homes and homelands. It is no longer just geographical but existential.

In the literature of the past one hundred years, exile has become an axial category. There are two ways to approach it. The first is to recall the many poets, essayists, and novelists who have written *about* exile. A salient example is the late Palestinian literary scholar (credited with being the inventor of "post-colonial criticism") Edward Said, who wrote about it eloquently in *Out of Place*.[54] Another approach is to ponder the way the *experience* of exile has shaped the worldview of so many of our best writers, even when they were not writing about it explicitly.

When one thinks of the artists and writers who have been shaped by themselves being exiled, the list is nearly endless. T. S. Eliot, Oscar Wilde, Ernest Hemingway, and Henry James were self-imposed exiles. They might be better termed "expatriates." For a couple of decades in the early twentieth century Paris became the favored port of refuge for many expatriates, the people Gertrude Stein, herself a self-exiled writer, dubbed "the lost generation." In his autobiographical volume *A Moveable Feast*, Hemingway gives an absorbing, nearly day-to-day account of what life was like for these talented but "lost" denizens of the Boulevard St. Michele and the bookstalls of the Left Bank.[55]

> Exile need not be the result of finding oneself in a "strange land," unable to "sing the Lord's song." It is a spiritual disquietude, a sense of uprootedness that affects us even in our own homes and homelands. It is no longer just geographical but existential.

---

54. Edward Said, *Out of Place* (New York: Random House, 2000).
55. Ernest Hemingway, *A Moveable Feast* (New York: Scribner, 1964).

Can any good come out of exile? There is a continuing debate about the net effect of exile on writers and artists. On the one hand, it could be argued that their sense of rootlessness and loneliness, and the initial strangeness of the local customs, might make it terribly hard to engage in genuinely creative work.

On the other hand, the literary critic Edward Said has argued that tasting the bitter potion of exile is an absolute necessity in the shaping of a mature writer. He believed one must really grasp the inner essence of one's own native tradition, even become steeped in it. Then, however, one must step outside it and view it from a different perspective in order to reach the dimension of the universal.[56]

Said, an exile himself, was also one of the most eloquent writers on exile. An American citizen who lived in New York City and taught for forty years at Columbia University until his death in 2003, he was nonetheless almost the paradigm of a "man without a country." In his superb essay on Said, Tony Judt calls him a "rootless cosmopolitan."[57] He was a man of contradictions and ironies. A recognized spokesmen for Arabs and Muslims, he was the Episcopalian son of a Baptist father from Nazareth. A self-designated Palestinian, he lived most of his childhood in Cairo. He was a staunch defender of the rights of Palestinians but an adamant critic of their leaders, Yassir Arafat in particular. He was fond of pointing out that unlike other exiles, Palestinians were exiled in their own ancestral land, yet due to the Israeli occupation they had no land to call their own. Judt's essay includes a description of the Palestinian territories today that resonates vibrantly with the land The Poet of Lamentations describes:

> as the years went by, with half the occupied territories expropriated; and with the Palestinian community in shambles and the putative Palestinian territory a blighted landscape of isolated enclaves, flattened olive groves, and ruined houses, where humiliated adults were fast losing the initiative to angry, alienated adolescents. . . .[58]

56. See Said, *Out of Place*, 7.
57. Judt, *Reappraisals*, 163.
58. Ibid., 171.

When one considers the exile mentioned in Lamentations, it is important to realize that being in the "strange land" of Babylonia did not stifle the spiritual creativity of the Jewish people. Exiles though they were, they created the Babylonia Talmud. Some people may at times wish to become voluntary expatriates. But no one really wants to be exiled. Still, when exile happens, as it does throughout human history, those who, like The Poet of Lamentations, understand it within a wider frame of reference can actually sing by the waters of Babylon. And some of the music and poetry, and even theology, they have produced in a "strange land" have endured for many centuries.

14

Starvation and Cannibalism

When cities are conquered children starve and people turn desperate. Jerusalem was no exception. Lamentations describes the starvation in chilling terms, including the awful revelation that women were driven to devour their own children. Hunger roamed the streets, and those who might be expected to help did nothing.

> I called to my lovers,
> but they let me down;
> my priests and my elders
> perished in the city
> while seeking food
> to keep themselves alive.
> (1:19 REB)

As always in famines, it is the children who suffer most.

> With thirst the sucking infant's tongue
> cleaves to the roof of its mouth;
> young children beg for bread,
> but no one offers them a crumb.
> (4:4 REB)

But no one, high or low, escapes the devastation. Defeat and degradation can be great equalizers.

> Those who once fed delicately
> are desolate in the streets;
> those brought up in purple garments
> now gravel on refuse heaps.
>
> (4:5 REB)

Despondent, and with no one to help, the women of Jerusalem became so frantic they even cooked and devoured their own babies.

> With their own hands tender-hearted women
> boiled their own children;
> their children became their food
> on the day of my people's wounding.
>
> (4:10 REB)

It is not just the cannibalism itself that grieves The Poet, horrific as that may be. It is the overwhelming shame and guilt of the act that evokes a shriek that blames both God and the self. One can almost picture this woman shaking her fist in fury at the heavens.

> LORD, look and see:
> who is it you have thus tormented?
> Must women eat the fruit of their wombs,
> the children they have held in their arms?
>
> (2:20 REB)

Christian art flows with touching images of mothers and children. The Madonna with the Christ child is the most beloved. Along with it, of course, there is the image of the pietà, the sorrowing mother cradling the dead body of her adult son. But in the passage quoted above we find the ghastliest of all these mother-and-child scenes, the monstrous sight of a mother, desperate with hunger, eating her own child. This image is in the Bible, but I have never seen it depicted in art of any kind. If for no other reason, we should read Lamentations because it takes us into depths of horror we find nowhere else in Scripture.

15

Humiliation

How the Lord has covered the Daughter of Zion
With the cloud of his anger!
He has hurled down the splendor of Israel
From heaven to earth;
He has not remembered his footstool
In the day of his anger.
Without pity the Lord has swallowed up
All the dwellings of Jacob;
In his wrath he has torn down
The strongholds of the Daughter of Judah.
He has brought her kingdom and its princes
Down to the ground in dishonor.

(2:1–2 TNIV)

Lamentations can be read as a jarring journey through the blistering landscape of humiliation.

Lamentations can be read as a jarring journey through the blistering landscape of humiliation.

In addition to hunger, death, and exile, The Poet speaks over and over about "dishonor." What does it feel like to be humiliated? It means to be cast down, spat upon, tossed aside. What does the world look like to people who have been humiliated?

It is fascinating to recall that although people have felt humiliated for millennia, philosophers did little or no systematic study of humiliation until quite recently. This is probably because philosophers have almost always been men of the dominant class, those least likely to experience humiliation. It may also be why the thinker who has introduced humiliation into philosophical discourse is the French-Bulgarian feminist thinker Julia Kristeva, often thought of as a "postmodern" scholar. Kristeva seized upon the term *abjection* to describe the mental and spiritual condition of people who have been defeated, marginalized, or disinherited, and who see the world through that lens. With telling insight she expands the categories of traditional philosophy with its subject/object axis by using "abjection" as a concept that falls between "object" and "subject."

For Kristeva, the "abject," unlike the subject, is positioned outside the dominant symbolic order of the world. But the "abject" cannot avoid facing and coping with that order. The "abject" is embedded in it and cannot invent a whole new symbolic order without appearing to others, as well as to the "abject" him- or herself, as mad. This creates a crisis of meaning that can stoke anger, violence, or embittered submission. James Baldwin was both black and gay. He probably never heard the term, but he embodies what Kristeva means by the "abject." His works, especially *The Fire Next Time,* passionately convey this sense of crackling outrage, bordering on madness. His novels portray these feelings with powerful plots and images. The mood of much of his writing can remind the reader of the shrill complaints of Lamentations.

Kristeva also argues, however, that the "subject" in any symbolic order, the one who profits from its values and meanings and enjoys its privileges, must at times confront the abject. And this can be traumatic for the subject. Her example is the human response to a corpse. The first response is usually repulsion; although cultures teach us to harness this feeling, it always lingers under the surface, even as we honor the dead. We realize that this *object* was once a *subject* like us, and we could (and eventually will) become like it. In the riveting film *Platoon,* about the Vietnam War, a handful of American soldiers are ambushed by the enemy. They take cover, but one of them is badly wounded. They use all the medical equipment they carry to try to keep him alive, but he soon dies. The sergeant who has been leading the effort to save him quickly turns to the soldiers and says, "Now, do see that pile of dead meat there? Unless you do what I say, that is what you are going to be" (my paraphrase). The subject has become object, or possibly "abject," now to be cast off. But the living must live with the presence of the dead.

Kristeva believes that this experience of confronting our own mortality, our own inherent "abjectness," is what forces subjects to construct a symbolic order, to prevent slipping from "I" to "it." But encountering those who have already slipped, or been shoved, into being something less than subjects poses a constant threat both to the symbolic order and to those who are protected by it. This is why when confronting a corpse a live person is most likely repulsed—he or she is forced to face an object that is violently cast out of the shared world, having once been a subject. We encounter other beings daily, and more often than not they are alive. However, to confront the corpse of one that we recognize as human, something that *should* be alive but is not, is to confront the reality that we are capable of reaching the same state—we confront our own mortality. This repulsion from death, excrement, and rot constitutes the subject as a living being in the symbolic order. Religions often use rituals, specifically those of defilement, in order to maintain clear boundaries between nature and society, the semiotic and the symbolic, the accepted and the rejected. In Christianity, however, the rejection and defilement, death, abandonment, and humiliation are all loaded onto the figure of the crucified One.

The concept of abject is often coupled (and sometimes confused with) the idea of the uncanny, the idea of something being "un-home-like," or foreign, yet weirdly familiar. The abject can be uncanny in the sense that we can recognize aspects in it, despite its being "foreign." An example, continuing on the one used above, is that of a corpse of a loved one. We will recognize that person as being close to us, but the fact that the person is dead, and "no longer" the familiar loved one, is what creates a sort of cognitive dissonance, the abjection of the corpse.

Humiliation is hard to bear. A key part of the Roman execution of Jesus, as it was with other prisoners of the day, was to subject them to a calculated program of humiliation. Stripping naked, ridiculing, insulting, and forcing them to carry the instrument of their own death all figured into the pitiless procedure. We sometimes use the phrase "bearing the cross" a bit too easily to refer to any burden or difficulty people must live with. But for the Romans it was a consciously devised tactic designed to rob their victims of their last bit of self-esteem.

But when people are humiliated and survive, they rarely forget it. As human beings we often nurse the memory of our humiliating experiences and continue to loath the people who inflicted them on us. Students of twentieth-century history claim that it is impossible to understand the rise of Hitler without taking into consideration the enormous humiliation to which the German people were subjected after World War I. On the other hand, one of Gandhi's key maxims was that one should avoid at all costs humiliating one's opponent since it always makes reaching some agreement enormously harder. Humiliation is another of the nearly unavoidable fruits of war, so the best way to avoid it is to avoid the wars that produce it.

16

Pornography and War

Rape, torture, humiliation, exile, cannibalism? Many of us who were weaned on the nicely expurgated Hurlbut's *Story of the Bible* would be dismayed to discover such things in the Good Book. Still, they are indeed there. But are they really unexpurgated? It is a central thesis of Paul Fussell's magnificent book, *The Great War and Modern Memory*, that no matter how graphic and detailed ex post facto descriptions of war are, they can never recreate the depth of its hideousness.[59] The sheer act of reducing war and conquest to writing, even the finest writing, has a distancing effect: "You still cannot smell it!" You cannot actually hear the groans of the wounded and dying, the ravings of those driven mad, or the hysterical weeping of the survivors. Lamentations may come close to enabling us to smell the aftermath of war, but like even the best of its genre, it cannot fully succeed.

Do films succeed any better in conveying the carnage and absurdity of war? In one sense they do. Their mixture of vivid visual images and sounds can come closer. Seeing a whole beach strewn with dead soldiers in *Saving Private Ryan* or watching bullets tear holes in human flesh in *Platoon* can move us into a kind of proximity to the reality. But at the same time, the overall theme of the film may still be to celebrate heroism, patriotism, or death-defying loyalty to one's comrades. What would our literary canon be without *The Iliad*, the *Chansons de geste* (e.g., the *Song of Roland*), the medieval epics, or Tolstoy's *War and Peace*? The last, of course, hardly celebrates war.

59. Paul Fussell, *The Great War and Modern Memory* (New York: Oxford University Press, 1975).

One of its central characters, Pierre, is at first romantically drawn to war, but after actually witnessing a battle, he changes his mind. He is in some measure an echo of Tolstoy himself, who served in Russia's wars in the Crimea, but later became one of the most famous pacifists. His influence reached to Gandhi and through the mahatma to Martin Luther King Jr.

Scattered in the canon of world literature are some luminous examples of the antiwar perspective. The most ingenious is Aristophanes's *Lysistrata,* in which the women go on a sex strike to try to convince their men not to forge into battle. But there are few examples of this countercurrent. During the past century, however, we have seen the emergence of masterful antiwar novels. Erich Marie Remarque's *All Quiet on the Western Front* is one of the most powerful. Hemingway's *Farewell to Arms* is an American classic in this genre, and his *For Whom the Bell Tolls* is written from a similar perspective. Kurt Vonnegut assays the same territory through science fiction in *Cat's Cradle.* Some have argued that Norman Mailer's merciless *The Naked and the Dead* becomes an antiwar book as it unfolds.

Is Lamentations an antiwar text? The question is debatable. Perhaps it is only an elegy about defeat. What if the Israelites had successfully resisted the Babylonian attack? What if they had "won"? What if Babylon had been captured and sacked? Would The Poet of Lamentations have risen to such eloquence about the starving children and violated women of that "enemy" city? The answer is, probably not. It is a long step from grieving our "fallen ones" to grieving those who died on the other side. Sometimes, however, this does happen.

We have already heard the archbishop of Canterbury in this connection. But for me another example is closer to hand. When the Memorial Church at Harvard was built in memory of the Harvard students, alumni, and faculty members who died in World War II, several professors insisted that a plaque also be installed to honor the students who died fighting on the German side. There was fierce opposition. But the professors, most of them on the Divinity faculty, persisted, pointing out that to leave these men unacknowledged would relegate the building into a Valhalla instead of a Christian church. They prevailed and, today, on the left inside wall stands a small tablet stating (in Latin) that Harvard does not forget these sons who "died under a different banner."

Writing about war, says Paul Fussell, contains a built-in irony because "every war is worse than expected." Any war, he continues, "constitutes an irony of situation because its means are so melodramatically disproportionate to its presumed ends."[60] In World War I, for example, eight million lives were destroyed presumably because the Archduke Francis Ferdinand and his consort were assassinated. The disproportion in World War II was "even more preposterous." A war to guarantee the sovereignty of Poland cost some 35 million lives (27 million of them Russian) and resulted in a Warsaw reduced to rubble and decades of Polish peonage to Moscow. A war to secure the freedom of Poland ended in its captivity. Irony was piled upon irony. Within a few years of the end of World War II, the two major enemies of the Western allies, Japan and Germany, were booming (they prospered in part because they were not permitted to rebuild their armed forces and did not have to support a military budget). Great Britain and France, on the other hand, slid into long slow declines.

Rightly perceived, war arouses disgust and repulsion. There is something fundamentally indecent about it. Yet this obscenity has provided the raw material for centuries of epics, heroic legends, romantic poetry, and novels. Human beings are somehow drawn to the obscene at the same time as it repels us. Once in a small French village on the western front during World War I a group of British soldiers came upon a church cemetery that had been shelled, opening some of the tombs and spilling rotted corpses onto the ground. The local authorities had placed "No Trespassing" signs around the site, but the soldiers crowded in to gawk at the ghastly exhibition. One soldier who kept a diary asked himself in it later why they had done that. Why did men who lived cheek to cheek with death every day, and who sometimes crouched under the bodies of dead buddies to escape machine-gun fire, give way to this morbid curiosity?

There may be no answer to this question, and if there is one, it can hardly be an attractive one. The German philosopher of religion

60. Ibid., 7.

Rudolf Otto in his famous book, *The Idea of the Holy,* argued that the holy (*das Heilige*) elicits in us both fear and fascination.[61] When it appears, it shakes us but somehow draws our attention to itself. In a so-called secular age, when what were once considered spiritual sentiments have been displaced by profane surrogates, we are drawn to horror and slasher films. Vampire movies have burgeoned into a multimillion dollar industry. This may be because, after all, Dr. Frankenstein's monster, Count Dracula, and the other creatures inhabit a murky netherworld between the living and the dead. They seem to defy that unknown country "from whose bourne no traveler has returned." The problem, of course, is that no traveler has in fact ever returned. Christians hold that Jesus Christ was resurrected from the dead. But Christian teaching makes clear that this was the promissory foreshadowing of an eschatological resurrection. Jesus was fully dead, the gospel states, until God "raised him up." He did not return as a Dracula-like mutant, one of the horror genre's "living dead."

This topic raises a key question about Lamentations. What effect does it have on the reader? Does it lure us into hating the Babylonians (or their current equivalents)? War always produces atrocities, and they are nearly always committed by both sides. But it seems they are never quite enough to quench the insatiable thirst of the public and to stoke patriotic indignation. Consequently, atrocities are also invented. One of the most notorious is the case—long since disproved—of the "crucified Canadian," which circulated on the western front and then on the home front during the early years of World War I. There are many versions of this canard, but one account has it that the Germans had captured a Canadian soldier alive and then in full view of his comrades stretched out his arms and pinned him with bayonets to the trunk and crosslike branches of a tree. He died, so the rumor held, slowly. There is something deeply perverse about this human tendency to make an already outlandishly repulsive reality even worse.

Does portraying the grisly awfulness of war and sometimes even grislier aftermath really turn us against war? Once again the answer

---

61. Rudolf Otto, *The Idea of the Holy: An Inquiry into the Non-rational Factor in the Idea of the Divine and Its Relation to the Rational,* trans. John W. Harvey (London: Oxford University Press, 1923).

is not obvious. Splashing the atrocities of the enemy across the front pages during World War I and II mainly resulted in lengthening the lines at the recruiting stations. This may be due in part to the well-known facility of young males to deny their mortality, to consider themselves invulnerable. It is always "the next guy," not me, who will "get it." Ironically, it is always "the next guy," since only the survivors live to remember. What would happen, the poet Siegfried Sassoon once mused, if all the war dead could vote on going into another struggle? But their voices are silenced. They cannot vote.

PART 4

INTERROGATING LAMENTATIONS

17

Prosperity and Liberation

As we approach the conclusion of our twenty-first-century reading of Lamentations, many questions remain. One has to do with its portrayal of a "golden age" before catastrophe struck, which carries with it hints of what may sound like the "prosperity gospel" that has gripped so many Christians today.

True, Lamentations begins with a soaring lyric conveying a human emotion that always arises when tragedy hits: contrasting the blighted present with the bright past.

> Those who once ate delicacies
> are destitute in the streets.
> Those nurtured in purple
> now lie on ash heaps.
> (4:5 TNIV)

But the reader immediately wonders. Was everyone eating delicacies? Tragedy often makes people paint the past in brighter colors than it actually had, and that is fully understandable. Irish immigrants, fleeing to America from the Great Hunger, still sang of the "old sod" as "a little piece of heaven" that "fell out of the sky one day." Parents for thousands of years have complained about the deteriorating behavior of youth "nowadays" as opposed to how much better things were in their day, at least in their rosy reconstruction. Legends of a golden age or a garden of Eden ripple through the stories of all peoples: "There were giants in the land then."

Literary scholars who have studied the English novels, short stories, and poetry produced after World War I have noticed that often the traditional trope of the "pastoral" appears. This is a very old literary strategy, especially in the midst of war or in its aftermath. Describing the ruination somehow required a framing device, a structure of contrast. Memories, real or imagined, of bucolic settings, often rural or drawn from village life, fulfill this function. But in World War I there was a glaring difference between the classes in this regard. The officer class may have had genuine memories of such rural settings. If they had not actually lived in the countryside, they had vacationed there or had summer cottages there. But the vast majority of the actual soldiers on the front lines were drafted not from hinterlands but from Liverpool, London, Glasgow, or Leeds, and knew little about village life. Very few had country homes where they might have watched plowmen or smelled honeysuckle or listened to birds (although many may have had window boxes, a favorite among the English). For the war poets, however, the pastoral contrast was far too strong to resist. Here is perhaps the most familiar example:

> In Flanders fields the poppies grow
> Between the crosses row on row.

Even in America, the poppy became the symbol of having served in the war, and red paper poppies on green wire were sold to be worn on what for many years was called "Armistice Day." Other poets contrasted the roses blooming on fences at home with the bits of bloody human flesh hanging from barbed wire.

One thinks also of Allen Tate, who relies effectively on the same contrast, in this instance with tombstones and leaves, in "Ode to the Confederate Dead."

> Row after row with strict impunity
> The headstones yield their names to the element,
> The wind whirrs without recollection;
> In the riven troughs the splayed leaves
> Pile up, of nature the casual sacrament.[62]

---

62. Allen Tate, "Ode to the Confederate Dead," *Collected Poems 1919-1976* (New York: Farrar Straus Giroux, 1977), 20.

It is worth noting, however, that in Lamentations the contrast does not turn to the pastoral. Here the contrast is drawn between being at home and wandering but also between affluence and impoverishment.

> In the days of her affliction and wandering
> Jerusalem remembers all the treasures
> that were hers in days of old.
>
> (1:7 TNIV)

Also in the case of Jerusalem there is some genuine justification in the lament. Jerusalem had indeed been a great city and had in truth been defeated and sacked. Its inhabitants had in reality been impoverished and humiliated. As we have seen in the course of Lamentations, however, this mood of mourning and hopelessness will not last forever. Perhaps the point here is that people cannot jump immediately to the task of rebuilding their lives or their cities after a disaster without a period in which they acknowledge the full scale and import of what they have lost.

> People cannot jump immediately to the task of rebuilding their lives or their cities after a disaster without a period in which they acknowledge the full scale and import of what they have lost.

"Just get on with your life" may eventually be sound advice for a grieving mother or a defeated people. It might one day be good counsel for the victims of a tsunami, the enraged citizens of New Orleans, or the numbed survivors of Port-au-Prince. But it will sound banal, even dismissive, until the full depth of the loss has been sounded.

Another question arises from The Poet's wistful recollection of what has been lost. At times it sounds almost crudely materialistic.

> Peace has gone from my life
> and I have forgotten what prosperity is.
> Then I cry out that my strength has gone
> and so has my hope in the LORD.
>
> (3:17–18 REB)

What does all this talk of purple garments (4:5), delicacies on the table (4:5), and unspecified "treasures" (1:7, 10–11) mean? With all this suffering everywhere in sight, why does The Poet sob about losing "prosperity"? Do we see here a preview to what is now called the "prosperity gospel"? In responding to this question the modern reader should bear in mind that material goods are in fact vital to life. The victims of hurricanes or of military pillaging do, of course, miss their lost loved ones. But they also miss their homes, their fields, the crops they had planted. The excesses of the "prosperity gospel" preachers have sometimes evoked a disproportionate condemnation. Biblical faith has nothing against either prosperity or abundance. A bountiful life on earth in addition to eternal salvation has always been integral to the good news. Notice again the words of Jesus in the Gospel of John (10:10 KJV):

> I am come that they might have life, and that they might have it more abundantly.

Indeed, at times the emphasis on abundance as a blessing seems too close to excessive.

> Thus the Lord blessed the end of Job's life more than the beginning: he had fourteen thousand sheep and six thousand camels, a thousand yoke of oxen, and as many she-donkeys. (Job 42:12 REB)

It is not abundance but inequality that the Bible condemns, the denial of distributive justice. One of the benefits of Job's unmerited suffering in mind and body was that though he was a rich man, he was able, for the first time, to realize how the poor live all the time. In chapter 24 he registers an indictment of what the rich and privileged have done, and continue to do, to the poor, the fatherless, and the landless:

> Some remove the landmarks; they violently take away
> flocks, and feed thereof.
> They drive away the ass of the fatherless, they take the
> widow's ox for a pledge.

They turn the needy out of the way: the poor of the
earth hide themselves together.

Behold, as wild asses in the desert, go they forth to
their work; rising betimes for a prey: the wilderness
yieldeth food for them and for their children.

They reap every one his corn in the field: and they
gather the vintage of the wicked.

They cause the naked to lodge without clothing, that
they have no covering in the cold.

They are wet with the showers of the mountains, and
embrace the rock for want of a shelter.

They pluck the fatherless from the breast, and take a
pledge of the poor.

They cause him to go naked without clothing, and they
take away the sheaf from the hungry;

Which make oil within their walls, and tread their
winepresses, and suffer thirst.

Men groan from out of the city, and the soul of the
wounded crieth out.

(Job 24:2–12 KJV)

One wonders whether, when The Poet of Lamentations and her people recover from the tsunami that has drenched them, they will have a deeper sympathy for others who suffer from war and destruction, including even the enemies of Israel.

Jesus' warning about the rich man and the camel can be and has been deployed against prosperity preachers. But grasped in the full context of the prophetic heritage within which Jesus preaches, clearly the reason it is hard for a rich man to enter the kingdom of God is not that he enjoys worldly goods. It is that he enjoys them at the expense of the poor. To the man who had two coats, the exhortation to give one to the poor might move him to share, but to the person who has no coat it states a claim he can legitimately make on someone who has a closetful.

In the Bible, prosperity trumps poverty. The *voluntary* poverty of Saint Francis or of Vincent de Paul was admirable. And it no doubt helped them to understand the bereft people they sought to serve. But both knew quite well that *in*voluntary poverty is ugly and degrading. When it is voluntary, poverty is a choice; but when it is not, it feels like a curse. Can anyone expect a hungry mother of three in a fetid slum of Recife or Lagos to respond to a message about the spiritual benefits of poverty?

Liberation theology advocates a "preferential option for the poor," but the option is to join in the struggle of the disinherited against their impoverishment and to reach out for what is rightly theirs. Television evangelists did not invent the prosperity gospel, but they have gravely distorted it. Still, they are half right. It is vital to tell people that God does not *will* them to be jobless, bereft of health insurance, and unable to make mortgage payments while the banking elites pocket millions of dollars in bonuses. But the mortal sin of these preachers is to teach their people that if they are poor, it is their own fault for not praying or tithing ardently enough. The Bible is clear that it is not their fault, but that in order to change the rotten system that creates such lopsided injustice something more is needed.

> The prosperity gospel preachers should take the next step. Only when we see them leading demonstrations outside the doors of Goldman Sachs and Citigroup can we believe that they have gotten hold of the real gospel and not the counterfeit version they now pander.

The prosperity gospel preachers should take the next step. Only when we see them joining demonstrations outside the doors of Goldman Sachs and Citigroup can we believe that they have gotten hold of the real gospel and not the counterfeit version they now pander.

The God of Mary of the Magnificat does send the rich away empty, but the same God fills the hungry with good things. Let us not condemn the yearning for these good things of life, but let us not trivialize what we need to do in order to put them within the reach of those who need them.

Yes, legends of a golden age ripple through all cultures, and the culture that produced Lamentations is no exception. But, as we have seen, these legends of a golden age carry a double meaning. The past contains a rich trove of images that can be retrieved and projected into the future. A people with no past has no future. A treasured past, even one with imaginary dimensions, can motivate people to imagine and even work for a better future.

18

Catastrophe and Community

Another question Lamentations leaves us with is this: Is there ever a positive side to calamity? The answer is that there often is, but sometimes there is not, and we are hard put to understand why there is this difference. When I spent a summer working at a church in one of the poorest sections of East London a few years after that area had been devastated by the blitz of World War II, the main theme recalled by those who had lived through it was not bitterness. They talked, sometimes almost wistfully, about the cheerfulness, defiance, and mutual helpfulness that kept them going. People had to rely heavily on one another, and they became innovative and at times even heroic. Yes, there were flames and destruction and death. But disaster brought out an often-subdued range of generous human impulses. There is hardly a shred of evidence in Lamentations that the cataclysm it describes elicited these often-hidden inclinations. One cannot help wondering why.

In *A Paradise Built in Hell: The Extraordinary Communities That Arise in Disasters*, Rebecca Solnit delves into this quandary.[63] Informed by what is now called "disaster sociology," but filling in the cold theory with warm bodies and real faces, she insists that disasters do often bring out a side of human nature that our quotidian existence normally obscures. Her examples include the San Francisco earthquake of 1905, the Mexico City quake of 1985, New York City on 9/11. One might also add the feeling of facing a common disaster

---

63. Rebecca Solnit, *A Paradise Built in Hell: The Extraordinary Communities That Arise in Disasters* (New York: Viking, 2009).

together generated by the 2010 oil spill in the Gulf of Mexico. Solnit points out that in "normal" times, which in fact might be quite abnormal, our competitive, consumer/market economy tends to pit us against one another, undermine our sense of a common community, and generate fear and loneliness. But at least in some disasters this dehumanizing incarceration is temporarily relieved. We know we have to cooperate and help one another. We help and we expect help. And to some degree this seemingly miraculous change actually occurs. Ordinary individuals take risks and improvise in ways that often surprise themselves. No wonder people become wistful when they remember it later, after "normalcy" has returned.

Solnit also points out the stark difference between how a disaster feels to those caught up in it and those who hear or read about it or who watch it unfold on television. During the coverage of Katrina, audiences heard over and over about a few violent incidents among the thousands of people confined to the Superdome while the bravery of hundreds of everyday people who jumped into swirling waters and climbed into disintegrating houses to rescue their fellow citizens was only treated episodically. Only later did we learn about the college students who, entirely on their own, packed their car with water containers and drove 500 miles to distribute it in New Orleans. Some of this distortion can be attributed to the media's insatiable thirst for the spectacular, but Solnit believes there is a deeper cause.

The view of human beings as somehow inherently competitive, self-centered, and even ruthless, she believes, has largely been foisted on us by a market society that places a premium on beating the other guy. Whatever values the market has, no one believes that it rewards tenderness or compassion. This cultural ethos prompts officials to think that what will inevitably happen in a disaster are panic and a cutthroat zeal to save oneself at any cost. Hence the first thing governments must do—according to this hellish scenario—is to send in the troops to prevent looting and killing. The problem is that those responsible for maintaining order often become the lawbreakers. Three New Orleans policemen have been convicted for the killing of an innocent man and the subsequent cover-up in the wake of Katrina. Several other law enforcement officers are under indictment.

Underlying this negative view is a pop version of Thomas Hobbes's description of human life as "nasty, brutish and short," and an equally bankrupt social Darwinism predicated on the survival of the fittest. But what actually happens after such events is quite different. By the time the emergency "first responders" get there, local people on the scene have already responded in multiple ways. Social philosophy has progressed since Hobbes and the social Darwinians. We now know that cooperation and altruism are also "survival traits" and that human beings are capable of a kind of self-sacrifice that is anything but brutish.

What about panic? The sociologists who have studied disaster behavior have discovered, sometimes to their own surprise, that it only rarely happens. Those who panic, so the studies show, are not usually the people on the ground. They are the officials who are *afraid* those people will panic. Consequently the steps the officials sometimes take make matters worse. After Katrina, officials kept health workers away from where they were needed because of false reports of violence that turned out to be rumors, often recirculated by media reports. Officials keep at a distance volunteers who are trying to help so that the allegedly better prepared professionals can do the job. Solnit holds that at the base of these self-destructive attitudes is a typical elite distrust of ordinary people and even a fear that spontaneous activity can get out of hand and threaten the elite's grip on power.

Perhaps in the end Lamentations sets the stage for what is to follow—the insistence by the prophets Amos and Jeremiah on equity and justice, the vision of a beloved community spelled out by the Sermon on the Mount and by the new Jerusalem envisioned in the book of Revelation.

What about looting? It is often the first thing that enters the minds of officials after a disaster. Again, however, careful studies of Katrina have shown that, although some looting did take place, most of the entering into closed stores and shops was carried out by people who had run out of food for themselves, their families, and their neighborhoods. When people are hungry and desperate they can scarcely be expected to walk past shuttered shops full of the sustenance they need. Human life is more important than material goods. We do not live on bread alone, but we do need bread.

After reading Lamentations, one cannot help wondering: What happened next? How did this wounded city pull itself together? Were there unprompted acts of kindness and sharing? Since the city did eventually recover, what were the resources its people called upon? Perhaps in the end Lamentations sets the stage for what is to follow—the insistence by the prophets Amos and Jeremiah on equity and justice, the vision of a beloved community spelled out by the Sermon on the Mount and by the new Jerusalem envisioned in the book of Revelation.

19

Revenge and Reconciliation

What about vengeance? It is another theme that appears time and again in Lamentations. What do we make of it? When people are hurt or misused they almost always want to strike back at their assailant. They want to see their tormenters tormented. They want *them* to suffer as *we* have suffered. They imagine the ugly events that will occur to them and they ask God to bring those events about.

> People have heard my groaning,
> but there is no one to comfort me.
> All my enemies have heard of my distress;
> they rejoice at what you have done.
> May you bring the day you have announced
> so they may become like me.
> Let all their wickedness come before you;
> deal with them
> as you have dealt with me
> because of all my sins.
> My groans are many
> and my heart is faint.
>
> (1:21–22 TNIV)

By the third chapter the fantasy of revenge, the craving for vengeance, becomes white hot. After all, these villains richly deserve the worst God can mete out to them.

> Give them, O LORD, their deserts
> According to their deeds.

> Give them anguish of heart;
> Your curse be upon them!
> Oh, pursue them in wrath and destroy them
> From under the heavens of the LORD!
> (3:64–66 JPS)

The thirst for revenge in the Bible is hardly restricted to Lamentations. It begins in Genesis with Cain's rage against his brother, Abel, whose sacrifice God has honored instead of his own. In that story God obviously disapproves of Cain's action. But God also protects Cain, who is rightly fearful of what people will want to do to him in revenge for his crime. The famous "mark of Cain" was originally a sign of God's protection, a divine recognition of how deep-seated is the craving for revenge in human beings. Throughout the Psalms the writers call to God to revenge them. They imagine inventive, sardonic punishments. They are especially drawn to seeing their enemies trapped in their own devices: "Let the wicked fall into their own snares!" (Ps. 141:10 NLT)

Apart from unrequited love, it is hard to think of any theme that is more pervasive in world literature than that of revenge. In a classic example, it drives the ongoing tragedy of Aeschylus's *Oresteia*, a sequence of dramas that relentlessly propel home the point that revenge begets further revenge in an endless spiral. The story is not an edifying one. The high point comes when King Agamemnon arrives home from his victory over Troy seated on a triumphal chariot. On another chariot, laden with spoils, follows Cassandra, his captive concubine, according to the laws of war in those times. Agamemnon's queen, Clytemnestra, greets him with a hypocritical show of joy and veneration, bids her maidens spread forth the purple carpets of the costliest golden embroidery, that the foot of the conqueror may not touch the ground. Agamemnon with wise moderation at first refuses to accept this honor, which belongs only to the gods. At last, however, he complies with her solicitations and follows her into the house.

Now the chorus begins to entertain dark forebodings. Clytemnestra returns to entice Cassandra, by saccharine persuasion, to the same destruction. At first Cassandra remains dumb and immovable.

But scarcely is the queen away when, seized by prophetic rage, the captive concubine breaks out into confused indistinct wailings. Presently, she reveals her predictions to the chorus more clearly; she beholds, in spirit, all the atrocities that have been perpetrated within this house: that Thyestean banquet in which the children were served up to the father and from which the son turned away his eye; the shades of the mangled children appear to her on the battlements of the palace. She sees the murder that is in readiness for her lord, and though shuddering at the reek of death, she rushes like a maniac into the house to meet her inevitable death. Behind the scenes are heard the groans of the dying Agamemnon.

The palace is thrown open; Clytemnestra stands beside the corpse of her king and husband, like an insolent criminal who not only acknowledges the deed but glories in it and justifies it as a righteous act of requital for Agamemnon's sacrifice of their daughter Iphigenia to his own vain ambition. Her jealousy of Cassandra and guilty union with the worthless Aegisthus, who does not make his appearance until the end of the play, are scarcely touched on as motives. They remain in the background, although we know they are there.

It is tempting to contrast Troy with Jerusalem, and Queen Clytemnestra with the broken and violated women depicted in Lamentations. The Greek queen is endowed with the traits of her epoch, an age drenched in bloody catastrophes, in which all passions spurted impetuously and men, both in good and evil, seemed to foreshadow the monstrous crimes of our own. No one is innocent here. The king has sacrificed his own child just to gain a military advantage against Troy. In the oldest narrative Iphigenia dies on the beach at her father's command. In a later version the goddess Artemis substitutes a deer in her place and carries her off to a distant land to become his priestess. At a superficial level this later narrative calls to mind the story of Abraham and Isaac. But the comparison quickly fails. God spares Isaac, and Abraham's progeny are blessed, and through them all the nations of the earth. In the Greek religious vision, the whole house of Atreus becomes the object of an unavoidable curse.

Sometimes the uniqueness of a biblical story can be highlighted by contrasting it with a structurally similar one that, however, conveys a much different view on the processes that occur between human beings and God and destiny. The following is the chorus of Argive elders singing of the death of Iphigenia and predicting the fall of Troy. Like Lamentations, it is a classical lament, but in this instance it is for the fated city of Troy ("Priam's city") instead of Jerusalem.

> In time old Priam's city wall
> Before that conquering host shall fall,
> And all within her towers lie waste;
> Her teeming wealth of man and beast
> Shall Fate in her dire violence destroy;
> May ne'er heaven's envy, like a cloud,
> So darken o'er that army proud,
> The fine-forged curb of Troy!
> For Artemis, with jealous ire,
> Beholds the wingéd hounds of her great sire
> Swooping the innocent leverets' scarce-born brood,
> And loathes the eagles' feast of blood.
> Ring out the dolorous hymn, yet triumph still the good!
> . . . .
> O Goddess! though thy wrath reprove
> Those savage birds, yet turn those awful signs to good!
> . . . .
> Of glory and of gloom.[64]

The "glory" here refers, of course, to the victory of the Greeks (the Argives) over the Trojans. Later the chorus sings, "Ring out the dolorous hymn, yet triumph still the good!" But in the midst of this forecasting, the chorus also at first bemoans the apparent disappearance or powerlessness of the gods who have contended with one another in the Trojan War. Then, however, the chorus catches a glimpse of this moment as the one in which Jove (or Zeus), the god charged with maintaining justice, will come to the fore.

---

64. Aeschylus, "Agamemnon," *Odes from the Greek Dramatists,* ed. Alfred William Pollard (Chicago: A. C. McClurg & Co., 1890), 23, 25.

Whoe'er thou art, Great Power above,
If that dread name thou best approve,
All duly weighed I cannot find,
Unburthening my o'erloaded mind,
A mightier name than that of mightiest Jove.

He, that so great of old
Branched out in strength invincible and bold,
Is nothing now. Who after came,
Before the victor sank to shame:
Most wise is he who sings the all-conquering might
    of Jove—

Jove, that great god
Who taught to mortals wisdom's road;
By whose eternal rule
Adversity is grave instruction's school.
In the calm hour of sleep
Conscience, the sad remembrancer, will creep
To the inmost heart, and there enforce
On the reluctant spirit the wisdom of remorse.[65]

But it seems that in the Greek view even Jove is not the supreme master. The chief of the Elysian gods indeed he may be, but he must still bow his head to the dictates of a higher power, that of Necessity (Fate). The dreadful end of Agamemnon's life turns out to be the punishment of Fate for his crime on the beaches of Troy, that "rite unblest" of which he was the sacrificing priest.

So 'neath Necessity's stern yoke he passed,
And his lost soul, with impious impulsive veering,
Surrendered to the accurst unholy blast,
Warped to the dire extreme of human daring.
The frenzy of affliction still
Maddens, dire counsellor, man's soul to ill.

65. Ibid., 25, 27.

So he endured to be the priest
In that child-slaughtering rite unblest,
The first-fruit offering of that host.[66]

Even the dead are not safe from the ravages of revenge. In Toni Morrison's novel *Jazz* a woman named Violet goes to a funeral in the Harlem of the 1920s. In the open casket lies the body of another young woman Violet's husband had murdered in a fit of jealousy. Violet walks to the casket, takes out a knife, and stabs the dead woman's face several times. Morrison claims she developed the story after reading an account of just such an incident in the newspaper.

But it is not just the plot of this wrenching novel that reveals the profile of revenge. The structure of *Jazz*—like Lamentations—is uneven, jumpy, and irregular. Like people bent on revenge, its throbbing focus leaps from one thing to another even though the underlying thrust is always on the grim satisfaction of revenge. The narrative voice never stops telling and retelling the awful tale, playing out embellishments (hence the title, *Jazz*), but never losing sight of the momentum of the basic purpose, like jazz musicians improvising on a theme.

As one might expect, there is no more acute cartographer of human passions than William Shakespeare. He not only charts it, he x-rays it. In *Hamlet* he turns his genius to the passion for revenge. He realizes that sometimes its insistent surging displaces all other emotions. The avenger is willing to set aside any consideration that might hamper its realization. People sacrifice homeland, family, safety, and anything else that stands in its way. But Shakespeare also knows about the convoluted complexity of revenge. *Hamlet* is one of the most powerful portraits of revenge in all literature. After his father's murder, the prince of Denmark's whole purpose in life narrows down to avenging his death. His love for Ophelia, his enjoyment of friends, his very love of life all seem choked off by his thirst for vengeance. But are they really? If he had acted on that passion at once, there would be no play. Instead he balks, reconsiders, and obsessively reexamines his own motives. The "native hue of resolution"

66. Ibid., 29.

grapples with "the pale cast of thought." As it must in Lamentations, revenge must also contend with other passions in *Hamlet*.

With characteristic mastery, the bard introduces into his tragedy two minor key reflections of the larger theme. Hamlet inadvertently kills Polonius behind a screen in his mother's bedroom when he mistakes him for the king. Then Polonius's son Laertes, who is Hamlet's old friend, becomes the one who is caught in the grip of revenge. But Laertes is not crippled by Hamlet's hesitation. In a justly famous scene, Laertes talks about the revenge he seeks and about all that he is willing to sacrifice to attain it.

> **Laertes**: How came he dead? I'll not be juggled with:
>   To hell, allegiance! vows, to the blackest devil!
>   Conscience and grace, to the profoundest pit!
>   I dare damnation. To this point I stand,
>   That both the worlds I give to negligence,
>   Let come what comes; only I'll be revenged
>   Most thoroughly for my father.
>   Shakepeare, *Hamlet*, act IV, scene V

The thirst for vengeance, it seems, is deeply set in the human psyche. The gospel, however, is about forgiveness and reconciliation. Lamentations has a lot about revenge and very little about reconciliation. Nowhere does The Poet express even the slightest inclination to forgive and forget those who have wreaked such havoc and depredation on her city. But, as I have pointed out in earlier sections of this commentary, we are ready for forgiveness and reconciliation only after we have recognized the destructive impulses that, often unbidden, course through our souls. In most church liturgies we confess our sins, against God and neighbor, before we receive the assurance of forgiveness. But even before confession comes the searching of the conscience. Lamentations could well serve as a guide for this search. How many people can read it without recognizing in its pages some of the same dark impulses that lurk within us all?[67]

---

67. See my chapter, "Repentance and Forgiveness: A Christian Perspective," in *Repentance: A Comparative Perspective*, ed. Amitai Etzioni and David E. Carney (Lanham, MD: Rowman and Littlefield, 1997), 21–30.

20

Healing

Lamentations need not leave a totally bitter taste in our mouths. It is true that, taken as a whole, it lays out a topography of trauma. But it also provides clues about how traumatized people begin the arduous process of healing.

Those who have worked with populations recovering from natural or human-made disasters in places like Indonesia, Bosnia, Burundi, and Uganda have noticed common features both in the nature of large-scale trauma and in what is needed for recovery and healing. As Lamentations shows, such catastrophes produce not only physical suffering but deep-seated psychological and spiritual dislocation. Victims lose their sense of direction, even a grasp of who they are. Their worlds are shattered. But the results of this psychic splintering vary from case to case. As we have seen in Solnit's research, often the victims of a disaster help and support each other in ways they might not have in the past. But sometimes they turn on one another in violence. Victim attacks victim. In Bosnia, for example, teenage vandalism and bullying increased. Numbed by all that had befallen them, adults often merely looked the other way. A culture seemingly indifferent to random violence emerged. What accounts for these differences?

> Lamentations need not leave a totally bitter taste in our mouths. It is true that, taken as a whole, it lays out a topography of trauma. But it also provides clues about how traumatized people begin the arduous process of healing.

But more importantly, whatever the aftermath of the calamity, how can healing begin?

In September 2008 the Mennonite Central Committee, which sponsors trauma response workers and programs in several different regions, gathered some of these workers in Salatiga, Indonesia, to compare notes. Insights from these varied experiences were published in the committee's *Peace Office Newsletter*.[68] This report explains some of the aspects of Lamentations that can be puzzling. A secularly oriented person might ask, for example, why in the biblical text does the loss of the temple and the priesthood feature so prominently. Don't people most need food, water, blankets, and medical supplies? But one of the things all these experienced trauma healers agreed on was that the restoration of customary symbols and rituals was utterly central to healing. Without them, the feelings of blind fury, disorientation, and helplessness merely deepen and the situation gets worse. People need both the space and the means to reclaim a sense of identity. Workers agreed that it was just as important to rebuild the local church or mosque as it was to rebuild homes.

Recovery from trauma—individual and collective—is a grueling trial. Survivors move through it at different speeds. Some never fully recover. But the response workers agreed that when people felt isolated the process took much longer. Therefore, they agreed, the restoration of a sense of community and of a spiritually grounded worldview was absolutely fundamental. They also agreed that the process should not be hurried along. Telling people to "just get over it" may actually make it more difficult and lengthen the time required. The workers also noticed that helping victims engage in a cognitive recognition of their trauma, what causes it, and how other people have recovered all help them to see their own plight in a larger context and to escape their paralyzing sense of isolation. They see themselves in other people's stories as they tell their own.

Since a sense of utter helplessness is one of the most common features in a post-trauma society, an essential part of the healing is that

---

68. Mennonite Central Committee, *Peace Office Newsletter* 39, no. 3 (2009), published by Mennonite Central Committee, 21 South 12th Street, Akron, PA 17501-0500.

victims must begin to *take action*. Even small steps help. They must, as a vital dimension of their recovery, engage in tasks that rebuild a sense of meaning, community, and agency. This in turn begins to rebuild their sense of interdependency. People move from being victims to being survivors. Otherwise the spiral of isolation, fear, and vulnerability continues downward.

21

Jerusalem Today

Lamentations is a paean to ruined cities. But as we close this commentary we must not forget that the particular city it focuses on, Jerusalem, is a city that still exists today as a vexed and conflict-ridden metropolis on the eastern shore of the Mediterranean Sea. Recall again what The Poet of Lamentations wrote about Jerusalem 2,500 years ago:

> How lonely sits the city
>   that was full of people!
> How like a widow has she become. . . .
> She weeps bitterly in the night,
> tears on her cheeks;
> among all her lovers
> she has none to comfort her.
> (1:1, 2 RSV)

Today, paradoxically, Jerusalem is hardly lonely, and she may now have too many lovers. In fact, her sadness is that so many people "love her to death." For the ancient Israelites, the "City of David" was the center of their kingdom, the site of the majestic temple. For Jews ever since it has been the subject of countless prayers and poems, and the "Zion" from which the Zionist movement derives its name. But Palestinians also love the city they call *Al-Quds* in Arabic. It has for centuries been their center for health services and governance, the place where generations of their most prominent families, the "venerables," have lived, and the city they hope will become the capital of an independent Palestinian state. Christian pilgrims still flock to the sites associated with Jesus' final week. Both the blessing and the bane of Jerusalem is that it is a city "holy to three faiths."

Today, as in the era of Jeremiah, it is not easy to separate the religious from the political conflicts that fuel disagreements about Jerusalem. The Poet of Lamentations even pauses in her lament to express regret that her people and leaders had once forged ill-advised alliances with foreign powers, and now her generation is paying the price for their folly.

> We have made a pact with Egypt and Assyria,
> to get enough bread.
> Our ancestors sinned; they are no more,
> and we bear their iniquities.
>
> (5:6–7)

Still, although it is impossible to separate religion from politics completely, it is important not to confuse the two. Today the picture is further complicated because over the centuries the word *Jerusalem* has been attached to many different entities. King David's Jerusalem lay completely outside the present walled "Old City" and was much smaller. During the Arab Muslim period (638–1099) there were Christian, Jewish, and Muslim "quarters" in the Old City. But, to the shame of Christians, during the century of Crusader rule (1099–1187), Jews and Muslims were prohibited from residing there. During the long era of Ottoman rule (1517–1917), the "quarters" returned and they remain today, although Jews have settled in previously Muslim-Arab parts. In 1883 Jerusalem consisted of an area of only one square kilometer, and everyone lived within the walled area. Theodor Herzl and the early Zionists saw Jerusalem as a musty, desiccated symbol of what they hoped their project could overcome. They preferred the coast, and Tel Aviv. But after the Israeli capture of East Jerusalem in the 1967 war, the city took on a new significance. Then, by 1990, due to Israeli annexations and extensions of the municipal boundaries, it had expanded to over one hundred times its previous size. It now covers 123 square kilometers.

The "Jerusalem question" has exasperated the international

community for nearly a century. During various discussions of the partition of Palestine after World War II, the UN General Assembly suggested that in addition to a Jewish and an Arab domain, Jerusalem itself should be a *corpus separatum,* administered internationally. Instead, at Israel's independence in 1948, after a pitched battle between their armed forces, the United Nations divided the city between Israeli and Jordanian control. But the Old City with its Jewish, Muslim, and Christian holy sites was entirely on the Jordanian side, divided from West Jerusalem by sinister barbed wire. Then, after their successful 1967 war, the Israelis annexed East Jerusalem and expanded the city's boundaries to include the airport to the north and suburbs to the west for several miles. They also razed the old "Moroccan" quarter adjacent to the Western Wall to create a plaza. The southern city limits reached nearly to Bethlehem.

These historical snapshots demonstrate that what we call "Jerusalem" has meant different things to different people at different times. *Demographically,* today's Jerusalem's population, consisting of a mixture of Jews (Ultraorthodox, Haredi, and secular), Muslims, and Christians, is vastly larger than that of ancient Jerusalem and has been changing substantially over the past century. Today its population of nearly 800,000 is about two-thirds Jewish and one-third Muslim. But within fifteen years it will be half and half, and after that the Palestinians may outnumber everyone else. Due to emigration the Christian population, which traces its roots to the first century CE, will have declined to less than 1 percent, a prospect viewed with sadness by Christians around the world.

Today Jerusalem's political status is still in question. On December 5, 1949, Israel's first prime minister, David Ben-Gurion, proclaimed Jerusalem as Israel's capital, but it became the legal capital with the passage of the Jerusalem Law of 1980. This law, however, was found to be a violation of international law by UN Security Council Resolution 478, which also declared that no embassies should be located there. Since then most branches of the Israeli government have resided in Jerusalem. But most of the world's countries, including the United States, have not recognized it as the capital since under international law the status of the whole area is still to be settled by a peace accord. Meanwhile the embassies remain in Tel Aviv. In

October 2008 retiring Israeli prime minister Ehud Olmert stated that in order to reach a peace accord Israel would have to withdraw from most of the West Bank settlements and share Jerusalem with a Palestinian state. But today the building and enlargement of settlements, many in East Jerusalem and some cutting deep into the West Bank, continue unabated.

Jerusalem is known around the world as a holy city, in fact, holy to three faiths.[69] One thinks immediately of the Western ("Wailing") Wall, the Haram al-Sharif (Temple Mount), and the Church of the Holy Sepulcher as well as many other Jewish, Christian, and Muslim "holy sites." But "holy to three faiths" also raises a number of more basic questions pertinent to the future of Jerusalem, and its "holiness" cannot be overlooked if there is to be peace in the Middle East. The meaning of "holiness" varies from one religious tradition to another, and so therefore does the holiness of Jerusalem It is thus important to notice the different ways in which Jerusalem *became* holy to Jews, Christians, and Muslims and to realize that its holiness refers mainly to the Old City, not to all of it. It is also well to remember that at times in the past the city was not holy to any of them, or was holy to more than these three faiths.

"Holy city" is a multivalent and mutable term, and it is still changing. The holiness of the city has waxed and waned over the centuries due in some measure to political circumstances and to developments then current among the three Abrahamic traditions. The meaning of Jerusalem's holiness is responsive to human influences, and it could change again. It is possible that all three traditions (and eventually others as well) could work with one another and with the political powers to deepen and expand the meaning of the city's holiness.

From its first days under David (ca. 1000 BCE), Jerusalem was "holy" to at least two religions, ancient Judaism and the religion of the Jebusites. At that time the city was located outside—just south and east—of the present walled Old City. The Bible says little about how David came to occupy Jerusalem, only that he wanted it to be called "City of David" (cf. Constantinople, Washington, and Ho Chi

69. Karen Armstrong, *Jerusalem: One City, Three Faiths* (New York: Ballantine, 1996).

Minh City). However, the residents still referred to it by its previous pre-Hebrew name, Jerusalem. According to the biblical account, David purchased the central religious site of the city, the "threshing floor," where the priests prepared the sacred grain for their ceremonies, from the Jebusites. Then he allowed their priests, who had previously occupied the site, to remain and to continue to use it for worship, alongside (or perhaps mixed with) the worship of Yahweh, the deity of the Jews, that he introduced. In short, under David Jerusalem was not a city marked by an exclusive monotheism.

David's successor, King Solomon, consecrated his temple about 950 BCE, but he also allowed, even welcomed, other spiritual practices into Jerusalem, many of them imported along with his many wives. The Jewish prophets railed against this practice, but the fact that they complained demonstrates that it went on. For many years the Hebrew YHWH religion remained decentralized, with centers in various places in Canaan. But eventually, more for political control than for religious purposes, worship was centralized in the temple of Jerusalem, which Solomon had built. Other religious centers were outlawed.

During the exile of the Jewish elites to Babylon in the early sixth century BCE, "Zion," the poetic equivalent of Jerusalem, became a symbol not just of a city but of a whole way of life that had been lost and that the exiles—like exiles ever since—romanticized and longed to regain. Seventy years passed. When the Persian ruler Cyrus allowed the Jews to "return" in 537 BCE, they rebuilt the city walls and the temple under Ezra. A powerful temple-centered priestly religion, closely integrated with the political ruling class, was set up. In 63 BCE the Romans under Pompey conquered Jerusalem and ruled through their collaborators in the priestly class, centered in the Jerusalem temple, which was built by Herod, the king the Romans installed.

This largely puppet regime kindled a variety of protests from the Jewish people, ranging from the armed rebellion of the Zealots, to the desert withdrawal of the Essenes (who hid the Dead Sea Scrolls, which were discovered in the Judean desert in the 1940s and 50s), to the nonviolent "Jesus Movement," which opposed both the Romans and the temple leadership but did not withdraw. This movement was centered first in Galilee, but when Jesus led his followers to Jerusalem he was executed by the Romans. His movement continued to grow and spread, soon including many Gentiles, but—to the surprise of many Christians today—these early Christians did not hold Jerusalem to be holy. Rather, as the site of the crucifixion, they despised and avoided it.

After the initial success, then defeat of the Jewish rebellion against Roman rule in 68–70 CE, the temple (except for the Western Wall) was razed and the city itself destroyed. The Jews were deported from the city, creating a huge diaspora. The Roman emperor Hadrian renamed the city "Aelia Capitolina" and built a temple to Zeus there, making the city "holy" in the Roman imperial polytheistic religion. But even in exile, Jews prayed facing Jerusalem, and for 1,900 years they sang and spoke about returning ("Next year in Jerusalem!").

With the "conversion" of the emperor Constantine in the fourth century and his deployment of Christianity as an imperial religion, the once-despised Jerusalem became yet another kind of holy city, this time of just one religion, Byzantine Christianity. Constantine and his mother, Helen, built several churches in the city, but Jews continued to be banned, though they were admitted once a year—on the Ninth of Ab—to mourn at the Western Wall for the destroyed temple. (I mentioned this holy day earlier as the one on which Jews today still read Lamentations.) Allowing them back in the city for this one day was not, however, a generous gesture on the part of the Byzantine authorities. They wanted the Jews to play an unintended role in a theological drama. As the Jews wailed, the Christians watched and were told that the sorrow of the Jews was a result of God's punishment on them for refusing to recognize their messiah. Ritual lament had been degraded into a politico-religious weapon. By the 600s, far from denigrating Jerusalem, Christians now viewed it as the holiest of cities, and the tomb of Christ as the navel of the cosmos, the very source of salvation. But they left the ancient temple in ruins as a stern reminder of God's punishment on the Jews.

In 637 Arab armies under Omar reached Jerusalem. Muslim rule in the city lasted, except for the Crusader Kingdom (1099–1187) and a few minor interruptions, until 1917. Whenever the earliest Muslims prayed, according to the instructions of the Prophet, they faced Jerusalem. It was their first *kiblah* (direction of prayer) since the Prophet honored the previous revelations that had been centered there. Shortly thereafter Mecca supplanted Jerusalem as the primary *kiblah*. But Jerusalem continues to be endowed with holiness because of its association with the Jewish prophets and because of Muhammad's "Night Journey" (*al-Isra*) during which he met Abraham, Moses, and Jesus (the previous prophets) after ascending (*al-Miraj*) from the Temple Mount. The stone from which he ascended is preserved under the golden Dome of the Rock, which has become a postcard trademark of Jerusalem. The city changed hands among various Muslim factions until 1517, when it was captured by Ottoman Turks, who held it until General Allenby led the British forces through the Jaffa Gate on December 11, 1917. English newspapers proclaimed that Jerusalem was now "back in Christian hands."

Changing patterns of political rule have often altered the religious profile of Jerusalem. During the centuries of Arab and of Ottoman control, and the three decades of British mandate, Jerusalem was open to all faiths. When the western section of Jerusalem became part of the newly created state of Israel in 1948, the city was divided by barriers. The "Old City" remained in Jordanian hands. Most Muslims moved or were forced out of the western part, which now lay in Jewish hands, while Jews were forbidden to visit their holy sites in the Jordanian-controlled eastern section. Then, in 1967, the Israelis captured the eastern half, including the old walled city, changing the religious patterns of the city once again. Despite the urging of some Israeli zealots to destroy the Dome of the Rock, cooler heads prevailed: the Israelis wisely preserved it and promised to continue the equal rights approach. Today the Haram al-Sharif is administered by the Muslim Waqf subject to the constraints of the Israeli occupation. Jews pray at the Western Wall, but are forbidden by Israeli security agents to pray on the Temple Mount. They are, however, settling in the traditionally Arab eastern parts of the city, both inside and outside the walls. Christians still maintain a deep religious interest in the city but make no claim to political sovereignty.

The term *holy* refers to something set aside, made special, for sacred purposes. The history of Jerusalem shows that although it is considered holy by three faiths, "holiness" is a mercurial concept, and its meaning varies both among the three religions and also within different wings in each of them. History also suggests that while the city has been the site of horrendous violence, nonetheless for significant periods the three faiths have been able to live together in relative harmony.

When Caliph Omar and his Muslim army conquered the city in 637 he allowed the Christians to continue to worship, and he invited the banished Jews to return. Saladin, who recaptured the city from the Crusaders in 1187, welcomed Christian pilgrims and Jews to the city, if they entered peaceably. One of General Allenby's first acts when he entered the city on December 11, 1917, was to assemble the leaders of the three religions and assure them that he would guarantee access to all holy sites. Some religious leaders suggest that these periods of religious amity in Jerusalem's past could be drawn upon imaginatively today to move toward a peaceful future.

Sacred spaces can be shared. All three faiths honor the Tomb of the Patriarchs in Hebron. Muslims and Christian pilgrims visit the "milk cave" outside Jerusalem where Joseph and Mary are believed to have stopped with the infant Jesus on their way as refugees to Egypt. Holy cities can also be shared. If Jerusalem is a key issue to finding peace, it will be necessary to take both political and religious factors into consideration. An agreement will require sensitive negotiations, including how the Temple Mount/Noble Sanctuary can be shared. Then, if this highly charged symbolic issue can be resolved, sharing the rest of the Old City—which already has its separate quarters—seems more possible.

The blessing and curse of Jerusalem is that, like no other city on earth, three major faiths, and people from virtually every nation on the globe, feel a sense of kinship and veneration for it. They also have legitimate claims to access to

> The blessing and curse of Jerusalem is that, like no other city on earth, three major faiths, and people from virtually every nation on the globe, feel a sense of kinship and veneration for it. They also have legitimate claims to access to the sites associated with their faiths. Like no other city Jerusalem does in some sense "belong to the whole world."

the sites associated with their faiths. Like no other city Jerusalem does in some sense "belong to the whole world."

Some have suggested that since the walled Old City (*not* the entire city) of Jerusalem already belongs spiritually to the world, it could be declared a world heritage site and administered by the United Nations in cooperation with an interfaith council.

Sadly, today Jerusalem is still suffering. The Israeli "wall" or "security barrier" snakes through its neighborhoods, dividing and fragmenting the city. A future border between the two sections should be as porous as possible and supervised by either joint Israeli-Palestinian teams and/or international units. Recent polls suggest that a majority of Jerusalemites (both Israeli and Palestinian) would welcome some such arrangement. An accord on Jerusalem could generate some of the trust and goodwill that is needed today in order to move ahead on the other issues. If that happens, the appropriate biblical passage for the Holy City might not be the doleful one that opens the book of Lamentations but these words from the prophet Isaiah: "Comfort, comfort my people, says your God. Speak tenderly to Jerusalem, and cry to her that her warfare is ended" (Isa. 40:2 RSV).

Conclusion: Lamentations Today

The late German philosopher Theodor Adorno was a Jew who survived World War II and the Holocaust. In 1950 he wrote a sentence that has been quoted more than any of his other words: "To write a poem after Auschwitz is barbaric." Obviously Adorno was overstating his case. Much artistic and literary work has been written since Auschwitz—including poetry, novels, testimonies, film scripts, history, and painting. Some of these, such as the novels of Primo Levi and Steven Spielberg's epochal film *Schindler's List,* must be accounted as masterpieces. Still, Adorno's words send a signal and pose a question to anyone who seeks to interpret the biblical message today. How can we respond to the titanic tragedies of our era, and maybe even to the ones we could still confront in the future, without cheapening them? When *should* words fail? When *must* we try to express the inexpressible?

Lamentations violates Adorno's warning. It is a poem, a superb poem, that was composed after the conquest and rape of Jerusalem at the hands of the Babylonians, which at that time felt to the survivors as something akin to a holocaust. But The Poet of Lamentations, in shouting out against the horror and amid thrashing about to grasp its significance in a world ruled by a just God, sets a high standard. This poem provides an example for anyone called to speak or to teach, to write or to preach in the name of that just God. It insists that, contrary to Adorno, we cannot remain silent. But it also makes painfully clear that in speaking out we must try desperately to avoid simplifying or trivializing.

What to say, what not to say, or whether to remain silent in the aftermath of catastrophe is always a dilemma. On the day of 9/11 I was scheduled to meet a large class in the afternoon. I anguished over whether I should simply cancel the class, talk with the students, encourage them to talk with one another, or sit in silent prayer and meditation. Finally I decided to play a long excerpt from Mozart's *Requiem*, then encourage them to express whatever fear, anger, or bewilderment was on their minds. I said they could do this in the form of a prayer if they chose. Some did. At the end I said a few words of my own and ended the class with a period of silent prayer.

I am sure this was not a perfect solution. Maybe there are no perfect solutions to such a dilemma. Still, if and when we do decide to speak or preach in the wake a tragedy, we do well to remember that we are not the first to have done so. We need not rely entirely on our own limited emotional, spiritual vocabulary. The Bible, and Lamentations in particular, provide us with a plentiful heritage of words and metaphors within which to wrap our intense feelings of terror, rage, and abandonment. To turn to such resources not only deepens and widens the reach of our outcries, it also reminds us—line by line—that we are not alone. Not only are there people who share our suffering today, but we join an ancient company of others who have grappled with the same demons. We ignore these scriptural resources at our peril. Not only can they provide the words we sometimes search for in vain, but they also deliver us from the danger of falling into self-pity and the road that goes nowhere called "why me?"

There may be no better way to be forced to grapple with a biblical text than to try to preach a sermon from it or write a commentary on it. This is especially true for Lamentations since, as I have written above, it is a book that largely speaks for itself. The commentator or the preacher often asks, "What else is there to say?" At least I found myself asking this question. But as a person who often has the privilege of preaching, I noticed in preparing this commentary that there are differences between a commentary and a sermon.

No commentary is ever timeless. It has to build a bridge between a text and the present. But sometimes both shores the bridge tries to connect are changing. Biblical scholarship is an ongoing enterprise. Archaeology, manuscript finds, and literary analysis often alter the profile of a given text. This is not as true for Lamentations as it is for some other biblical books. There is little dispute about the text itself. Still, research on the history of the lament or the sources of the whole Hebrew tradition could alter that side of the shore. The reader of this commentary is hereby warned to keep alert for such changes.

On "this side" of the chasm, the commentary writer must be content to write something that may last a few years, but he cannot be as up-to-date as the reader might like. For example, after I finished this commentary, shocking stories of how the Egyptian secret police tortured protesters and journalists filled our TV screen for days. The United Nations announced that deaths from malnutrition and starvation still threaten millions of the world's children. We are still far from having escaped from the danger of a devastating war in the Middle East. Even Jerusalem, on which I have devoted a concluding section of this commentary, might once again suffer the pangs of war. Since one never knows when the landscape will shift, the writer of a commentary must settle for a product that might be useful for a time but that will eventually—maybe even quite soon—find its way to the back shelves of libraries. It is a humbling experience.

Preaching, however, is somewhat different. The essence of a sermon is that it is spoken. Even the fieriest of yesterday's sermons can seem lukewarm on the printed page. In the Reformed tradition of Christianity the preacher takes on a huge burden. He or she recognizes that in that tradition the Word of God comes to life—catches fire—only when the preacher makes clear its relevance to the congregation gathered in the here and now. In this sense a sermon must always be contextual. Last year's homily or even last week's will not do. Can anyone imagine preaching the same sermon the week after 9/11 that one had planned the week before it? Karl Barth's famous dictum that the preacher must hold the Bible in one hand and the daily newspaper in the other has now been sped up. Nowadays news comes too swiftly for newspapers, which have become more and more organs of interpretation and opinion. Would Barth now suggest an iPod in one hand?

Pentecostals have made a valuable contribution to homiletical theology. With their insistent emphasis on the continuing presence of the Holy Spirit, they hold that the "inspiration" of a biblical text does not stop with its original writer. The Holy Spirit is also equally present when the preacher opens and interprets the text. There is inspiration "at both ends." I find this a suggestive insight as long as the preacher does not forget that interpreting a text is also a congregational, communal task. Many preachers have found it indispensable to work on a text with members of a congregation before preaching on it. This kind or sermon preparation laboratory uncovers insights the preacher may have overlooked, and it prevents him or her from getting sidetracked into a personal or transient preoccupation. I have come to think that Lamentations seems to cry out for such a workshop approach. Not every individual has experienced calamitous defeat, shattered hopes, abandonment, or exile, to say nothing of rape, starvation, torture, or cannibalism. But these are all themes that appear in Lamentations, and in a group study someone will have felt that particular form of wounding or at least know of someone who has. The sermon that results from this sort of searching preparation will probably be stronger and harder hitting than one prepared in the quietude of the pastor's study. Indeed, trying to grapple with Lamentations apart from people who can resonate with its graphic evocations of heartbreaking pain seems almost like a contradiction.

As I finished writing this commentary I found myself wondering why I rarely hear a sermon on Lamentations and why it seems overlooked in Christian education curricula. Is it because by and large the middle-class mainline churches have had a fairly easy time of it for the past several decades? We all experience personal and domestic tragedies, large and small. But as for societal ones, other than the domestically divisive Vietnam struggle, the wars we have fought have been shoved to the back pages. Even the trauma of 9/11 directly affected only a relative handful of people. We have not been forced to ponder the horrendous sides of history as other peoples and some of our own ancestors have. But will this sunny period continue? And can we feel so distant from the upheavals that wrack other countries? History does not trace a straight line of progress. There may be dark days to come. I do not wish for them, but if they do (or maybe even *when* they do) we may be ready to turn to Lamentations once again.

Selected Bibliography

Austin, Linda M. "The Lament and the Rhetoric of the Sublime." *Nineteenth-Century Literature* 53, no. 3 (1998): 279–306.

Barth, Karl. *Epistle to the Romans.* 6th ed. Oxford: Oxford University Press, 1968.

———. *A Shorter Commentary on Romans.* Hampshire, England: Ashgate Publishing, Ltd., 2007.

Bernstein, Richard J. *Radical Evil—A Philosophical Investigation.* Malden, MA: Blackwell Publishing, 2001.

Boff, Clodovis, and Jorge Pixley. *The Bible, the Church and the Poor.* Trans. Paul Burns. Maryknoll, NY: Orbis, 1989.

Bonhoeffer, Dietrich. *A Testament to Freedom: The Essential Writings of Dietrich Bonhoeffer.* Ed. Geffrey B. Kelly and F. Burton Nelson. Rev. ed. New York: HarperOne, 1995.

Caputo, John. *The Weakness of God: A Theology of the Event.* Bloomington: Indiana University Press, 2006.

Cox, Harvey. *The Secular City: Secularization and Urbanization in Theological Perspective.* 25th anniversary ed. New York: Collier Books, 1990.

Ellison, H. L. "Lamentations." In *The Expositor's Bible Commentary.* Ed. Frank E. Gaebelein, 6:695–733. Grand Rapids: Regency Library, 1986.

Freud, Sigmund. "Mourning and Melancholia." *Standard Edition of the Complete Psychological Works of Sigmund Freud.* Vol. 14. Trans. James Strachy. London: The Hogarth Press, 239–60.

Frye, Northrup. *The Great Code: The Bible and Literature.* New York: Harcourt Brace Jovanovich, 1981.

Gates, Henry Louis, Jr., and Nellie Y. McKay, eds. *The Norton Anthology of African American Literature*. New York: Norton, 1997.

Gottwald, Norman K. *Studies in the Book of Lamentations*. Studies in Biblical Theology 14. London: SCM Press, 1954.

Holst-Warhaft, Gail. *Cue for Passion*. Cambridge: Harvard University Press, 2000.

Hunsinger, George, ed. *Torture Is a Moral Issue*. Grand Rapids: Eerdmans, 2008.

Kierkegaard, Søren. *Attack upon "Christendom."* Trans. Walter Lowrie. Princeton: Princeton University Press, 1944.

———. *Fear and Trembling*. Trans. Alastair Hannay. Penguin Classics. London: Penguin Books, 2003.

Larrimore, Mark, ed. *The Problem of Evil: A Reader*. Malden, MA: Blackwell, 2001.

Leuchter, Mark. *The Polemics of Exile in Jeremiah 26–45*. New York: Cambridge University Press, 2008.

O'Connor, Kathleen. *Lamentations and the Tears of the World*. Maryknoll, NY: Orbis, 2002.

Niebuhr, Reinhold. *The Irony of American History*. Chicago: University of Chicago Press, 2008.

Ricoeur, Paul. *Time and Narrative*. Chicago: University of Chicago Press, 1988.

Rogerson, John W. *A Theology of the Old Testament: Cultural Memory, Communication, and Being Human*. Minneapolis: Fortress, 2010.

Schlingensiepen, Ferdinand. *Dietrich Bonhoeffer, 1906–1945: Martyr, Thinker, Man of Resistance*. Trans. Isabel Best. London: T. & T. Clark, 2010.

Severson, Eric R., ed. *I More Than Others: Responses to Evil and Suffering*. Newcastle upon Tyne: Cambridge Scholars, 2010.

Solnit, Rebecca. *A Paradise Built in Hell: The Extraordinary Communities That Arise in Disasters*. New York: Viking, 2009.

Sugirtharajah, R. S. *The Bible and the Third World*. Cambridge: Cambridge University Press, 2001.

Taylor, Charles. *A Secular Age*. Cambridge: Harvard University Press, 2007.

Tran, Jonathan. *The Vietnam War and Theologies of Memory.* Malden, MA: Wiley-Blackwell, 2010.

Warner, Michael, and Jonathan Vanantwerpen, eds. *Varieties of Secularism in a Secular Age.* Cambridge: Harvard University Press, 2010.

Yerushalmi, Yosef Hayim. *Zakhor: Jewish History and Jewish Memory.* Seattle: University of Washington Press, 1996.

THE SONG OF SONGS

for Kevin

This is my beloved and this is my friend
Song of Songs 5:16

Introduction:
Why the Song of Songs? Why Now?

The Song of Songs is a book like no other in the Bible. For centuries, readers approached it with a quality of hope and expectation that may be difficult for us to imagine. The Song inspired volumes of commentaries, midrashic interpretations, paraphrases, and homilies among ancient and medieval Jewish and Christian readers; indeed, medieval Christians commented more frequently on the Song of Songs than on any other book of the Bible.[1] By contrast, modern Christian readers often regard the Song as an oddity, useful only as a quarry for wedding liturgies. But for devoted readers over centuries, the Song was a key hidden at the heart of the Bible, capable of unlocking the Bible's central message of God's love for human beings.[2] It was a fathomless pool of meaning one could swim in one's whole life long and never sound the bottom. It was a garden in which one might encounter God walking in the cool of the day. For these readers, the Song of Songs was a devotional text surpassing all others: a text to be excavated through midrash and allegory, lingered over in *lectio divina*, prayed with individually and communally.

The Song of Songs may have fallen out of liturgical and devotional use among Christians, but it remains a rich source for Jewish prayer. Today, Jews still recite the Song of Songs on the Sabbath of Passover as a reminder that God delivered Israel from slavery, not only because God was covenantally bound to do so but because God

1. E. Ann Matter, *The Voice of My Beloved: The Song of Songs in Western Medieval Christianity* (Philadelphia: University of Pennsylvania Press, 1990), 6.
2. Bernard McGinn, *The Flowering of Mysticism: Men and Women in the New Mysticism 1200–1350* (New York: Crossroad, 1998), 80.

loved Israel, cherished her, and desired her good. Some Jewish communities recite the Song of Songs before Friday evening services, the better to welcome the Sabbath as a bride, and it is sung at the Western Wall in Jerusalem. The interpretations of the great rabbis and sages undergird these practices. Many saw in the Song an intimate retelling of the history of Israel and a meditation on the relationship between God and God's people. Others read it as a philosophical, mystical text about the desire of the individual soul for God. The eminent first-century sage Rabbi Akiba (ca. 50–135 CE) famously defended the inclusion of the Song in the biblical canon by insisting that "all the scriptures are holy, but the Song of Songs is the Holy of Holies."[3]

These readings profoundly influenced Christian interpretations of the Song. Christian readers heard in its verses a hymn to Christ's love for the church and a song about the soul's longing for the presence of God. The Song seemed a bottomless well of meaning: the Cistercian mystical writer Bernard of Clairvaux (1090–1153) wrote eighty-six sermons on the Song of Songs and barely got past the second chapter. Like many Jewish readers, Christians sought in the Song a path to intimacy with God. They prayed and studied the Song longing to hear God's voice, hoping to see God's face.

If you have ever read the Song of Songs, you may find this surprising. After all, the Song is unusual among biblical books for what it includes and what it leaves out. What it includes is erotic poetry that leaves no body part uncelebrated, no fragrance or taste of the beloved undescribed. What it leaves out is any reference whatsoever to God.

Although it is silent about God, the Song has exerted tremendous power over the religious imaginations of Christians and Jews. Perhaps that very silence opened a space for readers to seek God in unexpected places and in unexpected ways through their engagement with the Song. The medieval kabbalist Rabbi Ezra ben Solomon of Gerona (d. 1238 or 1245) taught that the Song belonged to God, and God sang it every day. The Carmelite mystic and reformer

---

3. Quoted in Marvin H. Pope, *Song of Songs: A New Translation with Introduction and Commentary*, AB (Garden City, NY: Doubleday, 1977), 19.

Teresa of Avila (1515–1582) wrote in her *Meditations on the Song of Songs* that, even when she heard the Song read in Latin and could not understand the meaning of the words, it stirred her soul nonetheless, even more than devotional books written in Spanish, her mother tongue, did. "Even when the Latin words were translated for me into the vernacular," she wrote, "I did not understand the text any more."[4] Teresa heard the Song the way we hear the sound of the ocean or a string quartet, the sound of someone weeping or the laughter of children. In the sound of the Song, she could hear God's voice, even when she could not understand the words.

Many readers of the Song found layers of meaning in it by reading it allegorically. That is, the literal meaning of the words did not represent, for these readers, the only meaning the Song contained. Images in the Song could point to other meanings entirely—for example, Rabbi Ezra ben Solomon of Gerona could imagine the Song as God's own song because, in his understanding of the range of meanings encoded into the Bible, the name "Solomon" referred to God. For the rabbi, the superscription at the beginning of the poem—"The Song of Songs, which is Solomon's"—meant that the Song belonged to God. When Bernard of Clairvaux and Teresa of Avila read the Song's first line—"Let him kiss me with the kisses of his mouth!"—they heard in the woman's desire for a kiss the desire of humanity for the incarnation of God in Jesus, the pressing of divinity into human flesh.

Early readers of the Song were much more comfortable with acknowledging multiple, hidden meanings of Scripture than we are. The great African theologian Augustine of Hippo (354–430) once articulated a principle for the interpretation of Scripture that made room for multiple meanings, a principle that has come to be known as the rule of love. If two or more interpretations of a particular text of Scripture all build up the love of God and the love of neighbor, he argued, we could not call any of them false.[5] "What harm does it do me," he asked in his *Confessions*, "if different meanings, which are

---

4. Teresa of Avila, *The Collected Works of St. Teresa of Avila*, trans. Kieran Kavanaugh, O.C.D., and Otilio Rodriguez, O.C.D., vol. 2 (Washington, DC: ICS Publications, 1980), 215.
5. Augustine, *On Christian Doctrine* 1.36, trans. D. W. Robertson Jr. (Indianapolis: Library of the Liberal Arts, 1958), 30.

nevertheless all true, can be gathered from these words?"[6] Many premodern readers expected to find several layers of meaning in Scripture—a historical, literal meaning; a moral meaning; an allegorical meaning; and a mystical meaning. In the case of the Song of Songs, however, the historical, literal meaning was frequently passed over in favor of deeper, more hidden meanings in both Christian and Jewish readings of the text.[7]

We contemporary readers of Scripture, on the other hand, tend to gravitate toward the historical, literal meaning and the moral meaning of Scripture.[8] We ask: What did this text mean in its time? And what might it mean for our lives, our context, our day? Since the Reformation, finding hidden meanings in Scripture, in words that point somehow to something other than what they literally express, has come to be seen as, well, premodern. Many contemporary readers regard such interpretations as artificial, excessive, or just plain wrong. When a medieval commentator on the Song interprets the woman's two thighs as a reference to the Jews and the Gentiles or her two breasts as references to the Old and the New Testaments from which we draw nourishment, we ask: isn't this just a way of avoiding the frank eroticism of the text?[9]

Maybe. But the desire to avoid the plainly erotic cannot begin to explain the outpouring of commentary on the Song. If solving the "problem" of the presence of a book of erotic poetry in the Bible were the motivation for all the interpretation it has inspired, why would the commentators keep returning again and again and again to the Song, finding new meanings each time? Why eighty-six sermons on

---

6. *The Confessions of St. Augustine* 12.18, trans. Rex Warner (New York: Mentor, 1963), 300.

7. For example, Matter observes, "There is no 'non-allegorical' Latin tradition of Song of Songs commentary. In the early Church, only the Pelagian theologian Julian of Eclanum is known to have written a non-allegorical interpretation; this is preserved only in the fragments which Bede refuted" (*Voice of My Beloved*, 4). Medieval Jewish commentators offer two ways of interpreting the Song: as a retelling of the history of Israel and as a mystical allegory about the individual spiritual journey. See Rabbi Shalom Carmy, "Perfect Harmony," *First Things* 208 (December 2010): 33–37.

8. A recent and important exception to this is Paul J. Griffiths's figural commentary, *Song of Songs*, Brazos Theological Commentary on the Bible (Grand Rapids: Brazos Press, 2011).

9. Quotation from Nicholas of Lyra's *Postilla Litteralis*, in Stephen D. Moore, "The Song of Songs in the History of Sexuality," in *God's Beauty Parlor: And Other Queer Spaces in and around the Bible* (Stanford: Stanford University Press, 2001), 28.

the first two chapters? Why has engagement with the Song been so generative?

When readers like Bernard of Clairvaux and Teresa of Avila read the Song, they recognized their own yearning for God. They heard in the verses of the Song so much that was true about their own search for God's presence: the beauty of the beloved that cannot quite be fully apprehended or described; the continual oscillation between yearning and fulfillment, absence and presence, not-knowing and knowing. Teresa of Avila said as much. Reading the Song is a consolation, she wrote, because a soul in love with God experiences the kinds of "swoons, deaths, afflictions, delights, and joys" that one encounters in the Song.[10] The readings of Bernard of Clairvaux, Rabbi Ezra ben Solomon of Gerona, Teresa of Avila, John of the Cross, and others do not represent a rejection of the erotic quality of the Song, but a recognition of the erotic quality of life with God.

In our day, scholars of the Song focus primarily on its literal, historical meaning. While it remains a difficult text to date (scholars have proposed dates ranging from 950 to 200 BCE), we know King Solomon did not write it. Most likely, it is the work of many hands. We know that the Song was probably redacted from several poems by an editor or editors with an ear for the resonances between them.[11] We know that literary parallels to the Song can be found in other cultures and languages of the Middle East, the Near East, and Tamil-speaking India. And, perhaps most importantly, the critical focus on the historical, literal meaning of the Song has made it impossible to ignore its celebration of erotic desire, sexual pleasure, and the beauty of the human body. Historical-critical study has been a tremendous boon for all who want to deepen their engagement with the Song.

But as the humanly erotic nature of the Song has come more insistently into view, its role as a text of devotion for Christians—a text to be prayed with and lingered over, a text that might profoundly shape our life with God—has diminished. The nineteenth-century American feminist Elizabeth Cady Stanton articulated a typical modern

---

10. Teresa of Avila, *Collected Works,* 2:218.

11. There are many theories about the origin of the Song of Songs. For a thorough survey see the introduction in Pope, *Song of Songs,* 22–33, 40–54 passim.

view of the poem in her *Woman's Bible*. The Song, Stanton wrote, is "merely a love poem." The "most rational view" to take of the Song, she argued, is as an erotic poem addressed by a king to his harem of available women. As for interpretations of the Song that find it an expression of Christ's love for the church, that was a "far-fetched" idea, "unworthy of the character of the ideal Jesus," used by the church as an "excuse" for including the Song in the Bible in the first place.[12] Stanton's view of the Song reflects the emphasis on the literal meaning of Scripture that historical-critical methods of reading the Bible have insisted on. Her assessment of the Song also reflects the profound discomfort that both the literal meaning of the Song and the allegorical interpretations of earlier readers have inspired in modern readers. Such an assessment of the Song does not leave much room for engaging it as a text of devotion.

Premodern readers were not oblivious to the literal meaning of the Song, of course, and they had their own anxieties about it. Origen of Alexandria (ca. 185–254) urged the reader who has "not ceased to feel the passion of his bodily nature to refrain completely from reading this little book."[13] Those who do read it, according to Origen, should take care "not to suffer an interpretation that has to do with the flesh and the passions to carry you away."[14] Teresa of Avila, on the other hand, had this to say to those who avoided the Song because it made them feel uncomfortable or because they were afraid of the effect it would have on them:

> It will seem to you that there are some words in the *Song of Songs* that could have been said in another style. In light of our dullness such an opinion doesn't surprise me. I have heard some persons say that they avoid listening to them. Oh, God, help me, how great is our misery! Just as poisonous creatures turn everything they eat into poison, so do we.[15]

---

12. Elizabeth Cady Stanton, *The Woman's Bible: A Classic Feminist Perspective* (repr. Mineola, NY: Dover Publications, 2002), 100.

13. Origen, *Commentary*, prol. 1, in *The Song of Songs: Commentary and Homilies*, trans. R. P. Lawson, ACW 26 (Westminster, MD: Newman Press, 1957), 23.

14. Ibid., III.9 (p. 200).

15. Teresa of Avila, *Collected Works*, 2:217.

If the Song seems inappropriate for devotion, Teresa suggested, maybe that has more to do with us, our anxieties and discomforts, than it does with the Song itself.

For centuries, the Song was the devotional text par excellence for many Christians. Can the Song once again become for Christians a text of devotion? Can this poem still help to shape our life with God, with one another, and with the world? What would it mean to read the Song prayerfully, with its literal meaning fully in view, in this day, in this time? What would we learn about our humanity? What would we learn about God?

Incarnation

The bride and groom of the first wedding at which I ever officiated chose a long passage from the Song of Songs to be read aloud during the ceremony. At the rehearsal, the reader—one of the groom's sisters, I think—tried to practice reading the passage in the fifth chapter of the Song where the woman praises every inch of her beloved's body: "My beloved is all radiant and ruddy, distinguished among ten thousand," she read. That drew broad smiles from the groom's friends and family, who were observing from the pews. "His eyes are like doves beside springs of water, bathed in milk, fitly set." A few titters drifted out of the family section. "His cheeks are like beds of spices . . . his lips are lilies, his arms rounded gold." This is where you could see the reader struggling to choke back her laughter. And by the time she got to: "His legs are alabaster columns, set upon bases of gold," we were all in such hysterics that we decided to abandon this passage altogether and went back to the safer, "Set me as a seal upon your heart" (Song 8:6).

We did what Christians so often do: we fell silent about the body. We chose abstract ideas about love over the specificity of legs and lips and eyes.

Why the Song of Songs? Why now? We need the Song because of the reverence for embodied life that shines through every verse. Our cultural confusion about the body does not help us honor our embodiment or teach us to treasure our bodies and the bodies of others. Certainly it does not help us protect the bodies of the vulnerable. The book of Lamentations documents the terrible violation of bodies in war, and, as Harvey Cox observes in his commentary on Lamentations, that violation continues, in ever more terrible ways. In a world in which bodies are regularly commodified and exploited, bought and sold, we need to be guided by the Song's reverence for the human body. In the midst of everything that makes us different from one other—our gender, our race, our vocation, our sexuality, our politics—embodiment is one thing we all genuinely share. Something very great is lost when we avert our eyes from the body.

Christianity does not always give us much help with the questions our embodiment poses, although it should. Christians worship a God who proclaimed all creation good, who came to us in human flesh, who rose from the grave, wounded but whole. Yet we remain suspicious of the body, its desires and pleasures and needs. We suspect deep down that it is the spirit that matters most. We feel we need to go beyond the body, transcend it, if we are to be spiritual people. But Christian faith bears within it a treasure, sometimes hard to see, but nevertheless there—the conviction that the body is sacred, that it is holy, that it is productive of its own kind of knowledge of God, that it is worthy of blessing and care. Where else in our culture can we go to hear such a message? To the Internet? To the glossy magazines? To the TV? If we do not hear it in church, it is a tragedy.

The Song of Songs resists attempts to transcend the body and even to interpret the body into invisibility. No matter how many meanings we excavate from its verses, thighs remain thighs and breasts remain breasts in the Song. It is impossible to read the Song and not confront questions about our embodied life: questions about desire and relationships and identity. Bringing the Song back into our liturgical life as a community and into our prayer life as individuals offers us a way to engage those questions in relation to the deeply incarnational core of our faith. With its loving attention to the body, its celebration of sexual pleasure, and its portrait of an intimate, exclusive relationship in which desire and vulnerability are mutually shared and expressed, the Song invites us to attend to the fullness of our embodied humanity and all the possibilities it holds.

With its unapologetic celebration of incarnate life, the life of the body that Christian faith proclaims God shared with us, the Song is a resource for Christian life that we very much need. Christians have long thought with the Song about the incarnational ground of Christian faith, as when Bernard and Teresa interpreted the kiss in Song 1:2 as the kiss bestowed on all humanity through God's incarnation. These interpretations will help us to pray the Song.

But even without the excavation of explicitly religious meanings, we find in the Song a profound understanding of incarnation. We do not need to move beyond the vision of human love portrayed in the Song in order to reach a deeply theological understanding of it. A truly incarnational theology, according to biblical scholar Dianne Bergant, "considers human love as both a value in itself and a sign or symbol of divine love and claims that we love God precisely in the act of loving others." To pray the Song is to be reminded of what Bergant considers the heart of incarnational theology: "God is not found beyond human endeavor but at the very heart of it."[16]

Mutuality in Love, Care for the Earth

The endeavor of the lovers in the Song of Songs is one that is mutually shared: the endeavor of loving and all that comes with it. Although this is a song sung by a woman and a man, their actions do not run along the lines of traditional gender roles. The poem opens unexpectedly with the voice of the woman expressing her desire, saying clearly what will please her—"Let him kiss me with the kisses of his mouth!" And as the Song unfolds, it becomes clear that everything depends on the woman's initiative. It is she who awakens and arouses her beloved under the apple tree (8:5b). It is the man who waits for her invitation before he enters her garden of delights.

In addition, both lovers are rendered vulnerable by their desire. We hear the woman's vulnerability when she begs her lover to tell her where she can find him: "Tell me, you whom my soul loves, / where you pasture your flock, / where you make it lie down at noon"

---

16. Dianne Bergant, *Song of Songs: The Love Poetry of Scripture* (Hyde Park, NY: New City Press, 1998), 21.

(1:7). But we hear the man's vulnerability as well when he compares her, in 1:9, to a mare among Pharaoh's chariots, driving the stallions wild. In your presence, he says to her, I am out of control. The woman's vulnerability is painfully visible when she is beaten by the night watchmen as she searches the city streets for her absent lover (5:7). We hear the vulnerability in the man's voice when he stands outside the walls of her house pleading, "let me see your face, / let me hear your voice" (2:14). The man and the woman move toward each other with energy; each holds the other in his or her gaze; each is made vulnerable by the desire to be loved in return. Neither one dominates; neither one remains passive. The man and the woman move through the landscape of the Song with equal energy, equal vulnerability, equal desire.

Just as the man and the woman share the experience of vulnerability, they also share the responsibility for cultivating their love and seeking the pleasure of the other as diligently as they seek their own. Each praises the other for her or his beauty in poems that describe every part of the other's beautiful body. Each is confident that they will be well cared for during their lovemaking: "his intention toward me was love," she sings in 2:4; "how sweet is your love, my sister, my bride," he sings back in 4:10. Even their play with language has an erotic dimension. They hand the same images back and forth across the verses of the Song, changing them just slightly each time, intensifying them with each exchange, mirroring in the trading back and forth of words their longing for each other's touch. "I am my beloved's and my beloved is mine," the woman sings in 6:3, celebrating the mutual trust between them.

The care that the lovers take with one another in their loving seems to grow organically out of their care for the life of the earth that makes a home for their love. The world gives them the images they use to describe each other: your eyes are doves, you are an apple tree among the trees in the woods, your cheeks are pomegranates, your breasts are two fawns; you smell like Lebanon; you taste like honey; you are a well of living water, a garden, a lily. The world also offers them places to meet for lovemaking: in the sheep pastures, among the cedars and pines, in the vineyards and gardens.

In return, they care for the world that supports and protects their love, from the does and gazelles to the private bowers of cedars and pines where they meet. They bring their love in line with the rhythms of the earth. The man calls to the woman in the second chapter: "It's spring! It's time to wake up and come outside where the vines are blossoming and the figs are appearing in the fig trees!" Their care for all the growing things in the world becomes an image of their care for each other. They speak of rising early to check on the grapevines and pomegranates. Have they budded, have they opened, are they ready? The tender care they give to budding plants is the same care they give to one another. As they plan to check on the readiness of the vines and fruits to bloom, the woman lets the man know that she also is ready. "There I will give you my love" (7:12), she says.

Living as we are in the increasingly visible emergency of climate change due to global warming, struggling to find the will to make the hard choices that might make a difference for future generations, the Song of Songs offers a vision of living gently in the world. Rather than exploiting the environment in order to make a home in it, the Song sings of making a home in the world through caring for it. The peaceful, agrarian world of the Song, of course, is not where we live. But crafting a vision of homemaking based in care rather than exploitation is an urgent need in our world. Praying the Song would help to keep that need before us. As the lovers call one another to come outside and see what new things the world is doing, they call us outside to look around as well.

Who Are You?

The lovers in the Song of Songs study each other closely. They catalog the glories of each other's hair, teeth, thighs, breasts, navels, cheeks, lips, bellies, eyes, noses, heads, feet, and fragrances. These lovers know what gives each other pleasure, and they offer it, generously. With his left hand under her head and his right hand embracing her (2:6; 8:3), they are as physically intimate as it is possible to be.

But as intimate as they are, they are also always losing each other. The Song is a song of love, and so it is also—inevitably—a song about separation, hesitation, missed meetings, vulnerability, misunderstandings, and the ache of absence. No matter how intimate our relationship with another, it is sometimes difficult for us to find each other, meet each other, recognize each other, and know each other.

The Song is punctuated by these kinds of difficulties. Where are you, the woman asks in chapter 1, and again in chapter 3, and again in chapter 5. Where are you? Why can't I find you? In chapter 6 the man asks a question about his beloved's very identity: "Who is this that looks forth like the dawn, fair as the moon, bright as the sun, terrible as an army with banners?" (6:10). And in chapter 8 the daughters of Jerusalem, who have borne witness to all the lovers' gorgeous descriptions of each other, ask: Who is this coming up from the wilderness, leaning upon her beloved?

Literary criticism of the Bible teaches us that these are rhetorical questions. They are not really asking, scholars tell us, who these lovers are. The questions are there to draw even more attention to the lover being described.

But I cannot help but hear a real question in these verses. Because no matter how intimate we are with one another, no matter how well acquainted we are with every inch of our beloved's skin, we remain mysteries to one another. The lovers in the Song are beautiful, to be sure, and the poet makes us see that beauty in all its shining glory. But they are also more than their beauty, more than the sum of their glorious body parts. And that *more* is difficult to comprehend.

That we cannot ever fully know each other, no matter how intimately we live, is one of the truest things about life: erotic life, family life, community life, life with God. The search for the beloved does not end with sexual union or marriage, baptism or final vows. Such moments are not the end of our search to know the other, but, in a very real way, a renewal of it, a chance to begin again.

You are ruddy and radiant, fragrant and glorious, your hair is like a flock of goats running down a mountain slope! You are so beautiful, my beloved, your eyes are doves. But who are you? Who are you?

O God, you are good, you are just, you are wise. You created us, and you sustain our lives. We know your stories, we have sung your songs. But who are you? Who are you?

Perhaps this is one of the things that drew readers like Origen of

Alexandria, Bernard of Clairvaux, and Teresa of Avila to the Song: its acknowledgment that, even in the midst of delighting in the beloved, even in the midst of loving and being loved, there is always something about the beloved that is, in Bernard's words, farther out or farther in. Maybe one of the things we learn through following them into the Song is that what we cannot know—about God, about our beloved, even about ourselves—is as worthy of reverence, adoration, and wonder as that which we can. The Song teaches us to love not only what we can see shining on the surface but also those depths of the other that are out of our reach. Honoring what is hidden in another, we learn something about ourselves as well. If even the most inaccessible parts of us can be loved, perhaps we are more than we know ourselves to be.

Whose Song Is This?

When I first accepted this assignment, I told a dear friend of my family's, a monk of the Abbey of Gethsemani in Kentucky, that I was working on a commentary on the Song of Songs. I gave him this news proudly, knowing the long monastic tradition of praying the Song, knowing how important the Song was to him. His first response was not encouraging. "What do you know about the Song of Songs?" he asked.

"Hey," I said, "I've been married for almost a quarter of a century! I know plenty about the Song of the Songs!"

"Huh," he replied, in a tone that made clear he was unconvinced.

I had been married for a quarter of a century, and my friend had been a monk for half a century, praying the Song and living it in ways I can only imagine. To whom does the Song speak most directly? To whom does it most truly belong? To the married woman in a heterosexual relationship? Or to the celibate man who has been praying the Song for most of his adult life? Are some readers better suited to understand the Song than others? Is there an ideal reader for this remarkable text? Must one be in a sexual relationship to engage it fully? Must one be heterosexual, like the Song's two lovers, in order to sing along with them?

There is a long tradition in the interpretation of the Song of saying who should *not* read it. Origen warned off those who had not
yet conquered their bodily passions. Two centuries before Origen,
Rabbi Akiba issued this stern warning: "He who trills his voice in
chanting the Song of Songs in the banquet house and treats it as a
sort of song has no part in the world to come."[17]

Commentators in our day seem less concerned with the profana-
tion of the Song that worried Rabbi Akiba and Origen. It is no longer well-enough known to be profaned. Some recent commentaries,
however, marked by the contemporary attention to the literal sense
of the text, valorize the heterosexual nature of the love relationship
in the Song in a way that seems to exclude homosexuality as a legitimate form of love to which the Song might speak. Robert W. Jenson,
for example, writes in his commentary, "If I manage confrontation
with the primal other whom the person of the opposite sex is for me,
I may be able to affirm otherness elsewhere also; if I do not, I will
remain the solipsist I was born as."[18] Jenson goes on to exempt celibate persons from this harsh judgment, but he remains loudly silent
on gay, lesbian, bisexual, and transgendered persons.

The history of Christian engagement with the Song, however, is
by no means a straightforward history of heterosexuality.[19] Origen
speaks for many when he says that God comes to him directly in the
Song—rather than through angels and prophets—to "kiss me with
the kisses of His mouth—that is to say, [to] pour the words of His
mouth into mine, that I may hear Him speak Himself, and see Him
teaching."[20] In his homilies on the Song, Origen urges his listeners to
take the role of the woman in the Song:

> join with the Bride in saying what she says, so that you may
> hear also what she heard. And, if you are unable to join the
> Bride in her words, then, so that you may hear the things that
> are said to her, make haste at least to join the Bridegroom's

17. Quoted in Pope, *Song of Songs*, 19.
18. Robert W. Jenson, *Song of Songs*, Interpretation (Louisville: John Knox Press, 2005), 62 and
    67.
19. See Moore, *God's Beauty Parlor*, 21–89.
20. Origen, *Commentary* I.1 (*Song of Songs*, 60).

> companions. And if they also are beyond you, then be with
> the maidens who stay in the Bride's retinue and share her
> pleasures.[21]

There are many places for a reader to stand in the Song. For Origen, the place most directly connected to the presence of God is the woman's; he puts himself in her place, and it is there that he hopes his listeners will stand. But if not, they can always identify with the man's friends. And if that does not work, they can identify with the daughters of Jerusalem who comment throughout the poem. Where one stands within the Song, whose words one makes one's own, depends not on one's gender or sexuality, but on having the capacity to meet God with the same energy, attention, and stamina with which the lovers meet each other. Gender and sexuality remain fluid in the history of the interpretation of the Song. From Bernard's comparison of his experience of the infusion of grace in prayer to the filling of a woman's breasts with milk[22] to the countless pleadings of commentators, both male and female, to be kissed with "the kisses of his mouth," gender and sexuality shift and change when readers engage with the Song.

Although the Song does not require that we be a particular gender or identify with a particular sexuality in order to enter into its dialogue of love, the Song does make demands on us. Bernard of Clairvaux summarized those demands best:

> the sacred love which is the subject of the whole canticle
> cannot be described in the words of any language, but are
> expressed in deed and truth. And love speaks everywhere; if
> anyone desires to grasp these writings, let him love.[23]

Whose Song is this? It is the Song of the one who loves.

---

21. Idem, *Homily* I.1 (*Song of Songs*, 268).
22. Quoted in Moore, *God's Beauty Parlor*, 24.
23. Bernard of Clairvaux, "Sermon 79," I.1, in *On the Song of Songs IV*, trans. Irene Edmonds (Kalamazoo, MI: Cistercian Publications, 1980), 138.

Reading and Praying the Song

Last year I met a woman who told me a story about the Song of Songs that I will never forget. Her husband had served on a submarine in the U.S. Navy during the 1970s. Family members were able to send messages to the sailors, but the messages could be no more than eight words long. A Bible verse, though, counted as only one word, so the loved ones on shore filled their messages with them.

"All the wives and girlfriends," she told me, "loved the Song of Songs." They would send messages like this: SoS 1:2—and the beloved, deep below the surface of the ocean, would look up Song 1:2 in the Bible. "Let him kiss me with the kisses of his mouth," he would read. Or SoS 4:7—"you are altogether beautiful, my love; there is no flaw in you." Or SoS 8:7, a message to a beloved submerged beneath miles of water—"many waters cannot quench love, neither can floods drown it."

Those women flung the words of the Song into the sea like a lifeline, where they entered the submarine like a secret code. Coiled within these SOSs were so many prayers: "I miss you. God be with you. Please come home to me." Bent over his Bible like a scholar, a sailor would search the Song for his beloved's voice. Together, they crossed the miles of water between them on the bridge of the Song.

Bernard, Teresa, Origen—they read this way too. They read the Song looking for a path to cross the distance between themselves and God. We too might turn to the Song looking for such a path—a path to cross the distance between ourselves and God, between ourselves and others, between ourselves and the world.

In a letter to his spiritual director, the twelfth-century Carthusian monk Guigo II wrote about a ladder of monks that stretched between earth and heaven, a ladder a monk could learn to climb. The first rung of the ladder was *lectio*, reading. Through reading, Guigo wrote, we focus all our powers of attention on a small portion of Scripture, a sweet grape that we put into our mouth. In meditation, the next rung of the ladder, we use all our knowledge and reason to understand what we read, chewing the grape. Reason and knowledge can get us only so far, however, and when we realize we cannot

learn everything we need to know about the passage through meditation, we turn to God in prayer. On this third rung of the ladder, we
extract the flavor of the passage. In prayer we try to cross the distance
between ourselves and God, and then, if we are lucky, God breaks in
upon our prayer before we have even finished uttering it and lifts us
up to the fourth and highest rung, contemplation. In contemplation
we receive nourishment from the grape of Scripture: "the sweetness
itself which gladdens and refreshes."[24]

This commentary invites you to read the Song in the way Guigo
taught, using every available resource, from reason to knowledge
to prayer, to understand it. In the pages that follow, I will comment
and meditate on the Song in smallish segments, some just a verse,
or even part of a verse, others a longer portion. Some of the longer
bits will tell a story; others will linger on descriptions of the lovers.
Guigo urges us to bring all the resources of our reason and knowledge to bear upon Scripture, and I will bring some of the key insights
of historical-critical study as well as interpretations from the long
history of Jewish and Christian commentary to bear on my reading
of the Song. I try to make visible the kinds of hopes and expectations readers over the centuries have brought to this text, hopes and
expectations we might share.

I hope you will find this commentary good company as you make
your way through the Song. But in the end I will not advocate one
way of reading the Song, because the meaning of any poem cannot
be captured by correct methodology. Poetry's meanings are expan-
sive, one thought or association leading to the next. Reading poetry
is itself an act of creation and an invitation to participate in God's
own creativity. If we let it, poetry can open our imaginations and
refresh our vision of God, ourselves, and the world.

I invite you to linger with the passages that speak most powerfully
to you and to compare what you read in the Song with what you
read, as Bernard of Clairvaux once put it, in the book of your experience.[25] I invite you, like Guigo, to pray your way into the mysteries

---

24. Guigo II, *The Ladder of Monks and Twelve Meditations*, trans. Edmund Colledge, O.S.A., and
James Walsh, S.J. (Kalamazoo, MI: Cistercian Publications, 1981), 69.
25. Bernard of Clairvaux, "Sermon 3," I.1 (*Song of Songs I*, 16).

that arise for you in the Song that historical-critical commentary cannot solve. I invite you to step into the wide circle of readers who have been thinking with the Song about the relationship between human beings and God, between human beings and other human beings, and between human beings and the world since the Song was first added to the collection of Wisdom literature in the Bible.

I invite you to think and pray with the Song about the life of the body, our life with one another, our life in creation, and our life with God. It is just one life, after all. One life that is even more than the sum of its parts. One life that opens onto depths that are spiritual, erotic, compassionate, and, on some level, not entirely knowable. One life touched and blessed by the kiss that has been sung about over centuries in language unutterably beautiful, from the Song to the midrash on the Song to Bernard of Clairvaux's eighty-six sermons on the Song to the song beyond language humming inside each of us.

1:1

The Song of Songs, Which Is Solomon's

The opening verse of the Song of Songs is not actually part of the Song itself. It is a superscription, added after the poems that make up the Song were compiled and edited. This means that the first voice we hear when we open our Bibles to the Song and begin reading is not the voice of the writer or writers. It is, rather, the voice of a reader—the first review, if you will. And it is a rave: "The Song of Songs, which is Solomon's."

The Song of Songs: can there be any higher praise? This is the greatest of all songs, our anonymous reader seems to say, a song surpassed by no other. Scholars who understand the Song to be an anthology of several poems (thirty-one, according to Marcia Falk[26]) have proposed "a song made up of songs" as a possible interpretation of the superscription. Most scholars, however, read "the Song

---

26. Marcia Falk, *The Song of Songs: A New Translation and Interpretation* (San Francisco: HarperSanFrancisco, 1990).

of Songs" as a superlative: the best of songs, the most sublime. Read in this way, the superscription seems to attest to the unity of the Song—or at least to the author of the superscription's experience of the unity of the Song. Indeed, the Hebrew word for song, *shir*, is used here in the singular. A multitude of readers down through the centuries has agreed: this is one song, and it is the greatest of all songs.

Rabbi Akiba intensified the praise of the superscription in the early first century CE when he defended the Song's place in the biblical canon. "The whole world is not worth the day on which the Song of Songs was given to Israel," he insisted, "for all the Scriptures are holy, but the Song of Songs is the Holy of Holies."[27] For Rabbi Akiba, the Song bore within its verses nothing less than the presence of the living God.

The *Midrash Rabbah* ranked the Song as the best among the three songs of Solomon in the Hebrew Bible: Proverbs, Ecclesiastes, and the Song itself. For the third-century Christian commentator Origen of Alexandria, the Song is the finest of what he considered to be the seven songs of Scripture: the song Moses and the Israelites sang to the Lord after crossing the Red Sea; the song the people of Israel sang at the well of Moses; the song Moses sang to the elders of the tribes of Israel after he finished writing down the law; Deborah's song celebrating the victory of the Israelites over the Canaanites; David's song of deliverance; Asaph's song of praise; and the Song of Songs, the greatest, according to Origen, of them all. The Targum on the Song, an Aramaic paraphrase that interprets the Song as a retelling of the sacred history of Israel, also places the Song among other biblical songs—ten to Origen's eight—the ninth being, "The ninth song of Solomon, king of Israel, uttered by the Holy Spirit before the Lord of all the World."[28] And Bernard of Clairvaux, in the twelfth century, wrote in the first of his eighty-six sermons on the Song that it is only right that a song sung in honor of the King of Kings and Lord of Lords should be called the Song of Songs.

Perhaps the most luminous reason ever given for the Song's claim to its title was offered by the medieval kabbalist, Rabbi Ezra ben

27. Pope, *Song of Songs*, 19.
28. Ibid., 296–97.

Solomon of Gerona. He believed the Song to be the greatest of songs because God sings it every day. Rabbi Ezra understood the name Solomon to stand, allegorically, for God, and so he interpreted the superscription to mean: "the song which the Holy One blessed be He recites daily."[29] For Rabbi Ezra, the words of the Song are God's own words, the Song itself God's own song.

The superscription not only sets the Song above all other songs, it also further honors the Song by associating it with King Solomon. Most early readers of the Song understood this to mean that King Solomon wrote the Song. But this is not the only possible meaning of the Hebrew phrase. As Marcia Falk has put it, the literal meaning of the phrase is, "The song of songs, which is by, OR to, OR of, OR about, Solomon."[30] It is hard to know what the author of the superscription intended by associating the Song with Solomon. Perhaps the author meant that the poem belonged to Solomon, or was written for him, or dedicated to him, or was about him. Most early readers, however, understood the superscription to mean that Solomon was the author of the poem, and they placed the Song among the rest of what they believed to be Solomon's writings: Proverbs and Ecclesiastes. These days, however, most scholars do not believe that Solomon wrote any of these books.

Why did the author of the superscription attach Solomon's name to the Song? Some have argued that the Song became associated with Solomon because he was a famous lover, with "seven hundred princesses and three hundred concubines" (1 Kgs. 11:3) in his harem. It is difficult, however, to see how Solomon's one thousand wives qualified him to be associated with a poem that celebrates a passionate, mutual relationship between two lovers who delight in loving each other exclusively—"my dove, my perfect one, is the only one," the man says of the woman (Song 6:9). Indeed, toward the end of the Song the male lover seems to poke gentle fun at Solomon's enormous harem. "My vineyard," the man sings, "my very own, is for myself; you, O Solomon, may have the thousand!" (8:12). You

---

29. Rabbi Ezra ben Solomon of Gerona, *Commentary on the Song of Songs and Other Kabbalistic Commentaries*, trans. Seth Brody (Kalamazoo, MI: Medieval Institute Publications, 1999), 39.
30. Falk, *Song of Songs*, 165.

can keep your vast, expensive vineyard, the man seems to say. My vineyard—my beloved—is enough for me.

Others have thought that it was Solomon's skill as a poet that led the editors of the Song to attach his name to it. First Kings 4:32–34 says that Solomon

> composed three thousand proverbs, and his songs numbered a thousand and five. He would speak of trees, from the cedar that is in the Lebanon to the hyssop that grows in the wall; he would speak of animals, and birds, and reptiles, and fish. People came from all the nations to hear the wisdom of Solomon.

It is easier to imagine how someone who loved the Song might associate it with Solomon's gift for poetry, especially his gift for describing nature in all its variety. In the Song nature is not something to be mastered or used or dominated. It is where lovers go to enact their love; it provides the fragrance and the beauty the poet draws upon to describe the lovers. The Song places the lovers *in* nature, creatures in creation. Solomon, who gave as much attention to the hyssop growing in the wall as he did to the great cedars of Lebanon, would seem to be the kind of author who might have celebrated both the lovers and their bower of cedar and pine (Song 1:15–17).

Some have argued that Solomon is a character in the Song, that perhaps he is the bridegroom himself—and, indeed, Solomon is mentioned seven times in the Song, including some verses about Solomon on his wedding day, his palanquin appearing in a fragrant procession, surrounded by sixty armed men (3:6–11). His procession is a beautiful sight as it makes its stately way across chapter 3, a vision of opulence and splendor. While Solomon's occasional presence in the Song may shed even more loveliness upon the bridegroom who lies in the vineyards with his beloved, they do not seem to be one and the same.

Whatever else we can say about the association of the Song with King Solomon, we know that his name "lends antiquity as well as authority" to anything it touches.[31] As J. Cheryl Exum and others

31. J. Cheryl Exum, *Song of Songs*, OTL (Louisville: Westminster John Knox Press, 2005), 89.

have noted, the appending of Solomon's name to the Song was "the first step in the religious appropriation of the book that would claim for Solomon the authorship of the Song, Proverbs, and Ecclesiastes."[32] Indeed, some commentators claim the association with Solomon as a primary reason for the Song's inclusion in the biblical canon. If Solomon wrote it, it belonged to the sacred literature of Israel, even though it did not refer explicitly to God.

But Solomon's name alone cannot begin to account for the devotion the Song has inspired through the centuries. Nor can it fully account for the Song's presence in the Bible. Dianne Bergant argues that the Song met the criteria of the rabbis who assembled the canon of Wisdom literature.

> The sages were humanists, concerned with human beings and attentive to human welfare, values, and dignity. They taught that whatever benefited humankind was a good to be pursued, and whatever was harmful should be avoided and condemned. . . . Placing the Song of Songs within the wisdom tradition suggests that it contains lessons beneficial for right living, insights that will enhance human life.[33]

Countless readers have followed the sages in seeking wisdom in their encounter with this greatest of all songs. And we, at the threshold of the Song's first verse, join them.

FURTHER REFLECTIONS
Christian Biblical Interpretation

One of the most urgent hermeneutical questions for early Christians was how to interpret the Old Testament in relationship to the Gospels. Augustine gathered up the results of early Christian thinking on this question when he wrote, "The New Testament lies hidden in the Old; the Old is enlightened through the New."[34]

---

32. Ibid.
33. Bergant, *Song of Songs*, 17–18.
34. Quoted in Sandra M. Schneiders, "Scripture and Spirituality," in *Christian Spirituality*, vol. 1: *Origins to the Twelfth Century*, ed. Bernard McGinn, John Meyendorff, and Jean Leclercq (New York: Crossroad, 1988), 14.

The NT writers themselves had sought to bind the story of Jesus as closely as possible to the Hebrew Scriptures. "If you believed Moses, you would believe me," Jesus says in the Gospel of John to those who accuse him of transgressing Moses' law, "for he wrote about me" (John 5:46). Early Christian interpreters followed the author of John's Gospel and found Jesus anticipated everywhere in the Old Testament. He was "the New Adam, the New Moses, the prophet promised in Deuteronomy, the promised heir to the Davidic throne, the Isaian Suffering Servant, and the mysterious Son of Man in the book of Daniel."[35] The interpreters who relied on allegorical or typological methods of interpretation and those who emphasized the historical, literal meaning of the biblical text both arrived at highly Christological readings of OT texts. Jesus himself became the hermeneutical key with which early Christians unlocked the meaning of the Hebrew Bible.

But what about the Song of Songs? Nowhere in its eight chapters is Yahweh mentioned or even the religion of Israel. God is silent and hidden in this biblical book. Did early Christian interpreters find Jesus there as well?

Drawing on the rabbinical tradition of finding the relationship between God and Israel described in the Song and following Paul's analogy of husband and wife to describe Christ and the church, Christian interpreters listened to the Song for a word about that relationship. Hippolytus of Rome was perhaps the first Christian commentator to see the woman in the Song as a figure for the church.[36] The many interpretations that followed in the path Hippolytus opened heard Jesus' voice calling out to his bride, *ecclesia*: "Arise, my love, my fair one, and come away." They heard him call the church beautiful. They heard him say with longing, "Let me hear your voice."

These early Christian interpreters also found in the Song their own longing for Jesus, their difficulty in finding him, and the ache they felt in the wake of his absence. Many interpretations, like that

---

35. Ibid., 4.
36. R. P. Lawson, "Introduction," in Origen, *Song of Songs*, 6–8.

of Origen, moved back and forth between readings that found the relationship of Christ and the church described in the Song and those that found a story of Christ and the individual soul.

With the advent of the historical-critical study of the Bible, such readings came to seem, at the least, anachronistic, and, at the worst, as attempts to supersede the sacred texts of Israel with Christian belief. And indeed, when such readings make claims about hidden Christian intentions of the authors of the Hebrew Bible, or attempt to erase the historical context out of which these texts arise, or replace rabbinical readings with Christian ones, they are both anachronistic and supersessionist.

The history of the Song's reception is a history of multiple readings that find in this erotic poetry about two lovers' fruitful ways of pondering the relationship between God and Israel, Christ and the church, God and the soul. The Song itself resists any absolute declarations about the intention of the author(s) or the final identity of the characters; it is poetry, after all. At their best, Christian readings of the Song enter the long conversation about this poem with humility and think theologically with the poem about the Song's own concerns: love, desire, the body, and the distance between even the most intimate of lovers.

1:2–4

Let Him Kiss Me with the Kisses of His Mouth!

Many voices cry out in the Bible, but none sound quite like the voice that opens the Song of Songs. Here is the voice of a woman speaking clearly about her desires, about what will please her. In a Bible full of stories in which women have very little control over their sexual lives, this comes as a surprise. Think of Sarah, taken into Pharaoh's bed when Abraham was too frightened to admit that he was the husband of such a beautiful woman. Think of Hagar, Sarah's servant, sent by her mistress into Abraham's bed in order to produce an heir. Think of Leah, property of her father, Laban, sent into Jacob's bed to make him think he had married her sister, Rachel. Think of Lot's daughters, offered to a gang of rapists in order to protect the male visitors to whom Lot had offered hospitality. Out of this grim context, the woman's voice in the Song shines unexpectedly: "Let him kiss me with the kisses of his mouth!"

The opening line of the Song sets the tone for the rest of the poem. This is a poem about love: sexual, urgent, and overwhelming. The lovers speak in the delicious language of desire, vulnerable and alive in their bodies.

> **This is a poem about love: sexual, urgent, and overwhelming. The lovers speak in the delicious language of desire, vulnerable and alive in their bodies.**

"Did I even know I had a body / before that kiss broke its boundaries?" the poet Karin Gottschall asks.[37] A kiss makes us vividly aware of our own body, open to the body of another. "Touch . . . makes the body real to us," the poet Mark Doty writes.[38] A kiss makes us feel just how embodied we are and how very much that matters. Even the woman's expression of longing for a kiss awakens us to the life of our body.

Because the woman speaks of her lover in the third person rather than directly to him—"Let him kiss me!" rather than "Kiss me!"—Phyllis Trible argues that the opening line of the poem draws us all into the orbit of the woman's love and longing. She invites us, Trible says, "to enter their circle of intimacy."[39]

Certainly many readers have felt invited to participate deeply in this poem, to make it their own. The woman's unexpected voice, expressing her longing so directly and uninhibitedly, has allowed readers over the centuries to hear the sound of their own deepest longings in the Song. Bernard of Clairvaux heard not only the sound of his deepest desires but the echo of "the intense longing of those men of old" who sensed, through their reading of the Song, "how profuse the graciousness" of the kiss would be and who longed to receive it on their own lips.[40]

---

37. Karin Gottschall, "The Bog Body," in *Crocus* (New York: Fordham University Press, 2007), 26.

38. Mark Doty, *Heaven's Coast: A Memoir* (New York: HarperPerennial, 1996), 123.

39. Phyllis Trible, *God and the Rhetoric of Sexuality*, OBT (Philadelphia: Fortress, 1978), 146.

40. Bernard of Clairvaux, "Sermon 2," I.1 (*Song of Songs I*, 8).

The Targum to the Song finds in the kiss an echo of God's giving of the Law to the people of Israel, an act of tender intimacy: "YHWH . . . spoke to us face to face as a man kisses his companion, from the abundance of the love with which He loved us, more than the seventy nations."[41] Many Christian readers, Bernard of Clairvaux and Teresa of Avila among them, heard in the woman's desire for a kiss the longing of humanity to draw near to God in intimate friendship. The desire for a kiss is the desire, according to these readers, for the incarnation of God in Jesus. The kiss is the pressing of divinity into human flesh, the kiss God bestowed on all human life.

Bernard of Clairvaux found in the words of the Song not only the longing of the whole human family for the incarnation but the longing of the individual soul for intimacy with God.

> For [God's] living, active word is to me a kiss . . . an unreserved infusion of joys, a revealing of mysteries, a marvellous and indistinguishable mingling of the divine light with the enlightened mind, which joined in truth to God, is one spirit with [God].[42]

What Bernard wanted, and what he went to the Song in prayer to find, was nothing less than an intimate relationship with the living God, a kiss that would break across the threshold of the firmament and dissolve the boundary between heaven and earth.

That is a lot to ask of this short book of love poetry. But by inviting readers of the Song into the lovers' circle of intimacy, the woman opens a space for us to express our deepest, fiercest longings as well.

The woman's yearning for her lover's kiss spills over into a song of praise for her beloved: his love, his fragrance, his name. The woman praises her lover's name (although his name remains hidden from us), which tastes better than wine on her tongue. She lingers over the fragrance of his body, and even the fragrance of his name is like "perfume poured out."

In these first two verses of the Song the woman engages four of our five senses: touch (the kiss), taste (the wine), smell (the fragrance of the beloved's name), and hearing (the name itself). Only sight,

---

41. Quoted in Pope, *Song of Songs*, 299.
42. Bernard of Clairvaux, "Sermon 2," I.2 (*Song of Songs I*, 9).

which will play an important part in the Song, goes unmentioned in the woman's opening words. The Song insists that we experience it as we experience love itself: with our whole body, every sense alert.

"The king has brought me into his chambers," the woman says in 1:4. This is the first royal reference in the poem (excluding the superscription, which is a later addition). Most scholars agree that the "king" the woman alludes to is simply her lover, whom she honors by comparing him to royalty. Marcia Falk renders the line, "Take me away to your room / like a king to his rooms," to emphasize the metaphorical nature of the image.[43]

The sometimes abrupt shift of persons makes the Song difficult to follow in places. The "we" of the end of verse 4 probably refers to the daughters of Jerusalem, who function like a chorus in the poem, commenting on the action, providing a dialogue partner for the woman, and opening a space for us, the readers, within the poem. Here they add their praise of the man to the woman's own praise, intensifying it.

The first few verses of the first chapter set the stage for the rest of this glorious song, from the woman's voice, startling in its clarity and unreserved in its passion, to her cascading words of praise for her beloved. We are not invited to ease into this poem; it impels us to experience it with every sense we have. Once we cross the threshold of the woman's longing for a kiss, we are in a world that seeks to overwhelm all our senses and capture our entire attention.

1:5–6

Black and Beautiful

The interpretation of these two verses of the Song has often been used as a measure of the racial bias of the culture within which the translation was produced. The "I am dark but lovely" of earlier translations (including KJV and RSV) seems to place the woman in the position of apologizing for her dark skin. More recent translations, like the NRSV, replace the "but" with "and," emphasizing the affirmative nature of the statement.

---

43. Falk, *Song of Songs*, 167.

There is a tension in these verses between darkness and beauty, but it is not a tension within the woman herself. The tension exists, rather, between the woman and those who gaze at her. The woman knows she is beautiful, as beautiful as the opulent tents of Kedar and the "curtains of Solomon." The woman uses images of wealth to describe the darkness of her skin, perhaps undercutting a class bias that regards dark-skinned women who work outdoors in the sunshine as less beautiful than privileged women who live sheltered lives, out of the sun.[44] But this passage is in no way an apology; rather it is the woman's assertion and celebration of her beauty. She delights in her body and in her skin. Even held in a critical gaze by others who might see her skin not as beautiful but as a marker of lower-class status, the woman continues to view herself through the eyes of her lover who, as he will soon declare, sees her as the "fairest among women" (1:8).

To the daughters of Jerusalem, whom she asks not to gaze on her and judge the darkness of her skin, she explains that her brothers sent her out to work in the vineyards, in the sun. "They made me keeper of the vineyards," she sings, "but my own vineyard I have not kept!" Because, throughout the poem, the woman is compared to a vineyard, Phyllis Trible argues that the woman here suggests that her lover is the keeper of her vineyard, her body. Dianne Bergant and others have heard in "my own vineyard I have not kept" a reference to the woman's sexual boundaries, breached. Whatever the case, her brothers disapprove and become angry. The woman herself, how-ever, is as pleased with her body and her sexuality as she is with her beautiful dark skin.

1:7–14

A Dialogue of Delight

In this section of the Song the dialogue between the lovers begins. What started out as a poem of the woman's yearning for her lover becomes here a poem of mutual longing, mutual desire, and mutual vulnerability.

---

44. Bergant, *Song of Songs*, 23.

In 1:7 the woman asks her lover where he pastures his flocks. Where can she find him? Such questions recur throughout the poem—Where are you? Where can I find you? Even: Who are you? The lovers meet and part, seek each other and find each other, miss each other by moments, and ponder the mystery of each other that is always just out of reach.

Here the woman seeks her lover at noon, when the sheep are resting and the shepherd can turn his attention to his beloved. The woman wants to know where to find him, rather than wandering around "like one who is veiled beside the flock of your companions" (1:7) The veil has stimulated a great deal of debate among readers of the Song. Is the woman veiled metaphorically, as Marcia Falk would have it, "wandering blindly" around looking for her lover?[45] Is the woman disguised so that she can pass by her lovers' friends and companions without notice? Would a veiled woman in the fields at midday be mistaken for a prostitute, as Bergant suggests?[46]

> What started out as a poem of the woman's yearning for her lover becomes here a poem of mutual longing, mutual desire, and mutual vulnerability.

It is impossible to know from the text what is intended. What does come through clearly, though, is that, whatever is meant by the veil, the woman wants to come to her lover by the shortest route. She wants to know where to find him so that she can join him where he is.

Her lover answers teasingly. If you don't know where to find me, he says, follow the tracks of the sheep and "pasture your kids / beside the shepherds' tents" (1:8). Is the woman a shepherd as well? Or is this the punning wordplay of lovers? Whatever it is, it is suffused with humor and delight.

In 1:9 the man continues speaking and reveals how vulnerable he has been made by his love for the woman. He compares her to a mare among Pharaoh's chariots. According to Marvin Pope, sometimes an attacking army would let loose a mare among the stallions of the opposing side's army to arouse and confuse them.[47] This is the

45. Falk, *Song of Songs*, 170.
46. Bergant, *Song of Songs*, 31.
47. Pope, *Song of Songs*, 338–39.

message of the man to the woman: You drive me wild. In your presence, I am out of control.

There is a long history in Christianity of feeling anxious about such loss of control. It is precisely because sexual desire is so powerful that Christians have expressed such suspicion of it. Sexual desire brings with it vulnerability. Like death, sexual desire can seem to rob us of freedom, asserting itself even when we will otherwise. But in the Song the power of desire to overtake us and set us spinning, like one of Pharaoh's stallions, is not something to worry over, at least not in this relationship, marked by mutuality in both pleasure and vulnerability. It is something to celebrate.

As he does throughout the Song, the man notices and praises not only the woman's body but also her adornments, which enhance her beauty. Her ornaments make her cheeks even more lovely; her neck looks even more glorious hung with strings of jewels (1:10). He promises to create for her even more ornamentation, made of gold and silver, to adorn her beauty.

An interesting feature of this dialogue and the rest of the dialogues between the lovers in the Song is that the man speaks *to* the woman directly (*you* are like a mare among Pharaoh's chariots, *your* neck looks beautiful hung with jewels) while she often speaks *of* him, as she did in the opening line of the Song (let him kiss me). J. Cheryl Exum notes that this tendency reflects the difference in the way the lovers experience each other and the language they use to describe those experiences. The man is concerned with the woman's presence, which he finds overwhelming. In order to cope with it, he praises her one part at a time: her eyes, her neck, her breasts. The woman is concerned with the man's absence. We often find her searching for him in the vineyards, in the fields, in the streets of the city. She uses language to "conjure" him, as Exum puts it, in stories in which she and he are the two main characters.

When the woman speaks *of* the man, rather than directly to him, we, as readers, are drawn further into their dialogue. The woman speaks to her lover and to us at once, drawing us in with stories and descriptions that seem addressed to us while at the same time keeping us at enough of a distance that we do not intrude upon the lovers' most intimate moments. Verses 12–14 are a vivid example of this. We are drawn in with erotically charged language that brings us into the warm, fragrant space the lovers inhabit. Here the woman again casts her lover as "the king."

> While the king was on his couch
>   my nard gave forth its fragrance.
> My beloved is to me a bag of myrrh
>   that lies between my breasts.

Her lover had praised her adornments; here she says that he is her adornment, lying close to her body, between her breasts. That is as far as we get, however. The next line—"My beloved is to me a cluster of henna blossoms / in the vineyards of En-gedi"—invokes the strong fragrance of henna, but it does not tell us much more of what is happening on the king's couch. Her language draws us in and veils our eyes at once.

1:15–17

Ah, You Are Beautiful, My Love

Reclaiming the Song as a text of devotion means learning to pray it. This little poem at the end of the first chapter is a good place to start. In these verses the lovers find themselves so enraptured with each other that all they can do is breathe in and breathe out one word: *beautiful.* The man says to the woman,

> Ah, you are beautiful, my love,
>   ah, you are beautiful;
>   your eyes are doves.

And the woman replies, speaking directly to the man,

> Ah, you are beautiful, my beloved,
>   truly lovely.

The whole orientation of the Song is captured in these few words.

> Ah, you are beautiful, my love,
>   ah, you are beautiful.

The Song is a song of lovers, a song of two people whom love has made attentive to the beauty of the world, lovers for whom the whole world is awash in beauty precisely because they are in love.

> Ah, you are beautiful, my love,
>   ah, you are beautiful.

Origen of Alexandria warned readers of the Song that they should read it only if they had overcome sexual desire in their own lives. If not, the text was too dangerous to read—its erotic power might sweep undisciplined readers away from the right path.

But Origen was not always so timorous when it came to engaging the Song. Fear did not ultimately drive Origen's reading of the Song; love did. In his first homily on the Song, he urged readers to "join with the Bride in saying what she says, so that you may also hear what she heard."[48] What will we hear if we join the lovers in noticing and praising the beauty all around us, breathing it in and breathing it out? What will we hear if we make the words of the Song our own?

> Ah, you are beautiful, my love,
>   ah, you are beautiful.

Breathing this prayer in and out of our bodies may teach us to expect to find beauty everywhere we look: in the faces of those we love and those we encounter, in their wondrous specificity. Ah, you are beautiful my love. Breathing this prayer may give us a lens to find beauty in unexpected places: in the crowded places of our cities, in the broken places of our lives, in the busy moments of an ordinary day: ah, you are beautiful. With these words, we can begin to knit what is inside of us to what is outside.

---

48. Origen, *Homily* I.1 (*Song of Songs*, 268).

Bernard of Clairvaux insisted that "only the touch of the Spirit can inspire a song like this, and only personal experience can unfold its meaning."[49] It is not enough to study the Song, Bernard believed. We have to live it. We have to pray it. We have to *breathe* it.

> Ah, you are beautiful, my love,
>> ah, you are beautiful.

The lovers in the Song find beauty everywhere they look: in each other's bodies, in the fields where they pasture their sheep, in the rooms and orchards where they make love, in the turning of the seasons, in the animals and trees and hills all around them. As for King Solomon, who lavished the same poetic attention to the hyssop that grows in the wall that he gave to the cedars of Lebanon, no beautiful thing is too small to be adored. The lovers let no beauty go unnoticed, uncelebrated, unpraised. Every time they exhale their reverence and adoration—ah, you are beautiful—they bind themselves ever more deeply to the life of the world that God created and called good.

This small section of the Song ends with the lovers lifting their eyes from each other and looking about them.

> Our couch is green;
>> the beams of our house are cedar,
>> our rafters are pine.

The home of these lovers, their bed, is the green world itself, as worthy of reverence as their beautiful bodies and fragrant smells. When they lift their heads to see the cedars and the pines towering over them, their posture of devotion does not change. The Song suggests that when we turn with reverence to another, bringing our whole attention to the other's

> The Song suggests that when we turn with reverence to another, bringing our whole attention to the other's uniqueness, the other's beauty, soon we will be turning to the world around us with a similar reverence. Soon we will see beauty everywhere we look.

49. Bernard of Clairvaux, "Sermon 1," VI.11 (*Song of Songs I*, 6).

uniqueness, the other's beauty, soon we will be turning to the world around us with a similar reverence. Soon we will see beauty everywhere we look.

2:1–3a
A Lily of the Valleys, a Tree in the Woods

Throughout the first chapter of the Song, the lovers trade descriptions of each other back and forth until, finally, words seem to fail them. Ah, you are beautiful, they say to one another, and the cascade of images of mares and stallions, bags of myrrh and henna blossoms, comes for a moment to a halt: ah, you are beautiful.

When the exchange of images begins again, at the beginning of the second chapter, the lovers seem to have sharpened their attention—not only to each other's beauties but to each other's words. They begin to build their contributions to the dialogue on words the other has spoken.

In 2:1 the woman describes herself as a flower, blooming. "I am a rose of Sharon," she sings, "a lily of the valleys." This description places her among the pine trees and cedars, the green world she invoked in 1:17 when she described the place where she meets her lover. She describes herself as a growing, changing, blossoming part of the creation that makes a home for their love.

Her lover receives the image she offers of a flower blooming and places it in a more inaccessible place than a valley. "As a lily among brambles," he returns, "so is my love among maidens" (2:2).

Taking up the man's image of an unexpected blossoming plant growing up, uniquely, among other, more ordinary growth, the woman offers this image of her beloved: "As an apple tree among the trees of the wood, / so is my beloved among young men" (2:3).

The lovers' intensifying exchange of words and images is one of the ways they cultivate intimacy across all that separates them: the woman's watchful brothers, the walls of her house, the boundaries of their own bodies. Receiving and returning each other's words, they draw closer to one another. For this exchange to succeed, poetically and erotically, they must seek not only their own pleasure but the pleasure of the other. They must be playful; they must listen carefully; they must respond organically, letting their words grow from the words of the beloved like the trees and flowers they celebrate throughout the poem. These are not easy words of praise, casually exchanged. These are words that build intentionally and creatively upon the words of the other, words that catch hold of what has already been said, turn it in a slightly different direction, and increase its possible meanings. Not only do the lovers conjure each other through their descriptions, they also reach out for one another, seeking to touch one another through language shared and heightened, just as they long to receive and return each other's touch. The pleasure they seek is a shared pleasure they each take responsibility to deepen. The rhythm of receiving a word, or an image, from the other and then returning it, transformed and intensified, mirrors the erotic exchange for which the lovers long.

The lovers' passionate attention to language and its intimate, erotic possibilities echoes in the works of many of the Song's readers. Bernard of Clairvaux spends a lot of time in his sermons on the Song considering the power of language and the importance of choosing one's words with care. He exhorts his monks—whom he worries offend the angels when they doze off during the night office—to "sing wisely" and seek after the sweetness at the heart of the words of the Psalms by chewing them "with the teeth as it were of the mind." The monk who prays the words of the Psalms with his heart wide awake will cause the angels to respond to him in the words of the Song of Songs and so draw him into its intimate dialogue. "What is this," the angels will ask, "coming up from the desert like a column of smoke, breathing of myrrh and frankincense and every perfume the merchant knows?"[50] If you pray the Psalms with attention, Bernard tells his monks, you might catch the attention of the angels. They will ask themselves who you are, opening the possibility that you are much more than you know yourself to be. To pray, for Bernard, is to open ourselves to a dialogue in which we encounter the other, and also ourselves, in unexpected ways, a dialogue in which intimacy is

---

50. Bernard of Clairvaux, "Sermon 7," IV.5–6 (*Song of Songs I*, 41–42).

cultivated and intensified with every loving exchange. For Bernard, prayer is a mutual act, like the lovemaking in the Song.

The theme of this particular dialogue is the hiddenness of the extraordinary lover among the ordinary: a lily among brambles, an apple tree among the trees of the wood. This was a favorite theme of Christian commentators because it suggested to them the incarnation of God in Jesus, the divine hidden in the human. Jewish commentators heard in the roses and the lilies a reference to Israel, hidden in the wilderness, yet seen and known and beloved by God. All allegorical interpretations, Jewish and Christian alike, grew out of a commitment to search for meaning hidden among the words of Scripture, a search that has its own erotic dimension. As that passionate reader of Scripture Augustine of Hippo insisted, hidden meanings are found with more pleasure than meanings that simply lie on the surface, waiting to be apprehended. Everyone knows "that what is sought with difficulty is discovered with more pleasure."[51] It is the search itself that lures one on, the search itself in which the pleasures of interpretation are found.

The theme of hiddenness, so beloved of the author(s) and readers of the Song, also recalls the hiddenness of the Song among the books of the Bible and the hiddenness of God in the poem. Just as one does not expect to find an apple tree in the woods or a lily among the brambles, we do not expect to find an erotic poem tucked away among the books of the Bible. We do not expect to find God between the lines of a poem celebrating the beauties of the human body, the bright ache of sexual desire, and the pleasures of lovemaking. But why not? One of the things we might learn if we pray this poem with devotion is that it is not God who is hiding, but we who have hidden ourselves from God, refusing to look for God in embodied human life. Like Adam and Eve, cowering naked in the shadows of the garden, we have hidden from God, believing that God will despise our nakedness, our desire, our vulnerability. But God made us this way: naked and vulnerable and longing for intimacy. Perhaps this is part of what it means to be made in the image of God: to long to cross the distance between ourselves and another, to cultivate love in the spaces between us.

51. Augustine, *On Christian Doctrine* 2.6, 38.

FURTHER REFLECTIONS
Imago Dei

At the heart of Christian thinking about human beings and human life is the idea, found in the opening chapter of Genesis, that human beings were created in the image of God.

> So God created humankind in his image,
> in the image of God he created them;
> male and female he created them.
>
> (Gen. 1:27)

When the first creation story is reiterated at the beginning of the fifth chapter of Genesis, the creation of human beings in the image of God is also reiterated (5:1). And when God's covenant with Noah is described in Genesis 9, humanity's creation in God's image becomes the measure of the value of a human life.

> Whoever sheds the blood of a human,
> by a human shall that person's blood be shed;
> for in his own image God made humankind.
>
> (Gen. 9:6)

The notion of the *imago Dei* gets picked up in the New Testament when Christ is described as "the image of the invisible God" (Col. 1:15) whose incarnation in human flesh restores God's original image, obscured by sin, in human bodies and human lives. "Just as we have borne the image of the man of dust," Paul writes, "we will also bear the image of the man of heaven" (1 Cor. 15:49).

Although Jewish anthropology did not posit a sharp distinction between body and soul, early Christians, influenced by Greek thought, focused on precisely such distinctions—the ways in which human beings carry within us both eternal life and certain death, the rational and the irrational, body and soul. The composite nature of human beings, these early theologians believed, made human beings a microcosm of God's entire creation. Formed from the dust of the earth, we are also animated by God's breath. In us, what is spiritual and what is material dwell together, and so our calling, as creatures made in God's image, is to mediate between the two.[52]

Early Christian theologians heard in God's words in Genesis 1:26—"Let us make humankind in our image"—a reference to the Trinity. Augustine found God's image imprinted in the many trinities human beings contain. Our being, our living, and our understanding mark us as made in God's image, Augustine believed. The human mind itself reflects God's Trinitarian image in its memory, understanding, and will. God's image, knit into the fabric of our humanity, remains even when we fall away from God.[53] In the language of the Song of Songs, it is the part of us that remains awake, even when the rest of us is asleep.

Many modern theologians have moved from the sense of the *imago Dei* as the capacity for reason hidden within each individual toward a more relational understanding of the image of God, although this relational understanding remains grounded in the doctrine of the Trinity. It is our capacity to live in relationship with one another and with God that marks us as created in God's image, who also exists in relationship. It is in relationships marked by love—including sexual relationships—that the *imago Dei* is most clearly reflected.[54] From this perspective, the Song can be read as a celebration of the image of God in which we were all created.

2:3b–7

Sweet Fruit

It is impossible to miss the erotic meaning of these next few verses. In the poetry of the ancient Near East, Cheryl Exum reminds us, the

---

52. See Lars Thunberg, "The Human Person as Image of God: Eastern Christianity," and Bernard McGinn, "The Human Person as Image of God: Western Christianity," in *Christian Spirituality*, vol. 1: *Origins to the Twelfth Century*, ed. Bernard McGinn, John Meyendorff, and Jean Leclercq (New York: Crossroad, 1985), 291–312, 312–30, respectively.

53. McGinn, "Human Person," 317 and 320.

54. See R. S. Anderson, "Imago Dei," in *Dictionary of Pastoral Care and Counseling*, ed. Rodney J. Hunter (Nashville: Abingdon, 1990), 571–72.

fragrant apple tree often had erotic associations, and certainly that is
the case here.

> As an apple tree among the trees of the wood,
>   so is my beloved among young men.
> With great delight I sat in his shadow,
>   and his fruit was sweet to my taste.

It is images like these that led Phyllis Trible to find in the Song the
redemption of the story of Adam, Eve, and the tree of the knowledge
of good and evil in Genesis 2–3. No trees grow in the lovers' garden
that must not be touched or tasted; the only consequence of tasting
the fruit of the tree in this story is pleasure and delight. The lovers
in the Song inhabit a "world of harmony,"[55] Trible argues, in which
creation—the trees, the flowers, the animals, the human beings—
supports and encourages love. No serpent hisses temptations in this
garden; there is no forbidden fruit. It is safe for the lovers to play
here, admiring, touching, and tasting.

Allegorical interpretations of the sweet fruit the woman tastes
include the Targum's reading of the fruit as the Law given by God on
Mount Sinai. "I longed to dwell under the shadow of His Presence,"
the author of the Targum writes, "and the words of his Law were as
spice on my palate and the reward for my observances stored up in
the world to come."[56] Origen also heard a reference to God's word in
the fruit of the apple tree, fruit whose sweetness is released through
"continual meditation on the Law of God."[57] Other Christian interpreters saw Jesus himself in the apple tree and gave thanks for the
fruit of the Eucharist.

In eighteenth-century New England, an anonymous poet wrote a
hymn called "Jesus Christ the Apple Tree." You may have sung it, or
heard it sung, during Advent and Christmas in a beautiful musical
setting by the composer Elizabeth Poston. Drawing on the images
found in Song 2:3, it transposes the erotic longing expressed in the
Song into a different key.

55. Trible, *God and the Rhetoric of Sexuality*, 155.
56. Quoted in Pope, *Song of Songs*, 373.
57. Origen, *Commentary* III.5 (*Song of Songs*, 181).

I'm weary with my former toil,
Here I will sit and rest a while:
Under the shadow I will be,
Of Jesus Christ, the apple tree.

This fruit doth make my soul to thrive,
It keeps my dying faith alive;
Which makes my soul in haste to be
With Jesus Christ the apple tree.[58]

The words of the Song have made room for the expression of all kinds of longing: the longing for love, to be sure, but also the longing for rest and the renewal of life and hope. As this hymn shows, one of the very great gifts of the Song is its ability to stimulate new songs, new poetry, new ways of describing what it means to be human. Like the world it describes, the Song seems endlessly generative, endlessly fruitful, rewarding meditation upon its words and images with more words, more images.

For Origen, the image of the shadow of the apple tree is even more interesting than its fruit, because he finds in that shadow an echo of shadows throughout Scripture, from the valley of the shadow of death in Psalm 23 to the Holy Spirit that overshadows Mary at the conception of Jesus. In a typically supersessionist reading, Origen argues that, while the Law used to give ample shade from the heat, it is no longer able to shield us, and we must turn to Christ, whose shadow he finds referenced in Lamentations: "Under his shadow / we shall live among the nations" (Lam. 4:20).

For Teresa of Avila, the shadow of the beloved is a place of secrets. "Who could say," she writes, "what the Lord reveals from it!"[59] As it does for Origen, the shadow of the beloved reminds Teresa of the Holy Spirit overshadowing Mary. This is a shadow, Teresa writes, that engulfs and protects, inspires and refreshes, a shadow that both quiets the soul and fills it with "ardent desires." For Teresa, the fruit the woman tastes in this shadow is the sweetness of the presence of God.

58. http://www.hymnsandcarolsofchristmas.com/Hymns_and_Carols/jesus_christ_the_
apple_tree.htm.
59. Teresa of Avila, *Collected Works*, 248.

Teresa's words show how, rather than undercutting the erotic meaning of the Song, the meanings that accumulate in commentary after commentary serve to illustrate the erotic draw of the Law, or of Scripture, or of the Eucharist, or of Christ, and the erotic pull of the practice of interpretation itself. "O souls that practice prayer," Teresa writes, "taste all these words!"[60] Teresa's reading of the Song, like many others, is not a rejection or an avoidance of its erotic power, but a recognition of the erotic in all attentive, devoted life.

The same dynamic is at work in allegorical interpretations of the banqueting house where the man brings the woman for love. It is the upper room where Jesus met with his disciples the night before his death, some Christian interpreters wrote. It is the altar of God where together we eat and drink the Eucharist in God's presence. It is Scripture, where we feast on the fruit of the word. Rather than drawing a veil over the sexual pleasure the man and woman seek in their banqueting house, these interpretations lift the veil on how physically and spiritually compelling life with God is.

"He brought me to the banqueting house," the woman sings, "and his intention toward me was love." Until now we have heard more about the woman's intentions than the man's, but now it is clear that the man seeks the same thing as the woman: love, and more love.

In the next verse the woman calls out for food—raisins and apples—because she is "sick with love." But is that because she is exhausted from their lovemaking? Or is she sick with longing and waiting? Is it satiety or unfulfilled desire that causes her to call out for these fruits that have a history as aphrodisiacs? Interpreters have read this verse both ways.

The ambiguity intensifies in 2:5 with another little mystery: to whom is she speaking? To her lover? To the women of Jerusalem, who never seem far from the scene? The words "sustain" and "refresh" are in the second-person-masculine-plural imperative, a form that is used for the women of Jerusalem elsewhere in the poem. "Ultimately," Exum argues, "the woman's words are addressed to the audience *of the poem*, its readers."[61] Once again, we are invited into

60. Ibid.
61. Exum, *Song of Songs*, 116.

the lovers' intimate circle, to experience firsthand the longing that love can inspire.

What Exum calls "the slippage between anticipation and experience so characteristic of the Song" is very much in evidence in 2:6.[62] The NRSV translates this verse in the subjunctive, emphasizing anticipation and longing: "O that his left hand were under my head, / and that his right hand embraced me!" But Bergant, Exum, Pope, and Trible translate this verse in the present tense, emphasizing the fulfillment of that longing: "His left hand is under my head / and his right hand embraces me." Several scholars have noted the resemblance of this description to pictorial depictions of lovemaking on Mesopotamian artifacts celebrating fertility deities; it was a familiar image in the ancient world. "Your right hand you have placed on my vulva," a Sumerian poem puts it, "your left hand stroked my head."[63] As Ariel and Chana Bloch point out, however, while it is possible to see the traces of fertility hymns in the Song, the Song itself is not concerned with fertility and reproduction.[64] It is concerned with love and love's pleasures.

Is 2:5 a description of the lovemaking that takes place in the banqueting house? Or is it the expression of a wish, a description of lovemaking for which the woman longs? The Song blurs the lines between anticipation and fulfillment on purpose, Exum argues. The words the woman speaks are intimate words, but they are also public words. She speaks them to the women of Jerusalem, the audience within the poem, and by extension to us, the readers.[65] The ambiguity of these verses both draws us into the intimate embrace of the lovers and shields it from our eyes. In this way we, as readers, are kept in a state of longing, and as the countless commentaries on the Song demonstrate, the Song becomes a place where our own longings can be expressed.

The woman concludes the dialogue by offering some practical wisdom about love to the women of Jerusalem and to us, who listen along with them.

62. Ibid., 117.
63. Quoted in Pope, *Song of Songs,* 384.
64. Ariel Bloch and Chana Bloch, *The Song of Songs: The World's First Great Love Poem* (New York: Modern Library, 2006), 34.
65. Exum, *Song of Songs,* 116.

> I adjure you, O daughters of Jerusalem,
>> by the gazelles or the wild does:
> do not stir up or awaken love
>> until it is ready! ·

She offers her wisdom with a combination of seriousness and playfulness, binding the daughters of Jerusalem by an oath made not in the name of God but by the animals who cavort across the landscape of the Song. These animals leap and play throughout the poem. She compares her beloved to a gazelle bounding toward her; he compares her breasts to two gazelle fawns. The gazelles and wild does suggest strength and agility, wildness and energy, movement and speed. The woman urges the women of Jerusalem, in the name of these beautiful, wild creatures, not to stir up love until it is ready. Love must be ready to meet the longing of the beloved with the same energy with which it comes bounding toward us. Meeting and returning that love will take all our strength and quickness. Don't rush it before you are ready, she seems to say. Let love awaken at the speed it will.

> Love must be ready to meet the longing of the beloved with the same energy with which it comes bounding toward us. Meeting and returning that love will take all our strength and quickness. Don't rush it before you are ready, she seems to say. Let love awaken at the speed it will.

Once it is aroused, we must rouse as well. Once it is awake, we must awaken, in the deepest possible sense. For love asks everything of us.

2:8–14

Arise, My Love

The Song is marked by the lovers' movements inward, into interior spaces, and outward, toward each other and the world. "The king has brought me into his chambers," the woman sings in 1:4, and in 2:4: "He has brought me to the banqueting house." Mystical interpreters have found themselves attracted to these passages. They seem to mirror the movement inside into secret interior places where one might meet God.

The Song's lovers have a gift for transforming exterior spaces into private, interior spaces. They find quiet places in the great, humming world where they can be alone together, as in 1:17: "the beams of our house are cedar, / our rafters are pine."

Unlike many other texts of devotion, however, the Song is as concerned with the lovers' movement outside as it is with their movement inside. To meet love, the Song seems to say, we must step outside: into the vineyards and fields, or the greening spring, or the night.

In 2:10–14 the man stands outside the wall that encloses his beloved and urges her to come outside. She will not be able to know the world as it is—blooming and blossoming—if she remains inside the walls of her house. To step outside is to join the earth as it turns and changes and comes to life again. To step outside is to declare one's allegiance to the life of the world and to find one's own life within it.

The lover who stands outside the wall, "gazing in at the windows, / looking through the lattice," has been a compelling figure for many readers of the Song. The *Midrash Rabbah* sees in the presence of the lover the presence of God, standing behind the Western Wall in Jerusalem.[66] Like the lover, God peers through the gaps in the wall, keeping a watchful eye on the ones God loves. The conviction of many that God's presence is palpable at the Western Wall is undergirded by the *Midrash Rabbah*'s reading of Song 2:9.

Bernard of Clairvaux also imagines God as one watching from outside the wall, a "hidden watcher of hidden things."[67] For Bernard, the wall is the human body, taken on by God in the incarnation, and the lattices and windows are "the bodily senses and human feelings by which he began to experience all our human needs." Christ's body opened a window for God onto human life, its pleasures and

---

66. Pope, *Song of Songs*, 393.
67. Bernard of Clairvaux, "Sermon 55," II.4, in *On the Song of Songs III*, trans. Kilian Walsh, O.C.S.O., and Irene M. Edmonds (Kalamazoo, MI: Cistercian Publications, 1979), 86.

its pains. By peering through this wall, Bernard wrote, God "learned mercy, although the mercy of the Lord is from eternity."[68] By living an embodied human life, God drew near to us and made our concerns God's own.

As the woman draws us into her story, her concerns, she urges us to listen: "The voice of my beloved!" she cries. But before we listen, we must look. Look, she says, he is bounding over the mountains and hills; look, he is standing behind our wall, looking in our windows. We watch as the beloved, with the speed and agility of a hero, moves across the landscape until he is speaking right into the ear of his lover: "Arise, my love, my fair one, and come away." If the woman used ambiguity to shield our eyes from the lovers' embrace in 2:4–6, she invites us back into their intimacy with her call to us to "Look! Look!"

The man echoes the woman's "Look!" as he urges her to look at all the signs of the changing of the seasons. (The NRSV translates the line as "now the winter is past," but Exum translates it, "look, the winter is past," and Bergant, "see, the winter is past.") He sings to her a hymn to the turning of the seasons, the awakening of the earth in early spring, and the fragrant blossoming of the trees and vines. This is the time of growth, of blossoming, of singing. Listen to the turtledove, he urges her; smell the fragrance of the blossoming vines; taste the figs. The winter is over, the rains are past; the migratory birds have returned to the land. Now is the time to come outside. Now is the time for love to bloom.

The man invites the woman to gaze at the world through a wide lens in the first part of his song, but in the second part he zooms in once more upon a specific part of the landscape—the clefts of the rock, the covert of the cliff. Once again, he looks for her in the most hidden of places, like the bramble patch where he found her, his lily, in 2:2. Here she is like a dove, hidden in the crevices of rocks and cliffs. Although he has bounded across mountains and hills with incredible energy and speed, he knows how to slow down, how to speak softly and lovingly, how to coax his beloved from her hidden places. "Let me see your face," he sings, "let me hear your voice; / for

---

68. Idem, "Sermon 56," I.1 (*Song of Songs III*, 88).

your voice is sweet, / and your face is lovely" (2:14). This is a lover who is both strong and gentle, eager and patient. Although he has raced to her side, once he is there he is able to wait until she is ready, as we will see in further chapters of the Song.

2:15

Catch Us the Little Foxes

The passage about the foxes is another of the Song's little mysteries. Some interpreters read it as part of the man's speech, and perhaps it is. Perhaps this is one of the ways he coaxes his beloved outside. Come, let's catch the foxes that are ruining our vineyards! I need your help! We can imagine the laughter and joy in the scene of the two lovers, chasing after those quick, red animals.

Exum hears the woman's voice in these lines, rather than the man's. The man has asked to hear her voice, Exum explains, and this is her answer. In Exum's reading, the woman herself has salted these ordinary words with a hidden meaning. "Young men can roam about freely in search of romance," Exum hears the woman saying to her lover, "like foxes romping through the vineyards. . . . The important thing for us is not to enjoy the random fox but to catch a fox for our very own."[69] I want to capture you, Exum believes the woman is saying. I want you for my own.

The Blochs add yet a third interpretation. They hear the voice of the woman's brothers intruding here, the guardians of the woman's "vineyard," her burgeoning sexuality. Like other interpreters, they speculate that 2:15 is a folk song that made its way into the Song. It recalls for them the scene in Judges 21:20–22 in which the men of the tribe of Benjamin come upon a group of girls dancing in a vineyard and abduct them. Later the men negotiate with the brothers and fathers of the girls to keep them as their wives.

Although the scene of the girls dancing in the vineyard fits in with the spirit of the Song, the abductions emphatically do not. The story from Judges is the familiar story of men—strangers, fathers,

---

69. Exum, *Song of Songs,* 130.

brothers—working out the sexual destiny of women, in which the women have no say. The Song, in strong contrast, reflects mutual attraction, mutual assertiveness. There are no abductions going on here. The man and the woman move toward each other with energy and desire; each acts on his or her own longings. The "catching" going on in 2:15 could be done by either the woman or the man. This is a chase full of joy and laughter, not threat and fear. As Bergant rightly insists, "There is no gender domination in this relationship."[70]

2:16–17
My Beloved Is Mine and I Am His

The mutuality that defines the lovers' relationship is summed up simply and beautifully in 2:16: "My beloved is mine and I am his."

Like the lovers' exchange in 1:15–16—"Ah, you are beautiful, my love; / ah, you are beautiful"— this verse captures, in a few words, the entire perspective of the Song and offers us a prayer to make our own. My beloved is mine and I am his. The confidence that her love is returned with the same strength with which she offers it shapes the woman's life toward boldness, generosity, and devotion. It makes her fearless. "He pastures his flock among the lilies," she continues: there is no fear of sexual intimacy here. She trusts her beloved to seek her pleasure as she seeks his. Knowing that he is hers and she is his gives her the confidence to meet his desire with her own. As we will see in 3:1–5, it makes her fearless in other ways as well, even to the point of searching through the city streets alone at night for her beloved.

> The mutuality that defines the lovers' relationship is summed up simply and beautifully in 2:16: "My beloved is mine and I am his."

There is considerable debate over the meaning of 2:17. When she calls out, "Until the day breathes / and the shadows flee, / turn, my beloved," does she mean: stay with me until the night is over? Or: come to me in the morning? Is she calling him to her? Or is she

---

70. Bergant, *Song of Songs*, 49.

sending him away? Is she doing both at once, calling him to love-making that will be both postponed and enjoyed, as Exum argues?[71]

Bernard of Clairvaux read "turn, my beloved" as "*re*turn, my beloved," a phrase that confounded him as much as contemporary scholars are confounded by "turn." For Bernard, of course, God is the beloved, and the word "return" puzzles him for this reason: how can God possibly return?

> Where can he come from? Where can he return to, he who fills heaven and earth? How can he who is spirit move from place to place? How can any movement of any kind be attributed to him who is God? For he is immutable.[72]

Bernard concludes that the movement of return does not reflect any movement on God's part but rather fluctuations of the soul. In order to explain this to the monks in his care, Bernard tells a story about himself and his own experience of God, a rarity in his writings. It is a risk to lay bear one's own experience, and Bernard clearly feels this. "I make this disclosure only to help you," he tells his listeners, "and if you derive any profit from it I shall be consoled for my foolishness; if not, my foolishness will be revealed."[73] But there is something about the Song that invites such risks, as centuries of its readers have long known.

Bernard describes the "fluctuations" of his own soul, a movement in and out of awareness of God's presence. It does indeed feel like God is "coming" and "going away," but it is impossible to be "conscious of the moment of his coming" or to locate where God is, even when he feels God's presence.

> If I looked outside myself, I saw him stretching beyond the furthest I could see; and if I looked within, he was yet further within.[74]

Even when God seems near, God remains out of Bernard's reach, further out and further in than Bernard is able to stretch.

71. Exum, *Song of Songs*, 133.
72. Bernard of Clairvaux, "Sermon 74," I.1 (*Song of Songs IV*, 86).
73. Ibid., II.5 (*Song of Songs*, 89).
74. Ibid. (*Song of Songs*, 90).

In this brief autobiographical account of his own experience of God, Bernard articulates one of the most important themes of the Song: that no matter how intimate we are with another, we can never fully know our beloved. There will always be something about the one we love that is just out of our reach. On some level we remain mysteries to one another. For the lovers in the Song, that mystery keeps them seeking after each other, trusting that what we cannot know is as worthy of reverence as what we can.

3:1–5

Seeking the One My Soul Loves

The Song of Songs is a poem about the pleasures of love, the beauty of the lovers, and the gorgeousness of the world that makes a home for them. But because it is a poem about love, it is also a poem about the risks of loving: absence, missed meetings, unresolved yearning, and seeking without finding.

The opening lines of the third chapter tell one of two stories about the sharp pain of absence that appears in the Song. These stories pick up and intensify the scene in 1:7 where the woman searches the hillsides for her beloved. But while that moment opens onto a loving, teasing dialogue, 3:1–5 and 5:2–8 cast the image of the woman searching for her beloved into a far more minor key.

The story in 3:1–5 is a continuation of the woman's speech begun in 2:8. She first tells a story about her beloved seeking her. He knows where to find her—she is at home—but a wall stands between them, and he cannot reach her. In this story, the man stands outside the woman's home and calls through the lattice for her to come outside. "Let me see your face," he calls, "let me hear your voice" (2:14). His longing is palpable.

The third chapter of the Song opens with another story of seeking and longing. While the man sought the woman in the daytime, urging her to come outside into the bright spring day, the woman seeks the man at night, in her bed. When she does not find him, she calls out to him, calling him inside, as he, in 2:10–14, had called her outside. He does not answer, and her words evaporate into the night.

When she receives no reply, the woman does what the man urged her to do as he called to her from outside the walls of her house: she rises and goes outside. But it is not the humming green springtime she enters as she leaves her bed and her room and her house. She steps out, instead, into dark city streets, patrolled by sentinels on their rounds.

"I did not find my beloved," she sings, "but the sentinels found me." A sense of menace hangs over this brief description of a lone woman encountering a group of men on the dark streets of the city, a reminder of the harms to which we are all vulnerable, even when we are on errands of love. But that menace is soon overcome by relief: "Scarcely had I passed them, / when I found him whom my soul loves." Having found him, she holds on to to him and will not let him go,

> until I brought him into my mother's house,
> and into the chamber of her that conceived me.
>
> (3:4)

And so this story about the pain of absence, the ache of longing, and the joy of reunion ends where it began: inside a bedroom, which is inside a house, which is inside the city walls. But this time the lovers are together.

The pattern of repetition in 3:1–4 reflects what Exum calls "the poetic preoccupation with conjuring—the drive to overcome absence with presence through language."[75] In the short space of four verses, the woman refers to "the one whom my soul loves" four times. This concentrated attempt to conjure the presence of the lover through language creates such a feeling of constriction that we almost sigh with relief when she finds him, and her language correspondingly relaxes. The effect, as Francis Landy puts it, is of the transition "from restlessness to rest, from solitude to companionship."[76]

"My mother's house" possesses associations with love and lovemaking. Twice in the poem the woman describes bringing her lover

75. Exum, *Song of Songs*, 134.
76. Quoted in ibid., 135.

into her mother's house and then further in, into her mother's bed-room. Trible draws on the many references—seven in all—to the mother and the lack of any mention of the father in the Song to point to the Song's subversive undermining of the patriarchy that so dominates the Bible. For Trible, the Song redeems the story of Adam and Eve in the garden of Eden. The mother is associated with erotic knowledge and conception ("her that conceived me" [3:4]; "the one who bore me" [8:2]), not with the pain of childbirth that is part of God's curse in Genesis 3:16. The woman sees her mother's chamber as a place for lovemaking; she herself was likely conceived there. This becomes even clearer in Song 8:2 when she imagines bringing her beloved into her mother's bedroom. In "the chamber of the one who bore me," the woman sings, "I would give you spiced wine to drink, the juice of my pomegranates."

Here in 3:4, however, the door of the mother's room closes on us, the readers, leaving us outside. Invited into the ache of the woman's longing and with her on her restless search around the city, we are not invited to follow the lovers into the mother's bedroom. But the woman knows we are nearby. At the end of the story, she addresses the women of Jerusalem, and us, with familiar words.

> I adjure you, O daughters of Jerusalem,
>   by the gazelles or the wild does:
> do not stir up or awaken love
>   until it is ready!   (3:5)

Once again, even as she embraces her lover with joy, the woman pauses to acknowledge the demands of love: the wakefulness it requires, the fearlessness, the stamina. We will see another form of this stanza once more in the Song, after the story in 5:2–7 that is parallel to this one.

The boldness of the woman's search is illuminated when we compare it to the description in Proverbs of the married woman whose "feet do not stay at home" but who seeks her lover "now in the street, now in the squares." When she finds him, she "seizes him and kisses him" (Prov. 7:12–13) and tells him she has made her bed fragrant "with myrrh, aloes, and cinnamon" (7:17). Proverbs warns against association with such a woman (7:10). The one who follows her to her perfumed bed, Proverbs cautions, is "like an ox to the slaughter" (7:22).

Although the woman in the Song is not a married woman looking for a lover outside her marriage, she does share some similarities with the woman in Proverbs. She is willing to leave her home in search of her lover and willing to roam the streets alone looking for him. She seizes him when she finds him and will not let him go. But while Proverbs tells this story with the woman in the role of the villain, the Song places the woman in the role of the brave heroine. Indeed, the woman in the Song gets to tell her own story, unlike the woman in Proverbs, who is described, somewhat leeringly, by the male speaker offering instruction to a younger man. The Song offers an alternative image of a woman searching the city for her lover and insists on a more complex and spacious view of female desire than Proverbs offers.

The story of the woman's quest for the absent beloved alone at night did not evoke condemnation or even discomfort among readers who cherished the Song as a text of devotion. Indeed, the story touched a tender place in the religious imagination of the Song's readers, a place of longing to overcome distance and separation. The Targum found in this story a retelling of the quest of Israel for the presence of God, withdrawn from them in God's anger over the golden calf (Exod. 33:3).

> Said the Israelites one to the other: "Let us rise and go and surround the Appointment-Tent which Moses spread outside the camp, and let us request instruction from YHWH and the Holy Presence which has been removed from us." Then they went around in the towns, in the streets and squares, but could not find (the Holy Presence).[77]

Other Jewish interpreters saw in this story a reflection of the longing of the people of Israel for Moses during the time he spent on Mount Sinai, receiving the commandments from God.

Christian interpreters most often viewed the object of the

---

77. Pope, *Song of Songs*, 417.

woman's quest as Christ. For some, the city represented the church through which we seek Christ, and the streets represented the Scriptures through which we run, searching for some sign of him. For others, the streets and squares represented mystery cults and various schools of philosophy that keep us chasing around in circles, while yet others saw the streets and squares as the marketplace, which contains only those things—fraud, deceit—that keep us separated from Christ.[78]

For Bernard of Clairvaux the watchmen, rather than a menacing presence in the woman's story, represent those who, like monks, watch and pray through the night. Their role is to teach, not to frighten. They appear in the story, according to Bernard, as the preachers who will prepare the woman to meet her lover, the Lord: "to teach her the faith and counsel her in the ways of holiness and true religion."[79] In the Song itself, though, the watchmen are not able to tell the woman where to find her lover. She finds him on her own.

This story of absence, longing, searching, and finding is so powerful that it has generated not only extensive commentary but also new poetry that both comments on the Song and extends the narrative of the woman's search into new territory.

John of the Cross, a Carmelite mystic, theologian, and poet of sixteenth-century Spain, wrote poetry that is suffused with the imagery of the Song. His "Spiritual Canticle" is a dialogue between a bride and a bridegroom. His "On a Dark Night" is a poem about leaving home in the middle of the night to search for the beloved. John's poetry is populated by the stags, shepherds, lilies, doves, hills, valleys, foxes, and vineyards that we know from the Song. The spiced wine, the bed of flowers, and the wine cellar all appear in John's lines, lending their erotic power to his poetry.

The poem inspired by Song 3:1–4, "On a Dark Night," is probably John's most famous poem, the foundation upon which his great works of mystical theology, *Ascent of Mount Carmel* and *Dark Night of the Soul*, are built. His poem provides a kind of commentary on the Song, and *Ascent* and *Dark Night* provide a commentary on the lines and stanzas of John's own poem.

---

78. Ibid., 418.
79. Bernard of Clairvaux, "Sermon 76," III.7 (*Song of Songs IV*, 115).

> On a dark night,
> Kindled in love with yearnings—
> oh, happy chance!—
> I went forth without being observed,
> My house being now at rest.[80]

From the first stanza, we see that we are in a world very similar to Song 3:1–4. Propelled from the safety of his house by desire, a lover goes out into the night. John plays the role of the woman; here, as in so many commentaries on the Song, gender is fluid and changeable.

For John, this movement outward into the night was the movement of the soul away from the things that prevent it from being united with God, a movement away from "all [of the soul's] sensual desires, with respect to all outward things of the world and to those which were delectable to its flesh, and likewise with respect to the desires of its will,"[81] a movement into a dark night where these desires would be purged and purified. How did John of the Cross find, in the Song, inspiration for a poem and a treatise that speak of the purgation of sensual desire and the pleasures of the flesh when the Song so clearly celebrates these desires and pleasures?

Like so many commentators, when John read the Song he found in its lines something true about life with God: that it is a passionate life, moving between yearning and fulfillment, absence and presence. If he missed the celebration of "sensual desire and the pleasures of the flesh" or, perhaps better, passed over them or under them to get to what he believed to be the deeper truth of the Song, it is not because he rejected erotic life. The invitation to step away from passions that did not satisfy him toward the great passion of his life— God—drew him as intently as the woman is drawn to seek her lover and led him to take the same kinds of risks.[82] He placed the erotic

---

80. John of the Cross, *Ascent of Mount Carmel,* trans. E. Allison Peers (New York: Image Books, 1958), 93.

81. Ibid., 104.

82. John's insistence on the need for reform in his own Carmelite order, a conviction he shared with Teresa of Avila, led to his being imprisoned and tortured by his fellow Carmelites in Toledo. For more about the life and work of John of the Cross, see Peter Tyler, *St. John of the Cross* (London: Continuum, 2010).

dimension of the Song in another context, another relationship than that between the lovers of the Song: the relationship between God and human beings, which is also marked by pleasure and wracked by painful yearnings.

3:6

What Is That Coming Up from the Wilderness?

The second half of the third chapter of the Song has generated a fair amount of scholarly debate. What is this wedding poem doing in the middle of the Song? Why don't we find it at the end, as the culmination of the couple's loving exchange? And why the reference to King Solomon? Is this another way to praise the male lover, or are we to take the reference literally? Might this be a poem used in one of Solomon's weddings? Furthermore, the second half of the third chapter contains Hebrew words that occur nowhere else in the Bible, making certain passages difficult to translate. For example, in 3:10 the NRSV states that the interior of the palanquin "was inlaid with love." Bergant's translation is "inlaid with ivory," Exum's "inlaid with precious stones," and the Blochs offer "the daughters of Jerusalem / paved it with love." All these translations are possible, and no translator can be wholly confident in her or his interpretive choices.

The Song is punctuated by questions about the lovers. The woman's question asked about the man tends to be: *Where are you?* The man's question about the woman is more often: *Who are you?* Sometimes these questions are asked by the lovers themselves. Sometimes it is the women of Jerusalem who give voice to the man's or woman's questions.

I take 3:6 to be the first of three questions asked about the identity of the woman, although students of the Song debate this verse a great deal. Although the interrogative pronoun *mi* is most often translated as "who" the NRSV translates it as "what" in order to support a reading of 3:6 that asks,

> What is that coming up from the wilderness
> like a column of smoke,

perfumed with myrrh and frankincense,
        with all the fragrant powders of the merchant?

This interpretation of 3:6 suggests that 3:7–11 provides an answer to this question. According to Exum, scholars are "virtually unanimous" in understanding "Solomon's litter" to be the answer to the question posed in 3:6.

There are exceptions to this reading, however. The Blochs translate *mi* as "who" and understand the answer to refer to the woman. For the Blochs 3:6 is completely separate from 3:7–11. They read 3:6 as a hyperbolic description of the woman as a kind of "supernatural phenenomen, a fantastic apparition that 'rises' from the east."[83] They understand the wedding poem proper to begin with 3:7. Pope also translates *mi* as "who" (his translation is, "Who is this ascending from the steppe . . . ?").[84] Unlike the Blochs, though, Pope does find the answer to 3:6 in 3:7 because he imagines the woman to be inside Solomon's litter, moving across the landscape toward her lover. Bergant, who translates the *mi* as "what," joins Pope in understanding the answer to the question as the woman.[85]

I find these exceptions to the "virtual unanimity" Exum reports compelling because 3:6 shares a grammatical form with two other questions about the identity of the woman that punctuate the Song. In 6:10 a voice, perhaps that of the male lover or the women of Jerusalem, asks,

Who is this that looks forth like the dawn,
        fair as the moon, bright as the sun,
        terrible as an army with banners?

And in 8:5a, a voice asks,

Who is that coming up from the wilderness,
        leaning upon her beloved?

---

83. Bloch and Bloch, *The Song of Songs*, 159.
84. Pope, *Song of Songs*, 412, 431.
85. Bergant, *Song of Songs*, 60.

That these three questions refer to one of the lovers in the poem seems to me a crucial point in understanding the Song and its vision of love. In a poem about a deeply mutual love—each lover knowing what will please the other, each reveling in the other's beauty—these questions remind us that no matter how close we are to another, we remain unknown, at some level, to each other. The lovers in the Song are beautiful: radiant, fragrant, queenly, kingly. But they are also more than all the attributes each celebrates in the other. And that *more* is difficult to capture in words. It can only be glimpsed across the distance that separates any two people from each other. Here that *more* that is beyond what we can know appears as "a column of smoke, / perfumed with myrrh and frankin-

> The lovers in the Song of Songs are beautiful: radiant, fragrant, queenly, kingly. But they are also more than all of the attributes each celebrates in the other. And that more is difficult to capture in words. It can only be glimpsed across the distance that separates any two people from each other.

cense, / with all the fragrant powders of the merchant." A column of smoke that cannot be wholly captured, an elusive presence that slips even through arms opened wide to receive it, escaping even the lush and lovely words that attempt to fasten it to the page.

Have you ever woken up next to someone you have known and loved for years and years and, as you watch them still sleeping, felt the question—*who are you?*—rise up inside you? Have you ever caught a glimpse from a distance of a child you have raised and won-dered: *who are you?* Sometimes this question floats up when we are disappointed, when our beloved has broken a promise or betrayed our trust, and we suddenly feel that the person we loved is not the person we thought them to be. But sometimes the question *who are you?* arises out of the ordinariness of daily life. Virginia Woolf once described as "moments of being" those rare occasions when we can see things clearly, as they are.[86] It is in such "moments of being" that we can see that the one we love—the lover, the child, the sibling,

---

86. Virginia Woolf, *Moments of Being*, ed. Jeanne Schulkind, 2nd ed. (San Diego: Harcourt Brace Jovanovich, 1985), especially 64–79.

the parent, the friend—is more than we can ever truly know. This is good news. It means that we might also be more than we know ourselves to be.

The column of smoke, rising up from the wilderness, not only suggests the elusive dimension of the other, it also carries resonances of the pillar of cloud that led the people of Israel through the wilderness, a sign of the presence of God with them. As Rabbi Ezra ben Solomon of Gerona put it in his commentary on 3:6: "When journeying before the Israelite camp, the *shekhinah* seemed like a column of smoke rising upwards and ascending. The verse states 'smoke' for she is derived from fire, as it is written: 'Now Mount Sinai was all in smoke, for the Lord had come down upon it in fire, the smoke rose like the smoke of a kiln' [Exod. 19:18]."[87]

So often in allegorical interpretations of the Song, the male lover represents God, the one who sees and loves and cherishes the woman, who represents the soul or Israel or the church. In this kabbalistic interpretation of 3:6, however, it is the woman who represents God, in the form of the *shekinah*. In this reading it is the fragrant presence of God that is coming up from the wilderness, a presence as elusive as smoke that yet permeates the life of the world.

3:7–11

The Litter of Solomon

Just as the Song urges us to turn our gaze toward the beloved standing outside the wall of the woman's house in 2:9 ("Look, there he stands . . ."), it focuses our imagination on the procession as it approaches: "Look, it is the litter of Solomon!" (3:7). Song 3:7–11 is framed by the invitation to look deeply, offered first to us and then to the daughters of Jerusalem, who once more make a place for us in the poem.

What do we see when we look? First, we see sixty armed men, "the mighty men of Israel," whose swords protect against "alarms by night." Like the sentinels who appear in 3:3, these soldiers—"equipped

---

87. Rabbi Ezra ben Solomon of Gerona,*Commentary on the Song of Songs*, 66.

with swords / and expert in war"—strike a harsh and jarring note in this song of love. They are a reminder of the dangers that do lurk in the night, a reminder of the terrors that the other book commented on in this volume, Lamentations, documents and mourns. They are a reminder that the peace that the lovers enjoy, both when they are outside and when they are inside, is a fragile peace. Just as the lovers are made vulnerable to each other by their hope that the other will return their love, so they also remain vulnerable to the harm that can befall human beings in this world.

What else do we see? A palanquin (again, the translation of this word is unsure) made of silver, gold, and purple, inlaid, as the NRSV puts it, "with love." The image here is of a beautiful bed being carried across the wilderness, a bed in which the woman awaits her lover, her king.

As the palanquin draws near, we are called outside to bear witness to the king's splendor.

> Daughters of Jerusalem, come out.
> Look, O daughters of Zion,
>   at King Solomon,
> at the crown with which his mother crowned him
>   on the day of his wedding,
>   on the day of the gladness of his heart.
> (3:10–11)

Like the woman in 2:8–14, we are being called outside to draw near to beauty and to joy. Solomon is beautiful and so is his crown; he stands before us, glad of heart. And a human being with a glad heart is indeed worth close study. This is part of the spiritual practice into which the Song invites us: to gaze upon human beings who are glad of each other and glad to be awake and alive in the world. Like the "Ah, you are beautiful" of 1:15, training our gaze upon the glad-of-heart king is another way of making the Song's posture of devotion toward the world and others our own. By constantly drawing us outside, the Song invites us to study the world as it blooms and flowers and folds itself protectively around the lovers. It also invites us to study the lovers themselves: their energy, their commitment to mutuality, their fearlessness, their devotion. By calling us to gaze with them at the world and each other, the Song teaches us to admire and delight in lives lived at full strength. As Irenaeus famously put it: "This is the glory of God: the human being fully alive."[88]

Once again, a mother makes an appearance in the poem: Solomon's mother, who crowned him on his wedding day. And, once again, fathers are strikingly absent. It is the mothers of the Song who celebrate the deepening intimacy between the lovers. There is no sense in the poem that the union of the two is desirable for any other reason than that they desire each other. There is no mention of any sort of political or social alliance enacted by these lovers. Like the woman's mother, into whose room she brings her lover in 3:4, Solomon's mother seems to bless their sexual union by rejoicing in the joy they take in each other.

Why does this poem appear in the Song? Perhaps to intensify the account of the relationship of the lovers, who meet and separate, lose and seek and find each other throughout the poem. In this account of a bride and groom being escorted into each other's presence, it is impossible for the lovers to miss each other. Although their coming together is assured in this little poem, their knowing one another fully and completely is not. "Who is this coming up from the wilderness?" remains a very real question.

The poem might also be here to increase our pleasure as readers. This little scene adds more beauty, more splendor, more gorgeousness to a poem in which beauty is already spilling over. As Solomon's litter moves slowly and majestically across the second half of chapter 3, we can rest our eyes on the horizon and watch the procession come into view: fragrant, richly ornamented, defended by the mighty men of Israel. It is quite a sight, but no more splendid than Solomon himself. The poem is crowned by the king and his joy. Glad of heart, he is a picture of a person fully alive, fully present to the moment, fully comfortable in his own skin—a man completely ready to meet his beloved.

---

88. Quoted in Mary T. Clark, R.S.C.J., "Irenaeus," in *Augustine through the Ages: An Encyclopedia*, ed. Allan D. Fitzgerald (Grand Rapids: Eerdmans, 1999), 456.

4:1–7

Altogether Beautiful

In a beautiful bit of allegorical reading of the first chapter of Genesis, Augustine sees in the firmament that separates earth from heaven an image of Scripture, "stretched over us like a skin."[89] The stars in the firmament are us, the readers of Scripture, clinging to it with both our hands, trying to see through its veil. The angels, who live above the firmament, have no more need of books; they read the very face of God. But for those of us who live below, the firmament of Scripture both draws us near to God while at the same time obscuring God's face, which the angels read so clearly.

As we have seen, language itself serves as a kind of veil in the Song, a skin stretched out between us and the lovers. The images used by the lovers to describe each other both draw us in close and keep us at a distance.

The man's long speech in chapter 4 offers a good example of this. He looks closely at his beloved, and we gaze along with him. He speaks directly to the woman, praising her body part by part: your eyes are doves, your cheeks are pomegranates, your neck is a tower, your breasts are two fawns. The images the man uses to describe her body are evocative, and we understand that he chants them in admiration. But what do we see, really? The man's speech does not leave the woman standing before us, exposed. Rather, she is clothed in images drawn from the world in which their love unfolds, shielded from any intrusive, voyeuristic gaze. The man's use of metaphorical figures, Exum argues, "preserves the mystery, the otherness," of the woman being described.[90] His gorgeous

> Language itself serves as a kind of veil in the Song, a skin stretched out between us and the lovers. The images used by the lovers to describe each other both draw us in close and keep us at a distance.

---

89. *The Confessions of St. Augustine* 13.15, 326.
90. Exum, *Song of Songs,* 23. Exum makes a distinction between a voyeuristic gaze, which "intrudes upon that which is seen," and an erotic gaze, which "participates in that which is seen" (p. 22).

descriptions both reveal and conceal, honoring not only what can be seen but also what cannot.

For the first and nearly the only time in the poem, an actual veil appears in the man's description of the woman. "Your eyes are doves behind your veil," he sings in 4:1; "your cheeks are like halves of a pomegranate behind your veil" in 4:3. There is some controversy over the translation of the word *tsammah* that the NRSV renders "veil." The Blochs, for example, translate the word as "hair": "The curve of your cheek / a pomegranate / in the thicket of your hair."[91] Whether "veil" or "hair" is the best translation, there is a sense here of something hidden. As Exum puts it, "the poet makes use of the veil not to conceal but rather to draw attention to the mystery that lies behind the veil, to what is not quite or not yet seen."[92]

In her reading of the Song, Exum finds that the man and the woman have distinctive ways of expressing their love for each other. The woman tells stories in which she and her lover appear as characters, seeking each other, calling out to one another, losing each other, finding each other. The man expresses his love differently. As he does in this passage, the man looks at the woman and describes both what he sees and how it makes him feel. As we know from his description of her as a mare among the chariots of Pharaoh in 1:9, he is overwhelmed by her. In her presence, he feels out of control. Although he can see and touch and speak to her, the woman still feels out of reach somehow, as if she lived among lions and leopards in the mountains (4:8). He is "held captive" (7:8) in her beautiful hair. He begs her to turn her eyes away, "for they overwhelm me!" (6:5).

According to Exum, the woman tells stories in order to make her beloved present. It is his absence that troubles her; she is sick with love and longing. It is not the absence of his beloved that troubles the man, however; it is her presence. His lover so overwhelms him that he must organize her into parts in order to cope with the power of her presence. If he can take her in bit by bit, perhaps he will not be utterly undone by her.

---

91. Bloch and Bloch, *The Song of Songs*, 73.
92. Exum, *Song of Songs*, 162.

The use of language both to render the absent beloved present as well as to keep the all-too-present beloved at a manageable distance is one of the characteristics of the Song that makes it so like a prayer. In the early fourteenth century, a mystical writer named Marguerite Porete described God in a way that would be at home in the Song as a description of how the lovers experience each other. She described God as *Loingprés,* "Farnearness."[93] In the Song, the lovers experience each other as both terribly absent and terribly present, and they use language to develop ways of moving between the far and the near, the unseen and the seen. Isn't this what we do in our life with God? Don't we tell stories that make God seem more present? Or invoke and gaze upon God's attributes one by one—love, mercy, grace—in order to make the overwhelming mystery of God more approachable?

In between two heartfelt professions of her beauty in 4:1 and 4:7, the man approaches his overwhelmingly beautiful beloved bit by bit. One by one, he lifts a part of her body to the light of his imagination and clothes it in images from the world all around them. Gazing along with the man, readers have wondered what hair that is like "a flock of goats, moving down the slopes of Gilead," might look like, or teeth that "are like a flock of shorn ewes that have come up from the washing, / all of which bear twins, and not one of them is bereaved." Perhaps her teeth all match, and none of them is missing. Perhaps her hair cascades past her shoulders, down to her waist. A neck like the tower of David might be adorned with golden jewelry; breasts like fawns feeding among the lilies might describe her breasts between his lips (which she describes as lilies in 5:13) or they might describe her breasts in relation to the rest of her body (which the Song often uses the image of "lilies" to describe). Like the veil obscuring some of the woman's features, the man's language obscures exactly what he means, but we are invited to involve ourselves in his erotic gaze, a gaze that does not trespass but adores.

Augustine was particularly fond of these verses, especially the description of the woman's teeth as sheep. For him, the image of

---

93. Marguerite Porete, *The Mirror of Simple Souls,* chap. 61, trans. Ellen L. Babinsky (New York: Paulist Press, 1993), 138.

teeth as sheep that are shorn is an example of how much pleasure he receives from reading and interpreting passages of Scripture that seem at first obscure and ambiguous.

> I contemplate the saints more pleasantly when I envisage them as the teeth of the Church cutting off men from their errors and transferring them to her body after their hardness has been softened as if being bitten and chewed. I recognize them most pleasantly as shorn sheep having put aside the burdens of the world like so much fleece and as ascending from the washing, which is baptism, all to create twins, which are the two precepts of love, and I see no one of them sterile of this holy fruit.[94]

This is the kind of creativity the Song inspired in Augustine. One idea arises organically from the one before, spinning a new story from the Song's shining threads.

The man's description of his beloved's body ends with lines that echo the woman's words to him in 2:17. She had sung,

> Until the day breathes
> and the shadows flee,
>   turn, my beloved, be like a gazelle
> or a young stag on the cleft mountains.

In 4:6 the man offers his response:

> Until the day breathes
> and the shadows flee,
>   I will hasten to the mountain of myrrh
> and the hill of frankincense.

The lovers speak their private language across the landscape of the Song, calling and responding. In 2:10–14 the man calls the woman out into the verdant day, and in 2:17 she calls him to her side for the night. In 4:6 he says: Yes, I am coming, as quickly as I can.

94. Augustine, *On Christian Doctrine* 2.6.7, 37.

Song 4:7 brings this portion of the man's speech full circle. He began with an exclamation of wonderment over his beloved's beauty, and he ends the same way. Having praised her in parts, he now seems able to raise his eyes to take her in wholly: "You are altogether beautiful, my love; / there is no flaw in you" (4:7).

FURTHER REFLECTIONS
Theology of the Body

Christian faith is rooted in convictions about the body: God created embodied human beings and pronounced them good; God lived an incarnate life among us, sharing in the needs and pleasures and vulnerabilities of embodied life; and, after his death, Jesus of Nazareth rose again, his body wounded yet alive. If the Christian story tells us anything, it tells us this: bodies matter to God.

Indeed, the body is one of our most important sources of knowledge about God. Like the "master hand" of the artist invoked by the man in the Song of Songs as he gazes in admiration at his lover's thighs (7:1), we see traces of God's own creating hand in our bodies and the bodies of others. We are, all of us, "fearfully and wonderfully made" (Ps. 139:14). It is through our bodies that we experience the world around us, reach out to one another, and offer ourselves in service. Our bodies are both strong and limited, miraculous and vulnerable. By making us this way, God ensured that we would always have need of one another. This is one of the most important insights into God's purposes that the body discloses: through the vulnerability of our bodies, God has placed us in one another's care.

As Christians, however, we inherit an ambiguous legacy about the body and about creation itself. What God called "very good" in the opening chapter of Genesis, Christians have often viewed as less than good and hence something to be dominated, brought under control, disciplined into submission. The body has often served as a place where religious ideas get tested and religious rules enforced.

Because, in the experience of sexual desire and in death, the vulnerability of our bodies can seem to diminish our freedom, some Christians have seen in the body our distance from God writ large.

Early Christian views of human beings that elevated the soul over the body persist in our own day. It is hard to resist Plato's notion that the soul is trapped in the body like an oyster in a shell and difficult to overcome the denigration of the body that has followed from that idea. There were even early Christians who believed that Jesus' own body was an illusion, a trick God played on us, because the idea that something as precious as divinity could be intermingled with something as messy and vulnerable as a human body seemed so outrageous. But it is precisely that outrageous idea that is the bed-rock of our faith.

Although Christian faith is indeed rooted in convictions about the goodness of the body, the Christian "theology of the body" is by no means always visible in practice. In every generation, Christians must think through the relationship of our embodied life and our life with God. The Song offers us resources, from within the very heart of our sacred Scripture, for the crucial, ongoing work of articulating a theology of the body that honors the body as part of God's good creation and undergirds an unwavering commitment to the care and protection of all human bodies, everywhere.

4:8–5:1

A Lover Who Contains the Whole World

There is a well-known story about the Hindu god Krishna, who, as a child playing outside, was accused by his playmates of eating dirt. When his mother pried open his lips to check, she saw inside the child's one small mouth the entire universe and all the life within it.[95]

A Christian woman in the late thirteenth century named Marguerite d'Oingt wrote of a vision of Christ standing before her, a closed book in his hands. As she examined it bit by bit—its clasps, its binding, the colors of the words inscribed on its cover—the book opened. Inside, she could see a place larger than the world itself, a place from which light and fragrance and wisdom poured.[96]

---

95. *Hindu Myths*, trans. Wendy Doniger O'Flaherty (Harmondsworth: Penguin, 1975), 218–21.
96. "The Mirror of St. Marguerite d'Oingt," trans. Richard J. Pioli, in *Medieval Women's Visionary Literature*, ed. Elizabeth Alvilda Petroff (New York: Oxford University Press, 1986), 292.

The man in the fourth chapter of the Song describes an experience similar to those of Krishna's mother and Marguerite d'Oingt, an experience of finding within one finite body the whole life of the world. As the man's speech continues, he shifts from praising his beloved in parts to considering her in her entirety. It is as if, having brought his lens in close the better to gaze upon and cherish her eyes, hair, teeth, lips, cheeks, neck, and breasts, he now draws his lens back to get a larger view of his beloved as a whole. What he sees when he stands back from his earlier close-up view is a woman who seems to contain the whole world, a woman who holds within her all that is fragrant and flowing and alive.

Rather than gazing upon what can be seen behind her veil, he looks up, toward the mountains, where he imagines her living, fierce and remote, among the lions and leopards. Some commentators have noted that the setting is more appropriate for a goddess than for a human being and find in this passage evidence for the Song as a remnant of a fertility liturgy.[97] But the passage makes poetic sense without appealing to cultic explanations. When the man considers her from a distance, rather than up close, in parts, her full presence overwhelms all his senses. If she views him as a king, he sees her as something even more awe-inspiring. She not only pleases him, she utterly destabilizes him. In 3:6 she appears as, or in, a column of fragrant smoke; here in 4:8 she appears among dangerous animals, as powerful and as overwhelming as a goddess. All he wants is for her to be with him, but she is the one who must choose. He will not, cannot, go into the lion's den to fetch her. All he can do is call to her: "Come with me from Lebanon, my bride; / come with me from Lebanon" (4:8).

She does choose to return his love, and the man is undone.

> You have ravished my heart, my sister, my bride,
>> you have ravished my heart with a glance of your eyes,
> with one jewel of your necklace.
>
> (4:9)

---

97. Pope, *Song of Songs*, 474.

With the intimate terms *sister* and *bride*, he draws her close to him, tries to make more familiar this awe-inspiring woman, this goddess whose presence overwhelms him and makes him feel out of control. Immersed in her sweetness and her scent, he begins again to praise her, but this time he intensifies his admiration into an even more erotic key. Echoing and responding to the woman's description of him in 1:2–3, he sings of "the fragrance of your oils," the "honey and milk" he finds under her tongue, the "scent of your garments" (4:10–11). As Exum notes, his words "are antiphonal across the space of the poem, building on the harmony of the lovers' voices to reinforce the mutuality of their desire."[98]

It is in 4:12–15 that the vision of the woman containing the world comes into view. Verse 12 imagines the woman as an enclosed garden: "a garden locked is my sister, my bride, / a garden locked, a fountain sealed." Commentators have heard in this image reference to the woman's sexual inaccessibility to all but her lover, who enters the garden only at her invitation (4:16). This image of inaccessibility, like the veil in 4:1–3, invites us to meditate on the parts of each other that are hidden even from our most intimate companions and honor those secret places with reverent language. Inaccessibility and hiddenness and not-knowing are as much a part of loving another as intimate union.

The man imagines his lover as a fertile garden of abundant fruits and spices, and as the spring that waters the garden, "a garden fountain, a well of living water, / and flowing streams from Lebanon" (4:15). Feminist commentators have powerfully interpreted the image of the garden as further evidence that the Song "reverses," in the words of Trible, the "tragedy" of the garden of Eden.[99] In the garden that is both the woman and the place where the woman and the man do their loving, there are no forbidden trees or fruits, no creatures urging the lovers to transgress divine commands. The man names all that he finds in the garden of his beloved—pomegranates, henna, nard, saffron, calamus, cinnamon, frankincense, myrrh, aloes—and each word sounds as delicious as the honey and milk he

---

98. Exum, *Song of Songs*, 172.
99. Trible, *God and the Rhetoric of Sexuality*, 160.

finds under her tongue. He names the living plants he finds in the garden not as an act of dominion but as a performance of ecstasy.[100] Like the garden fountain that waters all these living things, images spill out of these verses as if there is no end to them. The man cannot come to the end of describing the delights of the garden that is both his lover and the place where he meets her to make love. Those delights are in excess of anything he can say, and his language can barely keep up. Here, more than anywhere else in the poem, the lovers melt into their setting, becoming an almost indistinguishable part of the abundant earth.

One senses that the man's cascade of images would never stop unless someone put a stop to it. In 4:16 the woman interrupts. There is some scholarly debate over who invokes the winds and urges them to "blow upon my garden, / that its fragrance may be wafted abroad." Pope and Bergant, for example, understand the invocation of the winds to be spoken by the man; Exum and the Blochs think it more likely that the woman invokes the winds.[101]

I find it makes more sense to imagine the woman speaking these words. Why would the man want the fragrance of his garden—the garden locked to all but him alone—to be blown abroad into the world? Also, as his litany of the plants and spices of the garden intensifies, one senses that, without a deliberate interruption, it might never end. In 4:16 the woman reenters the dialogue through interruption. She breaks into the man's litany of praise with a plea that he come to the garden, even that he stop speaking and taste her fruits instead. It is she who wants her fragrance to be wafted abroad—she is calling out to her lover here with her scent, just as he has called to her with his voice.

The end of the verse everyone agrees belongs to the woman. Here is the same fervent tone we heard in 1:2: "Let my beloved come to his garden, / and eat its choicest fruits." As in "Let him kiss me with the kisses of his mouth" (1:2), the woman does not address the man directly but expresses her desire aloud to whomever is listening—God, the universe, her lover, the women of Jerusalem, us. "Let

---

100. Ibid.
101. Pope, *Song of Songs*, 498; Bergant, *Song of Songs*, 75; Exum, *Song of Songs*, 181; Bloch and Bloch, *The Song of Songs*, 178.

my beloved come to his garden," she says, offering the invitation he longs to hear. Let him eat its choicest fruits.

Her lover's answer is to come with haste: "I come, I gather, I eat, I drink," he sings. As always in moments that suggest sexual union in the Song, it is not clear whether the sexual play the man describes has already happened, or is happening, or will happen in the future. "Through both the blurring of temporal distinctions and the indirection of language," Exum writes, "sexual union is simultaneously anticipated, deferred, and enjoyed."[102] We are not invited to watch the lovers' sexual play, but we are invited to enjoy their delight and to seek our own erotic and aesthetic intoxication. Although there is, again, quite a bit of debate over who speaks the last words of 5:1— "Eat, friends, drink, / and be drunk with love"—I like to think of those words as spoken by both of the lovers to all of us.

Marguerite d'Oingt once told a story about a woman to whom God gave a vision of a tree and a river when she prayed to understand a word that had become lodged in her heart. While she was praying, she seemed to see a dried-out tree at the foot of a mountain. The tree had five branches, all bending downward. "Sight" was written on the leaves of one, "hearing" on the leaves of another, "taste" on another, "smell" on another, and "touch" on the last. Something that reminded her of the round bottom of a barrel rested on top of the tree, keeping out everything it needed to flourish—the sun, the rain, the dew.

As she stood there looking, a "great stream" came rushing down the mountain "with a force like that of the sea." When it reached the tree, the stream uprooted it, turned it upside down, and replanted it, top down, in the earth. The drooping branches reached instead toward heaven, all the leaves became green, all the senses were restored.[103]

For the man, the woman is such a stream—"a garden fountain, a well of living water, / and flowing streams from Lebanon." She has uprooted him, turned him upside down, and tuned his senses to

---

102. Exum, *Song of Songs*, 182.
103. Marguerite d'Oingt, *The Writings of Margaret of Oingt: Medieval Prioress and Mystic*, trans. Renate Blumenfeld-Kosinski (Newburyport, MA: Focus Information Group, 1990), 66–67.

such a pitch that he can taste the honey and milk under her tongue, smell the scent of her oils and her garments.

The Song itself is such a stream. As the lovers exchange words of praise, erotic invitations, and stories of seeking and finding and losing and seeking again, the Song nearly rushes off the page, awakening every sense we have.

Marguerite's vision suggests that, when our bodily senses are neglected, it is difficult to understand what is written on our hearts. Our bodies, no less than our spirits, need to be refreshed and renewed in order for us to engage wholly our life with God, our life with each other, and our life with the world.

> As the lovers exchange words of praise, erotic invitations, and stories of seeking and finding and losing and seeking again, the Song nearly rushes off the page, awakening every sense we have.

Reading and praying the Song offers that kind of refreshment—an awakening of our senses that reminds us that reading and prayer are practices of the body as much as they are of the mind and spirit.

5:2–8

I Slept, but My Heart Was Awake

In many ways 4:1–5:1 is the joyful, sensual center of the Song. The veil, the high mountains, the dens of the wild animals, the locked garden, and the sealed fountain do not seem truly to separate the woman from the man, but only to mark the fact that even her intimate lover can never know her completely. The man speaks in this passage from his ravished heart, piling words on top of words until finally the woman interrupts and calls him to her. The lovers call out to one another across this passage, drawing closer and closer, until they are together in the garden that is both the woman's body and the garden where they meet for lovemaking. Song 4:1–5:1 both describes and performs an intensifying pleasure that is aesthetic and erotic at once.

Paired with this joyful passage, however, is a story told by the woman about separation, absence, missed meetings, violence, and desire that is thwarted and left to fester. As in all her stories, the theme here is her lover's absence and her attempts to overcome it.

The story begins with the woman kept awake and watchful by love. Even while she sleeps, something inside her remains wakeful, some part of her keeps listening for the sound of her lover's voice, or the sound of his feet in the hallway, or his knock at her door.

"I slept, but my heart was awake." This quiet little sentence gets at something true about us, I think. It is a crucial part of the anthropology of the Song. Even when we feel more scattered than present in our own lives, even when we are distracted by many things, even when we are *asleep*, there is some part of us—even if it is a very small part and very hidden—that is awake and waiting. This is the place where love greets and addresses us—the part of us that stays awake longing and listening, the part of us that is reaching out for love, for God, for our beloved, even when the rest of us is too distracted to notice. The Song invites us to learn to be led by that most wakeful part of ourselves—to recognize it, excavate it, cultivate it. The Song invites us to learn to be kept awake by love.

Soon the woman's inner wakefulness is rewarded. Her lover comes to her, knocking at her door, calling her to let him come inside. But does she leap from her bed and invite him in? No, she hesitates. I've already undressed, she thinks. I've already bathed. Do I really want to let him come in? As she lies there, wondering what to do, her lover reaches through the opening of her door, and her whole body responds: "my inmost being yearned for him" (5:4). With her bodily senses now as fully awake as her heart, she rises from her bed and hurries to open the door, her hands dripping with myrrh. "I opened to my beloved," she sings, "but my beloved had turned and was gone" (5:6).

It is certainly true that the Song celebrates the pleasures of mutual, sexual love. But in this story of hesitation and absence and unfulfilled desire, the Song also sings of something true about even the most intimate, mutual, loving relationships: lovers are not always perfectly receptive to each other. It is not always the case that one lover calls out, "Come to my garden!" and the other answers, "I'm coming right now!" Lovers do not always yearn on the same timetable. The voice of the beloved does not always find an attentive, listening ear or a heart that is awake and waiting. Sometimes lovers hesitate a moment too long, and the opportunity for love passes.

Along with absence, misunderstanding, and separation, another risk of loving is regret. When she opens the door, her lover is gone. Perhaps she waited too long to open the door, or perhaps he sensed her hesitation and left. "My soul failed me when he spoke," the woman says. She seems to be remembering how it felt when she heard his voice through the door, how it stirred her. "How I wanted him when he spoke!" is the Blochs' translation. It seems to be an expression of regret and longing—his voice stirred me, but I hesitated, and now he is gone.

As in the woman's parallel story in 3:1–5, the woman's longing for her beloved propels her out into the city streets alone. Unlike the earlier story, though, her search is unsuccessful. "I sought him, but did not find him; / I called him, but he gave no answer." Having just left the garden of 4:12–5:1, where lovers' calls are answered with haste, the image of the woman calling and hearing only silence in return is particularly poignant.

In this version of the story, the consequences of the woman taking to the streets to look for her lover are graver than they were in the story the woman told in 3:1–5. Not only does she not find him, but the sense of menace that hovered over her encounter with the watchmen in the earlier story materializes in acts of violence in this one: "they beat me, they wounded me, / they took away my mantle, / those sentinels of the walls" (5:7).

This violent encounter is usually interpreted as an illustration of the risks the woman is willing to take for love and the suffering she is willing to endure for love, and surely it is. But it is more than that. The natural world the lovers inhabit in the Song is a garden of delight where everything—plants, animals, fruits, spices—supports and nurtures the love that the lovers share. But just as 5:2–8 is a reminder that love is not without moments of absence, unfulfilled longing, misunderstanding, and hesitation, it is also a reminder that the world in which we live and love is not wholly in our control. We can create, as the lovers of the Song do, intimate bowers of delight, but those bowers are not immune to the social and political forces at work in the world. The kinds of unexpected and heartbreaking reversals such as we find in the book of Lamentations—the lonely city that was once full of people, the princess who has become a vassal, the one with many lovers who has no one to comfort her (Lam. 1:1–2)—are possibilities, even at times of great joy, in this world of contingency.

The Song of Songs celebrates love that flourishes in a peaceful kingdom, but the woman's encounter with the watchmen in 5:7 reminds us that it might be otherwise. The beating and stripping of one woman in the Song is terrible enough. The terrors of Lamentations are even worse: "Women are raped in Zion, / virgins in the towns of Judah" (Lam. 5:11). The brief account—in one verse—of the attack of the watchmen on the woman serves to remind us not only of all that could threaten the lovers' joy but also that a world in which humans flourish among plants and animals, a world in which naked vulnerability is sheltered by mutual love, is a world worth our best energies to create and support and protect.

> We can create, as the lovers of the Song do, intimate bowers of delight, but those bowers are not immune to the social and political forces at work in the world. The kinds of unexpected and heartbreaking reversals such as we find in the book of Lamentations . . . are possibilities, even at times of great joy, in this world of contingency.

The story ends with the woman speaking, as she does at the end of the parallel story in 3:1–5, to the women of Jerusalem. But instead of speaking to them of love's demands, she asks them to deliver a message to her beloved:

> I adjure you, O daughters of Jerusalem,
>   if you find my beloved,
> tell him this:
>   I am faint with love.
>
>   (5:8)

This story, placed alongside the erotic account of the lovers' encounter in 5:1, leaves the woman in a state of unfulfilled longing. Verses 2–8 expose the shadow side of 4:1–5:1: calling with no answer, spices with no one to inhale their scent, desire with no fulfillment. We leave the woman faint with love at the end of this story.

The image of being "faint with love" recalls Psalm 63, where the psalmist cries out to God that "my soul thirsts for you; / my flesh faints for you, / as in a dry and weary land where there is no water" (63:1). For the psalmist, the soul's need for God and the body's need for God are one need. The body longs for God just as the soul does. With its loving attention to the body, the Song of Songs chips away at our tendency to divide the soul from the body and teaches us to bring all that we are to our life with God.

5:9–6:3

Making the Absent Beloved Present

This time, unlike the woman's two previous adjurations, the daughters of Jerusalem respond, initiating a dialogue with the woman that continues into the next chapter. Addressing the woman as the man did in 1:8—"O fairest among women"—the daughters of Jerusalem ask her: What makes your lover different from others? The Blochs point out that the form of this question is found nowhere else in the Bible, but it does echo in Rashi's paraphrase of 5:9, in which he turns the dialogue between the woman and the women of Jerusalem into a meditation on God's attributes: "How is your God different from all other gods?" Another echo can be found in the traditional question of the Passover haggadah, "How is this night different from all other nights?"[104]

This question gives the woman a way to satisfy her unfulfilled longing for her lover, by inviting her to sing of her beloved's charms until he is present once more. Feminist philosopher Julia Kristeva describes the woman's song of her beloved as an "amorous incantation" that allows the woman to experience her beloved's body even in his absence, a conjuring-through-language that allows her to "unite with him, sensually *and* ideally."[105] Such amorous incantations that

---

104. Bloch and Bloch, *The Song of Songs*, 184.
105. Julia Kristeva, *Tales of Love*, trans. Leon S. Roudiez (New York: Columbia University Press, 1987), 94.

attempt to make present what cannot be seen or touched are surely one of the reasons the Song has been taken up so often as a prayer that attempts to reach across silence and absence with language.

As we saw in 4:1–15, the man also makes good use of "amorous incantations." But he seems to sing his song of love directly to his beloved, addressing her as "you" and describing what he sees as he gazes at her. The woman, by contrast, sings her song to the daughters of Jerusalem and, by extension, to us. It is a song not of what she sees in front of her but of what she sees in her memory. She sings of her beloved's skin, his head, his eyes, his cheeks, his lips, his arms, his trunk, his legs, "conjuring" him, as Exum puts it, one part at a time.[106] Like her lover, she looks to the world around her for images she can use to describe him, seeking reminders of her lover in the world and its wonders.

> His eyes are like doves
>   beside springs of water,
> bathed in milk,
>   fitly set.
> His cheeks are like beds of spices,
>   yielding fragrance.
> His lips are lilies,
>   distilling liquid myrrh.
>   (5:12–13)

The woman also draws on sculptural images to describe her beloved, which some commentators hypothesize might reflect the poet/redactor's familiarity with Greek sculpture in Palestine. Because the second of the Ten Commandments forbids the creation of "an idol, whether in the form of anything that is in heaven above, or that is on the earth beneath, or that is in the water under the earth" (Exod. 20:4), the sight of a Greek nude statue would have made a powerful impact, the Blochs argue, on a Hebrew poet.[107] The description of the beloved's arms as "rounded gold," his body as "ivory work," his legs as "alabaster columns, set upon bases of gold,"

---

106. Exum, *Song of Songs*, 187, 188, 189.
107. Bloch and Bloch, *The Song of Songs*, 26.

might indeed reflect the poet's experience of nude statuary. The effect these sculptural images have on the portrait of the beloved is one of solidity, presence—the very thing the woman desires.

The poet draws from both nature and art to create this "amorous incantation." Although it has been compared unfavorably to the man's litany of the woman's charms in 4:1–7—in comparison it seems generic to many readers—it still possesses an incantatory quality, moving part by part across the man's body until we see him whole, like a cedar of Lebanon (5:15), hard and strong and desirable.

The woman ends her description of her beloved with a reference to his sweet speech (although some commentators argue that this is really a reference to his sweet kisses), his desirability, and his friendship.

> His speech is most sweet,
> and he is altogether desirable.
> This is my beloved and this is my friend,
> O daughters of Jerusalem.

"This is my beloved and this is my friend." The conjuring is complete.

The daughters of Jerusalem take up the dialogue again at this point, asking a question the woman herself usually asks: Where is he? "Which way has your beloved turned, / that we may seek him with you?" (6:1). Having gazed along with the woman as she lavished praise on each part of his body, they are eager now to accompany her as she looks for him.

Having been conjured by her words, however, he is no longer lost.

> My beloved has gone down to his garden,
> to the beds of spices,
> to pasture his flock in the gardens,
> and to gather lilies.
>
> (6:2)

Her lover is in the garden, which is her own body; they are together once more. The erotic play described in the man's song of the garden in 4:9–15 echoes here as well. Rather than encouraging the daughters of Jerusalem to go with her as she looks for her beloved, she again draws the curtain over their lovemaking with a statement of exclusivity: "I am my beloved's and my beloved is mine; / he pastures his flock among the lilies" (6:3).

6:4–10

Terrible as an Army with Banners

With 6:4 the man reenters the conversation, and the daughters of Jerusalem fall silent. He returns to the beginning of his own "amorous incantation" in 4:1, with praise of his beloved's beauty. Here, though, he focuses on the overwhelming, awe-inspiring quality of her beauty: he compares her to the great cities of Tirzah and Jerusalem; he describes her as "terrible as an army with banners" (6:4). His response to the almost unbearable power of her presence is at its most intense in this speech. "Turn your eyes away from me," he pleads, "for they overwhelm me!"

As Exum points out, the awe-inspiring, devastating power of the beloved's beauty is a familiar topos in love poetry.[108] But the man sounds almost desperate here, especially when he begins repeating his speech, almost word for word, from 4:1–3. It sounds speeded up, as if he is so overwhelmed by her that all he can do is repeat, a little faster, what he has said before. It reminds me of the scene in Umberto Eco's *Name of the Rose*, when the young monk, Adso, is seduced by a young woman he encounters in the monastery's kitchen in the middle of the night. So overwhelmed is he by this unexpected erotic experience that lines from the Song of Songs begin running uncontrollably through his mind.

> And she kissed me with the kisses of her mouth, and her loves were more delicious than wine and her ointments had a goodly fragrance, and her neck was beautiful among pearls and her cheeks among earrings, behold thou art fair, my beloved, behold thou art fair; thine eyes are as doves (I said), and let me see thy face, let me hear thy voice, for thy voice is harmonious

---

108. Exum, *Song of Songs*, 218.

and thy face enchanting, thou hast ravished my heart, my
sister, thou hast ravished my heart with one of thine eyes, with
one chain of thy neck, thy lips drop as the honeycomb, honey
and milk are under thy tongue, the smell of thy breath is of
apples, thy two breasts are clusters of grapes, thy palate a heady
wine that goes straight to my love and flows over my lips and
teeth. . . . A fountain sealed, spikenard and saffron, calamus
and cinnamon, myrrh and aloes, I have eaten my honeycomb
with my honey, I have drunk my wine with my milk. Who was
she, who was she who rose like the dawn, fair as the moon,
clear as the sun, terrible as an army with banners?[109]

The lover chanting the praise of his beloved in chapter 6 sounds
a bit like young Adso. He experiences his beloved as beautiful, to be
sure, but as more than beautiful: to him, she is sublime, with sublim-
ity's heady mix of beauty and terror, a beauty that cannot be possessed or controlled.

The flowing praise of his beloved's hair, teeth, and cheeks ends
with a turn toward the royal court, which the man invokes in order
to highlight his beloved's uniqueness. Among sixty queens and
eighty concubines and "maidens without number,"

> My dove, my perfect one, is the only one,
>   the darling of her mother,
>   flawless to her that bore her.

My perfect one is the only one. She stands out among all other
women, even the queens and concubines of the king. The mother is
once more invoked as one able to see the unique flawlessness of his
beloved. He sees her through the eyes of love—but he also sees her
as her mother sees her: perfect, without flaw. The mother, whom the
poem has associated with sexual union and procreation, is here associated with the ability to perceive the beloved's unique beauty. She
is united to her daughter's lover through her powers of perception.

The maidens and the queens and the concubines also see his

109. Umberto Eco, *The Name of the Rose*, trans. William Weaver (1983; repr. New York: Warner
    Books, 1984), 292–93.

beloved. They see her and call her happy, recalling Solomon's gladness of heart in 3:11. They see her and praise her. For the man, it is impossible to look on his beloved and not be struck by her uniqueness. Just as the woman describes him as "distinguished among ten thousand" (5:10), he sees her as the lily in the valley, the lily among brambles (2:1–2), the only one for him among all other women.

The man's speech ends with a question, the same question Adso asked in *The Name of the Rose* as the young woman in the dark kitchen pressed her body against his: "'Who is this that looks forth like the dawn, / fair as the moon, bright as the sun, / terrible as an army with banners?'" (6:10). Adso truly did not know whom he held in his arms, but the question in the Song has been understood to be a rhetorical one. Whether it is being asked by the man or by the daughters of Jerusalem, he and they know the answer already: it is the beloved, she of the pomegranate cheeks, with eyes like doves, hair like goats flowing down a mountain, and teeth like a flock of newly washed sheep. Although the NRSV puts the question in quotes, as if it is being asked by someone other than the man—the women of Jerusalem, perhaps, or the women of the court who have seen his beloved—I like to think of it as being asked by the man himself. For although he has sought to know every single part of his beloved, from her eyes to her hair to her feet, although he has delighted in her garden and gathered his myrrh with his spice, he still asks: Who is this? Who is this? Surely this question honors her as profoundly as his praise of her body, for it acknowledges that though he has meditated on her from head to toe, there is still something inaccessible and unknowable about her, something that cannot be seen with the eyes in his beautiful head. She is still a mystery to him, and he honors that mystery with his question.

6:11–12

In the Nut Orchard

Speaking of mysteries, 6:11–12 is one of the most enduring mysteries of the Song. We understand almost nothing about these verses, especially verse 12. Who speaks here? What do the words mean?

The Blochs prefer a reading that identifies the male lover as the speaker.[110] It is he who goes to the garden throughout the Song; it is the woman who is the garden itself. The NRSV seems to understand the woman to be the speaker, for it translates the literally untranslatable 6:12 as, "Before I was aware, my fancy set me / in a chariot beside my prince," as opposed to the Blochs': "And oh! before I was aware, / she sat me in the most lavish of chariots." Bergant and Exum tentatively embrace a reading that identifies the woman as the speaker, but they both acknowledge that it is impossible to know to whom the poet/redactor intended to speak or even what the person was meant to be saying.[111]

I do not know who speaks here any more than these great scholars of Hebrew texts. But I do hear, as they do, an echo in this passage of the many visits to a garden that the two lovers have made together. Whoever is speaking here goes down to the nut orchard to see if things are growing: Have the vines budded? Are the pomegranates in bloom? One gets the sense of someone walking slowly through the orchard, holding a branch to his or her nose, trying to catch the scent of spring, rubbing a thumb across the buds just beginning to appear. If this orchard refers, like the garden, to the woman's body, then it is possible to imagine the woman attending closely to the stirrings inside of her: Am I ready for love? she might ask herself. Or the man, gently reaching out for her, gauging her response: Is she ready for love? he might ask himself.

Whoever is attending so closely to the orchard and its development—and let us say for the moment that it is the woman—her imagination ("my fancy") creates a scene where she is in a chariot with her prince. Perhaps this is the sign that the vines have budded and the pomegranates are in bloom: she is so ready for love that her mind spins out erotic fantasies of its own accord.

But 6:12 is the most untranslatable verse in the entire Song. No one really has any idea what it means.

---

110. Bloch and Bloch, *The Song of Songs*, 192.
111. Bergant, *Song of Songs*, 116-17; Exum, *Song of Songs*, 225.

6:13–14

Return, Return!

This is the first and only place in the Song where the woman is identified by anything like a name. Many commentators believe that "Shulammite" has some sort of association with a particular place—the woman from Shulam perhaps. Others have heard an echo of a Mesopotamian goddess of war named Shulmanitu, which would intensify the woman's association with bannered armies—although it does not fit well the overall sense of love unfolding in a peaceful time that the Song reflects. Others, like Bergant, have wondered whether Shulammite might be some kind of derivation of *shlm,* the Hebrew root for "Solomon" and "Jerusalem" and "peace."

Here again the identity of the speaker is uncertain. Exum attributes this verse to the man; Bergant and the Blochs to the daughters of Jerusalem, in part because of the plural "we" who wish to gaze at her.[112] Are they calling her back from the nut orchard? Or calling her back from her erotic reverie?

I like to imagine this verse spoken by the daughters of Jerusalem. They, and we, have been listening to the man's praise of the woman. We have been looking at her through his eyes, and when she leaves the scene to check on the growth in the nut orchard, we miss her. "Return, return," the daughters cry, and we along with them. "Return, return, that we may look upon you" (6:13).

Some commentators have found in 6:13–14 signs of a dance, another evocative way to read these verses. Imagine the daughters of Jerusalem lined up on either side, with the woman, the Shulammite, dancing from one end of the row to the other. "Return, return!" could be a call for her to come dancing in the other direction. Or she could be dancing in and out of view while the daughters call for her to dance in front of them so that they can see her.

If there are two lines of dancers in this dance, with the Shulammite dancing between them, it is possible that the second part of

---

112. Exum, *Song of Songs,* 226; Bergant, *Song of Songs,* 117; Bloch and Bloch, *The Song of Songs,* 195-96.

6:13 is one line of dancers responding to the other: "Return, return, O Shulammite," one side sings, while the other responds, "Why should you look upon the Shulammite, / as upon a dance before two armies?"

The Targum heard the "Return, return!" as a call to Israel from God: "Return to Me, O Assembly of Israel, return to Jerusalem, return to the House of Teaching the Law, return to receive prophecy from the prophets who prophesy in the Name of the Word of YHWH."[113]

Bernard of Clairvaux also heard in 6:13 a call from God to human beings. For Bernard, "Return, return!" is the cry of the Holy Spirit to the human being made in the image of God. For Bernard the Spirit's cry reflects "the great dignity of the soul's relationship with the Word."[114] It is our creation in God's image that evokes this "cry of admiration" from the Spirit. "Return, return!" is God's call to the part of us that is awake and waiting, even when we are asleep.

Bernard's reading of 6:13 is reminiscent of the "unceasing cry of the soul" to God that he heard in the woman's plea to her lover in 2:17 to "[re]turn, my beloved."[115] The cry of one voice to another to "turn" or "return" captures the longing that propels the Song across its eight chapters. The readings of 6:13 by the targumist and Bernard of Clairvaux remind us that this longing is a mutual one. It could be a call from the soul to God, but it could just as easily be a call from God to God's people. In either case, the message is the same: Turn around, and let me look at you!

Whether as part of a dance or not, a question is posed, similar to the question the daughters of Jerusalem asked the woman in 5:9 ("What is your beloved more than another beloved?"). Why should we look upon the Shulammite, they ask. Why should we call out to her to return so that we may gaze upon her?

Why is this a question at all? Is it because she is just an ordinary woman? Not in the eyes of her lover. When the daughters of Jerusalem asked the woman what was so special about her lover in 5:9,

---

113. Quoted in Pope, *Song of Songs*, 612.
114. Bernard of Clairvaux, "Sermon 82," III.7 (*Song of Songs IV*, 178).
115. Idem, "Sermon 74," I.2 (*Song of Songs IV*, 87).

they evoked from her a speech about the beauties of her beloved's body so powerful that it conjured his presence in the garden. Here the question sets the man to spinning another "amormous incantation," which initiates another erotic encounter.

7:1–5

Another "Amorous Incantation"

In 4:1 the man began with a description of the woman's eyes: they are doves, he sang, behind your veil. Here he begins with her feet, lovely and graceful in sandals. Perhaps his eyes are drawn to her feet this time because she is dancing. Bergant notes that the Hebrew word translated as "feet" in the NRSV is closer to "footstep," a word that implies movement.[116] Perhaps as she dances between the lines of the daughters of Jerusalem, he is drawn to the graceful movement of her feet. He calls her a "queenly maiden," perhaps a direct response to the implication that there is nothing special about this woman that we should all be calling for her return. In his eyes, she is anything but ordinary: she is queenly, unique, and endlessly rewarding to contemplate.

From her feet, he moves to her thighs, which he describes with artistic imagery—as the woman did in 5:15 when she compared his legs to alabaster columns, set in gold.

> Your rounded thighs are like jewels,
> the work of a master hand.
>
> (7:1)

Bergant notes that the phrase, "the work of a master hand," refers not to the woman's thighs but to the jewels to which they are compared. But I wonder if we might read that phrase as a glimpse of the God who is nowhere explicitly mentioned in the Song but perhaps lies hidden here like the lily hidden among the brambles (2:1). The

---

116. Bergant, *Song of Songs*, 120.

"master hand" that holds and turns and shapes materials until they take the beautiful shape the man admires might lead our imaginations to the God who created the world and all that is in it, the God who created the lovers themselves and everything they gaze upon and praise. For how else can we see the hand of God except by gazing upon what God has made?

The man's song of praise continues as he marvels over the wonders of the woman's body. The navel of "Your navel is a rounded bowl / that never lacks mixed wine" is sometimes translated, more explicitly, as "vulva" or "vagina." The description of her belly as "a heap of wheat" suggests softness, a place where her lover might lay his head. Taken as a whole, the descriptions mix softness and hardness ("your neck is like an ivory tower"; "your nose is like a tower of Lebanon"; "your head crowns you like Carmel") in a way that fits well the man's experience of the woman. She is both accessible and inaccessible, known and unknown, beautiful and terrible. Her eyes, which he describes as "pools in Heshbon / by the gate of Bathrabbim" (7:4), seem to gather up and reflect her deepest secrets. "It is deep water, mysterious," Bergant writes.[117]

This is the third poem of praise for the various parts of his beloved's body that the man utters in the Song. Each one moves through the catalog of beauty until it culminates in some kind of utterance that reveals how destabilizing the man finds his beloved's presence. His speech in chapter 4 culminates in his description of how overwhelming his careful study of her has been for him: "You have ravished my heart, my sister, my bride" (4:9). His speech in chapter 6 ends with the question, "Who is this that looks forth like the dawn, / fair as the moon, bright as the sun, / terrible as an army with banners?" (6:10). Here in chapter 7 his loving description of her body culminates in his praise of her head and her hair in which, he says, "a king is held captive" (7:5). Once again, his part-by-part adoration has ended with him losing control of himself—ravished, confronted by her terrible beauty, caught in the tresses of her hair.

---

117. Ibid., 124.

These "amormous incantations" serve many purposes in the Song. For the man, they help him cope with the woman's sublime presence by allowing him to focus on one small part of her at a time. For the woman, they help her cope with the man's absence by singing him into being. For both lovers, they provide a way to honor and adore each other. For us, as readers, they honor the goodness of the body. Rather than an impediment to a deep moral and spiritual life, something to be transcended or overcome, the body in the Song reveals the goodness of creation and is as worthy of our reverence and our care as the world around us.

These incantations seem to me to be deeply "religious," but not because they portray the body as a place where religious ideas get tested and religious rules enforced. These incantations seem like prayers because they honor the body as every bit the holy mystery that the soul is.

> Rather than an impediment to a deep moral and spiritual life, something to be transcended or overcome, the body in the Song reveals the goodness of creation and is as worthy of our reverence and our care as the world around us.

The "amorous incantations" of the man and the woman insist that the body is not just worthy of our best theorizing and theologizing but something beautiful to linger over. The songs of praise to the lovers' bodies in the Song are remarkable for many reasons, not least of which is their duration. Bernard of Clairvaux speaks in his seventy-fourth sermon of the "unwearying lovers" of the Song, "whose passion drives them on and gives them no rest."[118] They are unwearying indeed, not only in their loving but in their attention to each other. The repetition of praise, the looking and looking at the same body, coming to know its beauties and its mysteries, its soft places and its hard places, its deep similarity to the beautiful world all around, is as erotic and reverent an action in the Song as the lovemaking itself.

---

118. Bernard of Clairvaux, "Sermon 74," I.1 (*Song of Songs IV*, 85).

7:6–9

O Loved One, Delectable Maiden!

The man's praise of his beloved continues in the next section of the speech but shifts slightly to make room for the man to enter the world of his poem as an actor. No longer simply standing before his lover, describing what he sees and how it makes him feel, here the man imagines himself stepping into the scene. Having compared his beloved to a palm tree and her breasts to its clusters, he makes clear his erotic aspirations.

> I say I will climb the palm tree
>   and lay hold of its branches.
> O may your breasts be like clusters of the vine,
>   and the scent of your breath like apples,
> and your kisses like the best wine
>   that goes down smoothly
>   gliding over lips and teeth.
>   (7:8–9)

Exum notes that the man echoes here the opening words of the Song, where the woman cries out, "Let him kiss me with the kisses of his mouth! For your love is better than wine" (1:2). "These verses," Exum writes, "establish a network of associations across the space of the poem, linking desire and delight in lovemaking with wine and its inebriating effect."[119] The genius of the redactor who arranged the poems of the Song is visible here. The resonances that have accumulated over the course of the Song intensify in these lines, as we see once again the lovers playing on each other's language, returning the other's own words in a way that invites further play, both erotic and aesthetic.

The man's desire to climb the woman like a tree reinforces the awe he feels in her presence. She is the stately tree; he is the one who climbs up to her branches. Her "flowing locks are like purple"; he

---

119. Exum, *Song of Songs*, 238.

is a king "held captive in her tresses" (7:5). She towers above him; he hopes that when he reaches her mouth her breath will smell like apples and her kisses taste like wine. This passage is a prayer. He is all desire, all hope.

7:10–13

There I Will Give You My Love

The man's prayer is answered when the woman replies with an extended invitation to lovemaking. She begins by binding herself to him in language very similar to 2:16 and 6:3: "I am my beloved's," she sings, "and his desire is for me" (7:10). Following this declaration, she begins to speak directly to him, as he has spoken to her throughout the poem. "Come, my beloved," she begins.

Just as her beloved called her to come outside in 2:10–13, she invites him to "go forth" with her. She asks him to join her in the fields and the villages, to walk with her in the early morning through the vineyards to see what is budding and blooming. Once again, the lovers themselves seem to belong to the budding and blooming world: vines, grape blossoms, pomegranates, lovers. Throughout the Song, the woman has warned the daughters of Jerusalem: Don't awaken love until it is ready! Love is ready now, and so are the lovers, and so is the earth. It is no wonder that Trible and others have seen in the Song a return to Eden, a paradise where human life and the life of the earth turn together harmoniously.

At the end of 7:12 the woman speaks the words her beloved has longed to hear. These words are her gift, her promise, spoken directly to him: "There I will give you my love." Her love, her body, the kisses he has hoped to taste—all of this she offers him as her gift. She has been saving up for him, she says, new fruits as well as old. The form of "new and old" is a literary form that, according to Bergant, "implies totality by naming opposing poles."[120] And indeed, the woman seems to be saying that she has saved up everything for her beloved, all of herself, completely.

---

120. Bergant, *Song of Songs*, 135.

Mandrakes, a fruit used as an aphrodisiac in several cultures, make their only appearance in the Song here, perhaps because of their reputation as "love apples" and perhaps also because the Hebrew word for "mandrake" is very similar to the Hebrew words for "caresses" and for "my lover."[121] The only other place mandrakes appear in the Bible is in Genesis 30:14–17, where Leah's son, Reuben, finds mandrakes in a field. Rachel wants them so badly that she offers Leah a night with her husband, Jacob, in exchange for them. Leah walks out into the fields to meet Jacob as he returns from work, greeting him with these words: "You must come in to me; for I have hired you with my son's mandrakes" (Gen. 30:16).

Like the Song itself, the Genesis mandrake story offers a rare biblical example of a woman asserting her sexual desire. But the words "you must" are never spoken in the Song. The lovers express their desires clearly and passionately, but always in the form of wishes, invitations, and the sweetest words of persuasion. The lovers move quickly when they need to cover a lot of ground to reach their beloved: think of the man "leaping upon the mountains, / bounding over the hills" (2:8), and the woman seeking her lost beloved in the streets of the city. But when they are in each other's presence, they are exquisitely patient, singing of each other's beauties, telling each other stories, waiting until all is ready, from the vines to the grape blossoms to the woman herself. No gesture is rushed or forced; no one is told "you must come in to me." The lovers draw near to each other, lose each other, seek and find and praise each other; and finally in 7:12 the woman says, "There I will give you my love." It is a breathtaking moment, a moment when the future seems to open and open, endlessly.

FURTHER REFLECTIONS
Creation

The great creation hymn that opens the book of Genesis sings of God speaking the world into being: "Let there be light. Let there be

---

121. Exum, *Song of Songs* 242.

land. Let there be great oceans. Let the waters and the earth bring forth creatures. Let us make humankind in our image." Speaking into a dark, formless void, God brings forth life in all its diversity and pronounces it all very good.

From this story of creation, the bedrock convictions of Christian thinking about creation took their shape: That one God made all that is and called it good. That everything that lives relies on God for existence. That in every moment of every day, God sustains our lives. And that just as we long for redemption and freedom, so does creation itself, "groaning in labor pains," longing for "the freedom of the glory of the children of God" (Rom. 8:19–22).

Furthermore, God's creation is like a sacrament, a visible sign of an invisible reality. God's "eternal power and divine nature, invisible though they are, have been understood and seen through the things God has made" (Rom. 1:20).

The Song of Songs is notable as only one of two biblical books—the other is the book of Esther—that does not mention God. But if creation is where we are to look for the invisible creator of all things, then traces of God are everywhere present in the Song: in the vineyards and henna blossoms, the foxes and the stags, the gardens and flowers and the lovers themselves.

Some Christian theologies have emphasized human dominance over creation. Because human beings are uniquely created in God's image, such theologies argue, we have the right to use creation for our own purposes, to extract what we need from the earth and the seas. We see the effects of this theology in the melting ice caps, in the mountaintops sheared away for coal extraction, in oil spills that wipe out hundreds of species of wildlife and whose effects are experienced for generations.

It matters how we understand creation and how we interpret our relationship to it. Contemporary theologian Sallie McFague has suggested that we use the language of "God's body" to describe creation. Thinking of the world as God's body, McFague argues, would remind us of the sacramental quality of nature—that it is a visible sign of the God we cannot see. It would resist our attempts to understand ourselves apart from creation, as masters who are in a position to dominate it. And it would increase our commitment to care for the earth and all the life the earth supports.[122]

The Song of Songs is an ancient resource for considering the relationship of human beings to creation. Here the human lovers are seen as creatures in creation, not masters of it. Their love is held and supported by nature—the cedar and pine trees that shelter them in their lovemaking, the pastures and gardens where they meet, the spices with which they adorn themselves. "The earth is the LORD'S and all that is in it," the psalmist sings, "the world and those who live in it" (Ps. 24:1). If the world is God's body, it is God who supports the lovers in their loving, God who shelters and protects them.

8:1–4

Love in the Open

In the Song the drawing together of the lovers in erotic play or sexual union is always followed by some sort of pulling away into absence or distance that the woman tries to overcome. The moment at the end of chapter 2 when the man "pastures his flock among the lilies" is followed by the woman's story of seeking her beloved at night in the streets of the city. The erotic encounter in the garden at the end of chapter 4 and the beginning of chapter 5 is followed by the woman's story of hesitating to answer her lover's knock, losing him, seeking him in the streets at night, and being beaten and stripped by the watchmen. At the beginning of chapter 8 her gift to him of her love in the vineyards is followed, not by a story of losing her beloved, but by her cry of desire to share their love in the open.

> O that you were like a brother to me,
>   who nursed at my mother's breast!
> If I met you outside, I would kiss you,
>   and no one would despise me.

122. Sallie McFague, *The Body of God: An Ecological Theology* (Minneapolis: Fortress, 1993).

Just as the brief references to the woman's brothers and the watchmen of the city remind us that the lovers are not wholly free to pursue their love in the open, so the woman's wish that she could kiss her beloved "outside" without being despised reminds us that the lovers' garden of delight exists within a larger world that judges women who kiss their lovers in the street quite harshly, as we saw in Proverbs 7:10–17.

The frustrated desire of lovers to express their love in public is both an ancient theme and a present dilemma in the history of love. As the Song illustrates, lovers want to express their love in the open—to their friends , their family (like the supportive mothers of the Song), and to the world around them. Having one's expression of love constrained is agonizing, as the woman's cry here illustrates. Couples whose love crosses boundaries—racial, religious, cultural, sexual—know this all too well. In our day and in our culture, no one knows this better than gay, lesbian, bisexual, and transgendered people, who are all too often despised and mistreated for their love. The Song records the woman's desire to express her love in the open and claims it as a basic human desire for all of us.

The woman yearns to kiss her beloved outside without being despised. And she also yearns to bring him inside, "into the chamber of the one who bore me" (8:2). Once again, the mother is the one who holds open a space for love, the kind of loving for which the lovers desire privacy. In my mother's room, the woman tells her beloved, "I would give you spiced wine to drink, / the juice of my pomegranates" (8:2). She longs for or remembers or experiences his embrace—the Song makes it deliberately difficult to tell—in the same words she used to describe it in 2:6: "O that his left hand were under my head, / and that his right hand embraced me!" (8:3). Her desire for that embrace is as strong at the end of the poem as it was at the beginning, even after their intensely erotic encounters in the garden and the vineyard. The repetition of her words from earlier in the poem speaks of a desire that is never finally satisfied, a desire that renews itself again and again.

The woman's poem of longing ends with the familiar admonishment to the daughters of Jerusalem: "do not stir up or awaken love until it is ready!" (8:4). Once love awakens, it can bring with it the kind of intense joy described in the Song, but it will also open a well of longing that can never quite be filled. Do not stir that up, the woman tells the women of Jerusalem, until it is time. The woman's admonishment has accumulated meaning as the Song has unfolded. It reaches us here with greater force than it did in the second chapter. Having followed the woman through the dark city streets and felt the rising intensity of both lovers' desire, we now understand what is at stake.

8:5a

Who Is That Coming Up from the Wilderness?

In 8:5 the daughters of Jerusalem pose the third and last question in the Song about the identity of the woman.

> Who is that coming up from the wilderness,
>   leaning upon her beloved?

The daughters of Jerusalem, and we along with them, have listened to the woman singing of her desires, her pleasures, and the ache of her longing throughout the Song. We have gazed at her through the eyes of her beloved, studying her closely from her head to her feet and then from her feet to her head. We have heard her invitations to her lover; we have heard her offer herself, wholly, to him. We know how she smells and how she tastes; we know how beautiful her feet look in her sandals when she is dancing. We have called out to her to "return, return!" so that we might look at her some more.

And yet: Who is she? Who is she? Even at the end of a poem in which she has made herself vivid on the page and been described by her beloved in loving detail, she remains a mystery. There is something about her that is always just out of reach—our reach, her friends' reach; even her lover does not have access to all that she is.

This seems to me one of the most important contributions of the Song to our understanding of what it means to love and to be loved. Lovers, children, friends, God—all our love relationships are marked by both intimacy and mystery. Honoring this in how we live out those relationships is crucial to the vitality of them. If we think we have our spouse or our child all figured out, we leave our spouse or our child no room to move, no room to change, no room to experience transformation, no room to keep discovering—over a lifetime—who they are.

Isn't this what we want for ourselves as well, to be deeply known by our beloved but also to have our unknown dimensions—perhaps unknown even to ourselves—reverenced and honored? When our loved ones honor both what they know and what they do not know about us, they make room for us to move and change and grow. They hold open the possibility that we are more than we know ourselves to be.

> Isn't this what we want for ourselves as well, to be deeply known by our beloved but also to have our unknown dimensions—perhaps unknown even to ourselves—reverenced and honored? When our loved ones honor both what they know and what they do not know about us, they make room for us to move and change and grow. They hold open the possibility that we are more than we know ourselves to be.

Bernard of Clairvaux imagined the angels asking, "What is this coming up from the wilderness like a column of smoke?" (3:6), when they hear the monks singing their night office with attention and reverence. He also heard the voices of the angels speaking in 8:5. The angels look upon us "with joy and wonder," Bernard writes, whenever they see us leaning upon God and gaining strength through our struggle to allow reason to guide us "like a good charioteer."[123] "Who is this coming up from the wilderness?" they ask when they see us changing. It is our capacity for transformation the angels admire.

For many rabbinical interpreters, the shift of scene from the blossoming fields and vineyards of 7:11–13 and the mother's room of 8:2 to the wilderness of 8:5 suggests a powerful figural answer to the question: "Who is this coming up from the wilderness,

---

123. Bernard of Clairvaux, "Sermon 85," II.5 (*Song of Songs IV*, 201).

leaning upon her beloved?" For the rabbis, the answer to the question is Israel, who was never forgotten by God during her years in the wilderness of slavery and the wilderness into which she fled that enslavement. The image of Israel coming up from the wilderness, leaning on the Lord who has sustained her life over years of hardship, is a tender one, evoking an intimate relationship that has endured over time.

Christian readings of this passage often emphasize the ascent, through prayer and meditation, of the soul out of "the desert of earthly exile" toward God.[124] The targumist, however, found in this verse an image of bodily resurrection.[125]

> Said Solomon the prophet, "When the dead shall come to life, the Mount of Olives will be cleft and all the dead of Israel come forth from beneath it; and even the righteous who died in exile will come by way of subterranean caverns and will come forth beneath the Mount of Olives. . . . Then all the inhabitants of the earth will say, 'What was the merit of this people that have come up from the earth, myriads upon myriads, as (on) the day when they appeared beneath Mount Sinai to receive the Law?'"[126]

The Song is full of new beginnings for the lovers. When they lose each other, they soon find each other again. They exhale their praise in long streams of words and then start over. The targumist heard in this verse an echo of the ultimate new beginning. These lovers not only come up out of the desert, they come up out of death itself, with Israel leaning on the arm of God. Here, at the end of the poem, is another new beginning, spilling over with life.

---

124. Pope, *Song of Songs*, 665.
125. For analysis of the concept of resurrection in Judaism, see Jon D. Levenson, *Resurrection and the Restoration of Israel: The Ultimate Victory of the God of Life* (New Haven: Yale University Press, 2006). For a consideration of resurrection in both Judaism and Christianity, see Kevin Madigan and Jon D. Levenson, *Resurrection: The Power of God for Christians and Jews* (New Haven: Yale University Press, 2008).
126. Quoted in Pope, *Song of Songs*, 664–65.

8:5b

Under the Apple Tree (Again)

In the second part of 8:5 the woman speaks again. "Under the apple tree," she sings, "I awakened you." Her words echo her song of the apple tree in 2:3 in which the apple tree is her beloved—"an apple tree among the trees of the wood"—whose "fruit was sweet to my taste." This recollection of her awakening and sexually arousing the man "serves as prelude," Exum argues, "for a permanent sign of their love in v. 6."[127] It is interesting to note, as the Blochs do, that this first erotic encounter takes place at the woman's initiative: *she* awakens *him*.[128]

Once again, the place of lovemaking is associated with a mother—the man's mother, this time. The NRSV identifies the apple tree as the place "where your mother was in labor with you," but many other translations (those of Bergant, Bloch and Bloch, Exum, and Pope, for example) identify what happens under the tree as the conception of the man. In any case, it is the ordinary miracles of the body that are celebrated here, from sexual awakening to conception to childbirth. As they are throughout the Song, the women here are full and active participants in their sexual lives.

8:6–7

Love Is as Strong as Death

The woman's hymn to love in the next two verses is perhaps the most familiar and cherished section of the Song. Often read at weddings, it is a potent meditation on love and death. For some commentators, 8:6–7 is the Song's proper end, and the verses that follow are merely a miscellaneous collection of poems. It is, for many readers, the high point of the Song.

The woman speaks here in the imperative mood, insisting that the man set her "as a seal" upon his heart and his arm. A seal is a

127. Exum, *Song of Songs*, 249.
128. Bloch and Bloch, *The Song of Songs*, 5.

mark of one's identity, worn close to the body. She wants to be like a seal on his heart, not just close to his body but within his body, completely intertwined with his sense of himself. The image of the marked or inscribed heart in the Hebrew Bible often points to a deep knowledge and a profound belonging. For example, in Jeremiah 31:33–34, God's inscription of the law on the hearts of the people of Israel marks the fact that "I will be their God and they shall be my people." With my writing on their hearts, God says, there will no longer be any need for the people to teach each other about God, "for they shall all know me, from the least of them to the greatest." Throughout the Song, the woman has celebrated a similar relationship with her lover—"My beloved is mine and I am his" (2:16). She has sought his presence, the kind of presence—immediate and full of knowledge—promised by God's inscription of the law on the hearts of Israel.

"Love is as strong as death," she sings, "passion fierce as the grave." The association of love and death has a long history and emerges from deeply human experiences of the power of both. Indeed, love can, in a sense, awaken death, or at least our bone-deep awareness of its inevitability. The poet Karin Gottschall associates a first kiss with the beginning of death.

> My death began when pleasure announced itself
> and burdened me with weight: ambitions
> built on bone and breath—so tenuously preserved.[129]

I remember standing in the back of the church on my wedding day, looking down the aisle at my husband-to-be, and suddenly knowing—really knowing—that one day I would die. There was something about being on the cusp of making a lifelong promise to intertwine my life with another's that made me feel my mortality in my bones. We were pledging ourselves to one another for a lifetime, and one day we would have to say good-bye. Life does not go on forever. But, the Song suggests, perhaps love does. Perhaps the relationships we have forged in love are as powerful as death itself.

---

129. Gottschall, "Bog Body," 27.

In many Christian writings, love and death have been associated as forces so irresistible that they override our will. "It is better to marry," Paul famously wrote, "than to be aflame with passion" (1 Cor. 7:9). Just as the power of death is overwhelming, desire can engulf us, turn us in new directions, undo us. This association undergirds a fearfulness about sexual desire in Christianity not found in the Song. The man speaks of feeling overwhelmed by the woman's presence, but the loss of control he experiences when he is with her is something he welcomes. The risks the woman takes to be with her beloved cause her to be focused, not anxious. She knows the risks of loving, of course. She knows that love is not something to handle casually, and she counsels us throughout the poem not to awaken love prematurely. She advises us not to rush in to love, but she does not teach us to be afraid of it.

> The Song offers a vision of love that finds goodness in sexual desire and cherishes the wisdom that can come from engaging it mutually and lovingly. . . . Rather than a limitation on our lives, desire can be an enlargement of our lives, involving us intimately in a life other than our own.

The Song offers a vision of love that finds goodness in sexual desire and cherishes the wisdom that can come from engaging it mutually and lovingly. As the American poet Mark Doty has put it, it is through desire for intimacy with another that "we are implicated in another being, which is always the beginning of wisdom, isn't it—that involvement that enlarges us, which engages the heart, which takes us out of the routine limitations of self?"[130] Rather than a limitation on our lives, desire can be an enlargement of our lives, involving us intimately in a life other than our own.

"Passion [is] fierce as the grave," the woman continues. Passion and death are, as Bergant puts it, "tenacious and undaunted in the pursuit of their goals."[131] The vision of love and passion here is intense: "flashes of fire," "a raging flame," "fierce as the grave," "strong as death." No wonder we read this portion of the Song at weddings.

130. Doty, *Heaven's Coast,* 20.
131. Bergant, *Song of Songs ,* 145.

Its language is robust enough to do justice to the radical promises people make when they pledge themselves to each other for a
lifetime.

The Hebrew word translated in the NRSV as "flame" ends with a
shortened form of the name of God: *yh*. Some commentators have
identified this as the one place where God is invoked in the poem
and have translated the phrase "flame of God" rather than "a raging flame."[132] There is, in the words of Pope, only "scanty and shaky
support" for such a reading.[133] God's name remains unspoken in the
Song, although some readers have heard it whispered here.

The woman's hymn to love ends with an affirmation of love's
strength, its unquenchability, and its ultimate worth. Bergant,
Exum, and other commentators see references to cosmic powers
in this verse. The "many waters" that cannot quench love seem to
hark back to the waters of chaos that raged before God ordered them
through the creation of the world. Bergant notes that the natural
forces named in 8:6–7—death, flame, sea, river, flood—all point to
Canaanite gods of destruction.[134] These are fierce, elemental powers,
but love is equal to them.

The hymn ends with the woman's conviction that love is price-
less. How ridiculous it would be to offer one's wealth in exchange
for it! Nothing we can make or sell or build is its equal. For something overpowering enough to compare with love, we must look to
death itself.

8:8–10

Little Sister

After the woman's powerful hymn to love's power and worth, a new
voice seems to speak up—a voice outside the lovers' "circle of intimacy." "We have a little sister / and she has no breasts," the voice
begins. "What shall we do for our sister, / on the day when she is
spoken for?" (8:8).

132. Pope, *Song of Songs*, 670–71.
133. Ibid., 671.
134. Bergant, *Song of Songs*, 146.

Who is speaking here? There is very little agreement among commentators. Bergant and the Blochs hear the woman's brothers' voices.[135] Exum reads 8:8–10 as another narrative told by the woman, paired with a story told by the man in 8:11–12.[136]

I think the woman's brothers do speak here, but they speak through the woman who reports the words they once uttered. Exum finds it strange that we would suddenly hear a voice that does not belong to the woman or the man or the women of Jerusalem, and so do I. It makes sense, though, that the brothers who appear in the beginning of the poem reappear for a moment at the end. Just as we heard of the brothers' anger through the words of the woman in the first chapter of the Song, so perhaps we hear their words recounted by her here.

In the first chapter the woman describes her brothers as "angry with me."

> They made me keeper of the vineyards,
> but my own vineyard I have not kept!
> (1:6)

It is her brothers who sent her out to work in the sunshine. "I am black and beautiful," she sang of her sun-darkened skin (1:5).

"My own vineyard I have not kept" could refer to the transgression of the woman's sexual boundaries by her lover. Certainly in 8:8–10 those boundaries are once again at issue. Describing their sister as "little" and sexually undeveloped, the brothers are concerned to make sure her boundaries are well defended.

> If she is a wall,
> we will build upon her a battlement of silver;
> but if she is a door,
> we will enclose her with boards of cedar.
> (8:9)

---

135. Ibid., 147; Bloch and Bloch, *The Song of Songs,* 214.
136. Exum, *Song of Songs,* 256–59.

Walls can be scaled; doors can be opened. The brothers seem intent on sealing off all her entry points, protecting her from potential lovers.

The brothers do not see the woman as her lover sees her or as she sees herself. The brothers say "she has no breasts"; the woman insists, "my breasts were like towers." In my lover's eyes, she sings, I am "as one who brings peace." The Blochs offer a richer translation of this verse: "But for my lover I am / a city of peace."[137] The woman uses images of city defenses to describe her body. With her walls and towers, she is protected against anyone who would breach her boundaries without her invitation. For her lover, though, it is not her excellent defenses that define her. For him, she is a place of peace and welcome.

The Targum hears the voices of angels in 8:8–9. The "little sister" of the passage is God's people, who lack the resources to defend themselves. What shall we do for our little sister when someone wants her, the angels ask. How shall we reinforce her places of weakness?[138] This reading allows us to hear in the brothers' words a desire to protect their sister in a world where women are so vulnerable to men's desires. Parents may hear in the brothers' words something of their own desire to protect their children from growing up too soon.

In the end, though, it is the woman who prevails. I am no longer a child, she seems to say. I have grown up, and I have chosen my lover for myself.

8:11–12

Solomon's Vineyard

The woman's song about the distance between how her brothers see her and how she sees herself is followed by the man's song comparing Solomon's vineyard to his own. Solomon's vineyard is vast and fertile, requiring a large staff to keep it going. Farmed by "keepers"

---

137. Bloch and Bloch, *The Song of Songs*, 113.
138. See Pope, *Song of Songs*, 679.

who share in its profits, the king's vineyard is a complicated operation of workers and supervisors and accountants.

The man compares his vineyard to that of Solomon's.

> My vineyard, my very own, is for myself;
>   you, O Solomon, may have the thousand,
>   and the keepers of the fruit two hundred!
> (8:12)

Throughout the poem, the woman's body has been described as a vineyard. Solomon, of course, was known not only for the land that he possessed but the size of his harem: "Among his wives were seven hundred princesses and three hundred concubines" (1 Kgs. 11:3). The man here seems to say to the king: You can have your many wives and concubines. My beloved is enough for me. She is all that I want and all that I need.

> The man here seems to say to the king: You can have your many wives and concubines. My beloved is enough for me. She is all that I want and all that I need.

As Bergant notes, the man's "boasting song" reemphasizes the woman's hymn to the strength and worth of love in 8:6–7.[139] There is nothing stronger than love, nothing worth exchanging for it, not even the vineyards of Solomon. Vast wealth is nothing compared to love. "If one offered for love / all the wealth of one's house / it would be utterly scorned" (8:7).

8:13

Let Me Hear Your Voice

The Song ends with one last exchange between the two lovers, an exchange that suggests that their dialogue will go on and on.

The man speaks first, addressing his beloved as "you who dwell in the gardens." Like the lily and the rose to which she compares herself

---

139. Bergant, *Song of Songs*, 149–50.

at the beginning of the second chapter, the woman is a creature in creation. The last place we see the lovers in the Song is where we so often found them: outside, in the green and growing world.

Just as the woman's brothers reappear at the end of the Song, so do the man's companions with whom, in the first chapter, he pastured his flock (1:7). Here the man sings to the woman: "my companions are listening for your voice." Exum understands the companions to function as the daughters of Jerusalem do: as a placeholder for us, the readers, who are also listening for the voice of the beloved.[140] But the man's song turns more intimate in the next line. "Let me hear it!" he cries, with a familiar urgency we remember from the woman's first words: "let him kiss me with the kisses of his mouth!" It is true that we are all here, listening; the man has invited us to listen along with him. But in the end the deep ache he feels to hear her voice breaks through, an ache that we cannot reach or assuage. Once again, we find ourselves pulled into the lovers' dialogue, but ultimately we remain outside the intimacy that is theirs alone.

8:14

Flee!

Just as the first words of the Song belong to her, the woman also has the last word as the Song comes to a close. Like the man who cries, "let me hear it!" the woman's last words to her lover also take the imperative form. "*Berach!*" the woman cries, and commentators have been arguing about what she meant ever since.

The NRSV translates *berach* as "Make haste." But is the woman calling her lover to her, as many readers have supposed, or sending him away? The Blochs insist that *berach* always means to run away *from* and never toward.[141] Some readers have heard in the woman's cry a plea for her lover to flee from his companions and come to her alone. Others have understood the woman to mean, "Run away before we are discovered together!" All these readings make sense within the Song; all resonate with some part of the poem.

---

140. Exum, *Song of Songs*, 262.
141. Bloch and Bloch, *The Song of Songs*, 221.

I follow Exum in hearing the last verse of the Song as both an admonition for the lover to "flee" and an invitation to draw close, to be far off and near at once.[142] The verse opens with "flee" but ends by calling the man to "be like a gazelle / or a young stag / upon the mountain of spices." Throughout the poem, the "mountain of spices" has referred to the woman, fragrant and delicious. "Run away," she seems to say, and also, "come."

What better ending for this poem of seeking and finding and losing and seeking again? For it is an ending that is not an ending, an ending that ensures that the love play of the Song will continue, no matter how close the lovers become, no matter how well they know each other. There will always be distances to cross and absences to overcome with ever more inventive, ever more tender, forms of love. The lovers will never come to the end of their adoration and praise. They will never stop calling out to one another across all that separates them. Even as they draw closer and closer to each other, there will remain between them mysteries to be reverenced. There will always be unknown and unnamable places within each of them to be sought with gentleness and adored with awe.

---

142. Exum, *Song of Songs*, 262–63.

A Book of Devotion

I began this project wondering if the Song of Songs could once again become a text of devotion for Christians. What would we find if we turned to this poem listening for God's voice, as countless readers before us have done? What would we hear if, as Origen long ago urged, we made the words of the Song our own?

One thing we find when we pray with the Song is good news: good news about the glory of the human body, the joy of mutuality in love, the responsiveness of a world that is cherished and loved, and the longing to know and to be known. These are the Song's own concerns, the Song's own preoccupations. Bringing the Song into our prayer brings our bodies, our relationships, the earth, and our longings into our prayer as well. This is precisely where these concerns belong: at the intersection of our life and God's life, at the place where we turn toward God with all that we are.

The Song also has the potential to cultivate a deeper understanding of Christian convictions about incarnation. The Song is not a Christian poem; it was not created by Christians seeking to illuminate the incarnation of God in Christ. But Christian readers have been pondering the incarnation in its company for centuries, having found in its loving attention to the body a fresh way to consider all the possibilities that human embodiment holds. So when Teresa of Avila hears the woman cry out, "let him kiss me with the kisses of his mouth," she cannot help but hear the longing of humanity for a closer relationship with God, a longing, to her mind, for the incarnation, God's kiss bestowed on us. And when Bernard of Clairvaux reads about the man peering through the gaps in the lattice, hoping to catch a glimpse of his beloved, his mind is also drawn to the incarnate God, looking at the world through a human body, learning mercy through sharing in the human experience of embodiment. As Bernard's and Teresa's engagements with the Song show, the Song makes room for us to respond to its words and images with words and images of our own. Its power to generate new poetry, new thought, new theology is attested over centuries and is still available to us whenever we open its pages.

Finally, the Song offers us a way of reading that is also a way of receiving the world, a way that leads to prayer. By inviting us into the dialogue of the two lovers, we are encouraged to read as they love— lingering in the presence of the beloved, admiring the beloved's beauty and grace, and adoring both what can be seen and known and spoken of and what is beyond our sight, beyond our ability to know or describe. In a world marked by speed and overwhelmed by information, the Song offers us a space beneath the pine branches and cedar boughs to read slowly, admiringly, meditatively. As centuries of interpretation have shown, the Song does not rush us, as readers, toward one final meaning. Rather, it invites us to read and reread and read again, listening for unexpected resonances, allowing multiple meanings to accumulate. It is a banqueting house, a garden, a vineyard, a field: a place to be explored in every season, a place that discloses something new each time we move through it.

When the Sabbath next arrives to clothe the world in rest, the Song of Songs will be sung at the Western Wall in Jerusalem. And one day soon, in a synagogue or a church or the offices of a justice of the peace, the Song will be read as two people prepare to pledge themselves in love to one another for the rest of their lives. Somewhere a lover is tucking a verse of the Song into a message meant for a sailor on a submarine. And in some quiet room somewhere, someone is making the words of the Song her own.

I hope this commentary has inspired you to join those in the past and in the present who have sought in the praying of the Song a life of deepened intimacy with God, with another, with the world. Hidden like a jewel at the heart of the Bible, the Song of Songs waits for us to take it up again and so enter with other faithful people into a song that never ends.

Selected Bibliography

Augustine. *The Confessions of St. Augustine.* Trans. Rex Warner. New York: Mentor, 1963.

———. *On Christian Doctrine.* Trans. D. W. Robertson Jr. Indianapolis: Liberal Arts Press, 1958.

Bergant, Dianne. *Song of Songs: The Love Poetry of Scripture.* Hyde Park, NY: New City Press, 1998.

Bernard of Clairvaux. *On the Song of Songs I.* Trans. Kilian Walsh, O.C.S.O. Spencer, MA: Cistercian Publications, 1971.

———. *On the Song of Songs II.* Trans. Kilian Walsh, O.C.S.O. Kalamazoo, MI: Cistercian Publications, 1976.

———. *On the Song of Songs III.* Trans. Kilian Walsh, O.C.S.O., and Irene M. Edmonds. Kalamazoo, MI: Cistercian Publications, 1979.

———. *On the Song of Songs IV.* Trans. Irene M. Edmonds. Kalamazoo, MI: Cistercian Publications, 1980.

Bloch, Ariel, and Chana Bloch. *The Song of Songs: The World's First Great Love Poem.* New York: Modern Library, 2006.

Carmy, Rabbi Shalom. "Perfect Harmony." *First Things* 208 (December 2010): 33–37.

Doty, Mark. *Heaven's Coast: A Memoir.* New York: HarperPerennial, 1996.

Eco, Umberto. *The Name of the Rose.* Trans. William Weaver. 1983. Reprint, New York: Warner Books, 1984.

Exum, J. Cheryl. *Song of Songs: A Commentary.* OTL. Louisville: Westminster John Knox Press, 2005.

Rabbi Ezra ben Solomon of Gerona. *Commentary on the Song of*

Songs and Other Kabbalistic Commentaries. Trans. Seth Brody. Kalamazoo, MI: Medieval Institute Publications, Inc., 1999.

Falk, Marcia. *The Song of Songs: A New Translation and Interpretation.* San Francisco: HarperSanFrancisco, 1990.

Fitzgerald, Allan D., ed. *Augustine through the Ages: An Encyclopedia.* Grand Rapids: Eerdmans, 1999.

Gottschall, Karin. *Crocus.* New York: Fordham University Press, 2007.

Griffiths, Paul J. *Song of Songs.* Brazos Theological Commentary on the Bible. Grand Rapids: Brazos, 2011.

Guigo II. *The Ladder of Monks and Twelve Meditations.* Trans. Edmund Colledge, O.S.A., and James Walsh, S.J. Kalamazoo, MI: Cistercian Publications, 1981.

Hindu Myths. Trans. Wendy Doniger O'Flaherty. Harmondsworth: Penguin, 1975.

Jenson, Robert W. *Song of Songs.* Interpretation. Louisville: John Knox Press, 2005.

John of the Cross, Saint. *Ascent of Mount Carmel.* Trans. E. Allison Peers. New York: Image Books, 1958.

Kristeva, Julia. *Tales of Love.* Trans. Leon S. Roudiez. New York: Columbia University Press, 1987.

Levenson, Jon D. *Resurrection and the Restoration of Israel: The Ultimate Victory of the God of Life.* New Haven: Yale University Press, 2006.

Madigan, Kevin J., and Jon D. Levenson. *Resurrection: The Power of God for Christians and Jews.* New Haven: Yale University Press, 2008.

Marguerite d'Oingt. *The Writings of Margaret of Oingt: Medieval Prioress and Mystic.* Trans. Renate Blumenfeld-Kosinski. Newburyport, MA: Focus Information Group, 1990.

Matter, E. Ann. *The Voice of My Beloved: The Song of Songs in Western Medieval Christianity.* Philadelphia: University of Pennsylvania Press, 1990.

McFague, Sallie. *The Body of God: An Ecological Theology.* Minneapolis: Fortress, 1993.

McGinn, Bernard. *The Flowering of Mysticism: Men and Women in the New Mysticism 1200–1350.* New York: Crossroad, 1998.

McGinn, Bernard, John Meyendorff, and Jean Leclercq, eds. *Christian Spirituality.* Vol. 1: *Origins to the Twelfth Century.* New York: Crossroad, 1985.

Moore, Stephen D. *God's Beauty Parlor and Other Queer Spaces in and Around the Bible.* Stanford: Stanford University Press, 2001.

Origen. *The Song of Songs: Commentary and Homilies.* Trans. R. P. Lawson. ACW 26. Westminster, MD: Newman Press, 1957.

Petroff, Elizabeth Alvilda, ed. *Medieval Women's Visionary Literature.* New York: Oxford University Press, 1986.

Pope, Marvin H. *Song of Songs: A New Translation with Introduction and Commentary.* AB. Garden City, NY: Doubleday, 1977.

Porete, Marguerite. *The Mirror of Simple Souls.* Trans. Ellen L. Babinsky. New York: Paulist Press, 1993.

Stanton, Elizabeth Cady. *The Woman's Bible: A Classic Feminist Perspective.* Repr. Mineola, NY: Dover Publications, 2002.

Teresa of Avila, Saint. *The Collected Works of St. Teresa of Avila.* Trans. Kieran Kavanaugh, O.C.D., and Otilio Rodriguez, O.C.D. Vol. 2. Washington, DC: ICS Publications, 1980.

Trible, Phyllis. *God and the Rhetoric of Sexuality.* OBT. Philadelphia: Fortress, 1978.

Tyler, Peter M. *St. John of the Cross.* London: Continuum, 2010.

Woolf, Virginia. *Moments of Being.* Ed. Jeanne Schulkind. 2nd ed. San Diego: Harcourt Brace Jovanovich, 1985.

Index of Ancient Sources

Index of Subjects

Abel and Cain, 143
abjection, 121–22
Abraham, 144, 158, 194
Absalom, 29
absence of God, 47–53, 55
Abu Ghraib prison, 104
acrostic, 36–39
Adam and Eve, 206, 209, 221, 238
Adorno, Theodor, 161
Aeneas, 22
Aeschylus, 143–47
Aesop's Fables, 34
Afghanistan, 82, 84
African slaves, 112–14
Agamemnon, King, 143–44, 146–47
Aids and Its Metaphors (Sontag), 28,
    96–97
AIDS/HIV, 28, 42
Akiba, Rabbi, 172, 184, 189
allegorical reading of Song of Songs, 173,
    174, 174n7, 176, 206, 209–11, 228
Allenby, Edmund, 158, 159
All Quiet on the Western Front
    (Remarque), 125
al-Qaeda, 105–6
Altizer, Thomas, 49, 50, 51
American Civil War, 84, 86
American Revolution, 83–84
Amery, Jean, 102
Amnesty International, 100
angels, 205, 264, 271
animal imagery, 1, 199–200, 213, 216,
    222, 231–34, 237, 241, , 250, 2,
    260, 274
antiwar sentiments, 86, 90, 92, 125. *See
    also* wars

apple and apple tree imagery,
    179, 180, 204, 206,
    209–11, 266
Arafat, Yassir, 116
Arendt, Hannah, 80–82
Argentina, 81, 92, 109–10
Ariadne, 22
Ariadne auf Naxos (Strauss),
    22
Arianna (Monteverdi), 22
Aristophanes, 125
Artemis, 144
Asaph, 189
Ascent of Mount Carmel (John of
    the Cross), 223
atheism, 48–51, 53, 60–61, 80
atomic bomb, 12, 17, 80
"atrocity producing situations," 97
Attack upon "Christendom"
    (Kierkegaard), 52
Augustine of Hippo
    on biblical interpretation, 173–74,
        192, 206, 233–34
    on Eucharist, 106
    on evil, 72
    on fall of Roman Empire, 71
    on Genesis, 231
    on God's Trinitarian image, 208
    on hidden meanings in Scripture,
        206, 234
    on *imago Dei*, 208
    Niebuhr's reading of, 78
    on relationship between Old and
        New Testaments, 192
    on teeth as sheep in Song of Songs,
        233–34